Dear Sam

ls!

x

CHILLI, SKULLS & TEQUILA

Road Dog Publications was formed in 2010 as an imprint of Lost Classics Book Company and is dedicated to publishing the best in books on motorcycling and adventure travel. Visit us at www.roaddogpub.com.

Book cover design by Olwen Fowler

ISBN 978-1-890623-57-9
Library of Congress Control Number: 2017947912

An Imprint of Lost Classics Book Company
This book also available in eBook format at online booksellers. ISBN 978-1-890623-58-6

Chilli, Skulls & Tequila

Notes from Baja California

by

Zoë Cano

Publisher
Lake Wales, Florida

WHAT THEY ARE SAYING ABOUT
BONNEVILLE GO OR BUST—
ON THE ROADS LESS TRAVELLED

A thrill on two wheels! An up-close-and-personal tour of Americana —*MetroWest Daily News* USA

Best bits are the colourful local encounters! —*Wanderlust Travel Magazine*

An inspiring and motivational story —Back Street Heroes

Her written descriptions are vivid, detailed and engaging. —*Overland Magazine*

She passed her test and headed off for the USA. Straight away. Like you do! —*Motorcycle Sports & Leisure*

Her research is deep, the descriptions strong and her connections with other people are open and friendly. Each of these meetings is like a pearl on a necklace!—*Adventure Bike Rider*

Read the story, the tale of someone achieving her dreams. An accessible and entertaining read —*100% Biker* Magazine

An unputdownable tale! —*South East Biker* Magazine

A marvellous book. I hope we will see more from Zoë Cano; a talented author. —*Sam Manicom*, Travel Writer

To the Ones Who Dream

About the Author

Zoë Cano, whose name means "Life," is an adventurous traveller, writer, and photographer.

Born in Hereford, England, in the 1960s she moved to live and work in Paris for ten years before working in New York and finally Boston, with extended periods in Brazil and Asia for the international events and exhibition business.

Zoë started rowing competitively and took the challenge to skiff the entire length of the Thames from its source in the centre of England to Greenwich. She has crossed the Peruvian Andes on horseback, motorcycled solo across the American continent, and still travels extensively.

Zoë now lives in London and is also the author of the highly successful books *Bonneville Go or Bust—On the Roads Less Travelled* and *Southern Escapades*.

For more information on Zoë Cano, her books, and her travels, visit www.zoecano.com.

CONTENTS

CHILLI, SKULLS & TEQUILA

INTRODUCTION

As for me, I am tormented with an everlasting itch for things remote. I love to sail forbidden seas, and land on barbarous coasts.
Herman Melville, *Moby Dick*

I close the old laptop, which has once again irritatingly overheated, and stare outside the window noticing the first flurries of snow dancing and swirling along the pavement below. My beloved sets of two wheels, the Bonneville and little scooter, covered and parked next to each other out on the street, are also becoming whitened. I touch the cold external wall next to my desk-cum-dining table, to confirm what it must feel like outside. Freezing!

The plugged in heater is on but might as well be off. Next to my feet on the wall behind me is the air ventilator that I've covered with paper and duct tape around its edges to stop the leaking cold air from brushing around my ankles. I stroke the comforting furry-coated hot water bottle on my lap and dip the marmite toast into the mug of tea.

I smile. I am indeed literally living off "bread and butter," having created a much more frugal and simple way of living compared to what seems like another lifetime just a short while ago. But I'm happy.

It was almost exactly a year to the day that in early 2015 I'd had enough and handed in my notice to that godforsaken full-time job in London that I could no longer support and which stressed the hell out of me. I'd taken the plunge into a deep, bottomless sea of the unknown. I had no job to go to, very little savings, and no idea for what I was going to do to pay the bills.

All I knew was I needed to make a radical change in my life.

From the outset, I needed focus and direction in finding ways fairly quickly to create multiple revenue streams, remembering advice my father had once wisely said about not putting all my "eggs in one basket."

I take another sip of the tea and start to add up what I actually did achieve in the last year. It seems unbelievable.

From the outset and without much prompting, I'd quickly started to write *Southern Escapades* about my travel adventures through the Deep South at the end of 2014. In those cold days of winter, I became like a hermit—writing, writing, writing—sitting huddled close to the radiator in the lounge, the warmest place to be. Mike, my publisher and travelling companion, who'd ridden out with me on his bike for part of that 2,000 mile trip, nodded he liked it, and this second book got published that same year.

At the same time, maybe now with a different mindset, I had a sort of epiphany. I felt that maybe I could organise some book signings here in the UK. I should definitely contact Triumph and see if I could join them at shows to sign copies of my first book *Bonneville Go or Bust* about my original solo trip across America. It seemed like a crazy plan, highly unlikely that a big organisation like that would take on little old me, and plus, the London Motorcycle Show was only three weeks away at the end of February. But they stuck their thumbs up and said, "Yes, come and join us!" Lights in the tunnel were beginning to shine.

By early spring, I took a leap of faith. With my confidence growing from this amazing opportunity I'd just been given, I needed to find more shows to visit. I started to contact groups like the Triumph Owners Club, The Ace Cafe, Brooklands Motor Museum, Triumph dealers, and motorcycle show and rally organisers across the UK, suggesting I be a feature for them. As well as signing books, I could bring my Triumph T100 along with me to show my authenticity. One girl and one bike—more like a summer road trip across Great Britain!

I had to keep focused and not give up immediately on what I was trying to achieve. The "F" word—*Freedom*!

I also needed to keep living costs down as much as possible. No new clothes or things people simply take for granted like that daily cappuccino from Starbucks. The secret to this new way of life and to make this work was to minimize outgoings. Amazingly, by the end of that year I'd gone to thirty-three events around the country book signing. I clocked up more than 5,000 miles on my bike, taking everything I needed on it, including a tent.

Without a doubt, I experienced some of the best and unique times meeting the kindest people who all welcomed me and showed genuine interest in my story.

Every event I was invited to was eclectic, extreme, and different; from the corporate culture with Triumph to small village halls lost in the countryside, the Hells Angels welcoming me with open arms at the famous Bulldog Bash, being almost blown away by a sea storm at Bexhill-on-Sea, among the hordes along the seafront promenade at the Brighton Bike Show, Llangollen which is the most beautiful place anywhere, charity shows like Copdock, air shows, classic motorcycle shows, hill climbs, bike jumbles, and even signing books at Chelsea Football Grounds!

So the positive experiences far outweighed this new frugal lifestyle out on the road. One highlight, which will forever stay with me, confirms the reason for having jacked it all in. I was on my way back from the Llangollen Show in North Wales, and I'd packed and left early to take the scenic Welsh border roads down to Herefordshire. The summer morning was bright, warm, and sunny, with cloudless blue skies. As I climbed the hilly, narrow, and twisty mountainous roads towards Llandrindod Wells, I was overwhelmed by its pure unadulterated beauty. Real tears of joy came to my eyes. The hills spread out around and in front of me, with the freshest cleanest air. Hardy Welsh sheep nibbled at the grasses on the edge of the road, Welsh Mountain ponies and their foals inquisitively raised their heads to look at me and my iron horse. There was a complete feeling of true contentment. I felt privileged to be there, and it was one of those special moments that I breathed in deeply, not wanting the moment to disappear.

By the end of the year you could say I'd "survived" and got by. I had to pinch myself that this was for real. The pinch hurt, so it must have been true.

Nothing is perfect, but I had in some way gained and found my freedom, which had been taken away from me for so long in the corporate world. It had been, without doubt, one of the best summers, perhaps even the best year of my life.

Once again, I look out of the window and see the snow flurries still merrily dancing to the wind's tempo. With the hot water bottle gone cold and my hands now under my bum to keep them warm, my mind wanders off, dreaming of warmer climes.

When am I going to "really" travel again? Last year I was out on the road nearly all year with no respite. The initial idea of travelling down through Alabama and Georgia back in 2014 was to create a set of unique travel journey stories "on the roads less travelled" through and around each corner of the American continent. That was, therefore, my Southeast corner part, and although only a two-week escapade, it had thoroughly dug up some incredible adventures and experiences along the way. In my head, what I now had to somehow do were the three other corners—the Southwest, the Northwest and the Northeast—and not necessarily in any particular order. It was my choice, but it all hinged on the ticking clock of time and finding the money to make it happen.

I excitedly look at my diary. If I did anything or could even afford it, the summer wouldn't be possible due to me being on the road in the UK for shows. I desperately want to go somewhere warm, so it seems like the Southwest is the most interesting option. But where exactly? And for how long?

For some time, I'd heard about the mystical and legendary "Transpeninsular Highway" threading through the 800 mile Baja California Peninsula in Mexico, just 160 miles south of Los Angeles, that bohemian travellers wanting to get lost and surfer dudes looking for that perfect wave had long ago discovered. It was still up there as one of the greatest road trips.

I was already imagining the starry nights, vast deserts, empty beaches, fish tacos, and chilled beers. Or was I just dreaming? Was it more of a place for food poisoning, crooked cops, dilapidated roads, tourist traps, and violent drug cartels? I'd heard cell phones don't work, petrol stations were sparse, and to take as much water and provisions as possible. I preferred to sweep those less attractive issues "under the carpet," at least for the time being. Anyway, there's only one main road on the Peninsula, so what could possibly go wrong?

But the place became more intriguing the more I read about it. I was lucky to have grown up and travelled to remote places before the Internet. That was when there was still a sense of pure adventure. But at some point, with the rise of *Lonely Planet* guides, Sat Nav, apps like Yelp, and social media channels telling and showing you everything before you'd even arrived, road trips had lost that undiluted excitement and surprise of exploration and discovery. But not in Baja California. There the spirit of the place still seemed to be intact, and I was starting to also believe it was still a wild place with a lot of surprises.

The idea was to do the trip on a motorcycle, but as the budget was tight, the plan was to ideally find one through sponsorship, as I'd successfully done for the last US trip thanks to Triumph. It really shouldn't be a problem. At this stage, I was being very naïve.

Carried away with excitement, I immediately surf the net, telling myself I can plan everything else afterwards. Adrenalin pumping, I find the cheapest possible flight to fly out from Gatwick at the beginning of May. And with just three months to go, I press the button, and a note comes back confirming I've made payment for a non-reimbursable return flight to Los Angeles.

Crazy what the winter blues can do!

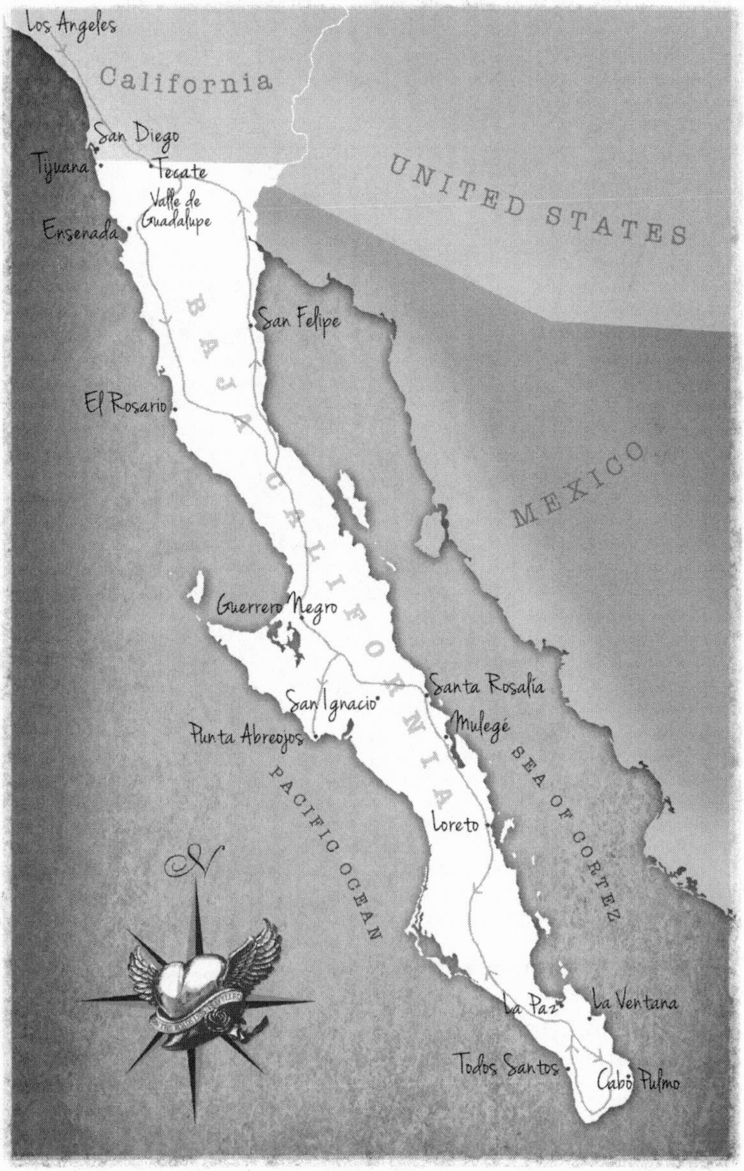
Los Angeles
California
San Diego
Tijuana
Tecate
Valle de Guadalupe
Ensenada
UNITED STATES
San Felipe
BAJA CALIFORNIA
El Rosario
MEXICO
Guerrero Negro
Santa Rosalía
San Ignacio
Mulegé
Punta Abreojos
SEA OF CORTEZ
PACIFIC OCEAN
Loreto
N
La Paz
La Ventana
Todos Santos
Cabo Pulmo

1

Just Give Me the Wheels!

Buy the Ticket—Take the Ride.

Hunter S. Thompson

The very next day after having spontaneously bought the air ticket from London to Los Angeles, I'm on a mission to find wheels to do a solo trip down to Baja California.

I'll be "on the road," leaving Los Angeles for just over three weeks. The cost of hiring a bike for that length of time is, unfortunately, well over my budget, so I quickly have to dismiss that option. No. Let's keep focused with the original idea and make contact with the guys at Triumph in Atlanta who provided the motorcycle last time and see what can be done.

I send a long explanatory email out about how unique and exciting this trip is going to be and great coverage for them and . . . wait and wait and wait for a reply. The days tick by. Now there's just under three months to go. Conscious that

1

I don't have much time to pull this all together, as well as creating an interesting itinerary, I decide to cheekily make contact with a few friends in California to ask about crazy possibilities of maybe taking their bikes. Unsurprisingly, I get a friendly but resounding negative reply back.

To be totally fair, at this stage I hadn't even considered how difficult it might be to take the dealer's or an individual's bike registered under someone else's name over the Mexican border. Even with the NAFTA agreement, I knew it wasn't as easy as travelling through the European member states.

The precious days go past. Still no reply. I'm getting impatient, frustrated, and just a little worried. I shoot another friendly note out to Triumph about a week later. Then another week lapses—no reply. I'm already thinking this isn't going to happen. I finally receive a short note from a Triumph dealership in Los Angeles simply saying that even for their PR they don't provide bikes, and none are ever allowed to go into Mexico.

That's fine; I accept that, but it means I have no motorcycle. I'm going to do this trip, whatever it takes, and anyway, reading the small print of the terms and conditions of the cheap air ticket I'd bought, I see there's no reimbursement there.

I breath in deeply, lean back in my chair, and turn the radio up in deep contemplation. Wilson Pickett's deep, raspy voice belts out *Mustang Sally*, forcing me to tap my foot. I smile. That's it! A compromise, but what could be cooler than doing the trip in a convertible Ford Mustang down this iconic route? I can already imagine it. A silk scarf wrapped around my head, large sunglasses, red lipstick, white leather driving gloves, and the warm desert air brushing past my naked arms on those long, lost roads to lost, magical destinations.

With a sudden burst of energy, I pull up names of rental car companies offering Mustangs from Los Angeles airport. Bingo. I find one for my dates, and although charging a bit above my budget, around $40 a day, it sounds good to me. I'll cut corners elsewhere. Anyway, it should be fairly cheap to eat and stay at places along the way. I hand over my card details, and my e-receipt is pinged back.

But it's only a few days later, after reading the small print I discovered with a shock that convertibles aren't allowed to leave the USA, mainly due to the ease of their theft. That's a problem, and things are starting to get complicated. With the disappointment of no motorbike, the cool ragtop option was the nearest "get your hair blown away" experience compromise.

Do I jettison the road trip down to Baja and do something within the US instead, but still with the Mustang? I stand back like a general on the battlefield, pulling out maps and looking at the tactical options of what's best. A road trip from LA would either be a circular route eastwards through Arizona to somewhere like Texas, or up the coast and back down, which I'd only done just a few years ago on the bike. That would involve a lot of repetitive mileage and was not the kind of trip I'd been prepared or interested to currently take on. Basically, I wasn't excited.

But the opportunity to explore Baja California, even without two wheels or a pull down top, was tantalizingly still too good to dismiss. The time of the year, in May, would be perfect, just lapping over from the end of the main tourist season, when I imagine large numbers of cumbersome camper vans had been travelling up and down the peninsula—not adding a very pretty picture to the landscapes. And it would also be a time before it gets excruciatingly hot, later on in the summer months. Hopefully, it should be pretty quiet down there.

I jump online and scroll down to see what other vehicles I can get with my small budget. I put my "sensible hat" on and decide on a "non-eye-catching" car, which although with a smaller engine size, should do the job. Oh well, I'll keep the windows down to bring in as much "outside" air as possible rather than the chilled, processed AC. I'm disappointed with not getting what I ideally wanted as a vehicle to have as my first experience down through Baja, but I'm grateful that the trip is still on. Maybe it's safer too. All my stuff can be locked inside without fear of the roof being ripped open. I could even lock myself inside if I felt in danger. I really don't know what to expect. Job done. The wheels are now ticked off the list.

I check that my travel two-year ESTA Visa Waiver authorization is still valid from the last trip and happy to learn I can use it for another five months, until the end of July. So at least I can get into the US, even if I am leaving the day after. Another tick, and I've saved $14.

Mexico's tourist visa I'll be able to get entering the country, about which I've already checked with the Embassy here in London. Apparently, anyone can enter and stay over the border in Mexico for a couple of days without a visa by just showing their passport, but for any longer you then have seven days to get the 180-day tourist visa. Most people get this at the border entry. I'd heard nightmares about the length of time getting through Tijuana, one of the main entry points in and out of Mexico from the US. So the plan was to travel further east and get in through a smaller, lesser-known border town.

And then the best part of it all, I started to pull together the travel plan and route. The way I'd prepared my solo trip across America in researching to stay at lost, interesting and remote places really paid off, so I'll try and do the same this time.

I hungrily read articles and research online to give myself an initial idea of the place. What I'd initially thought was just a remote, wind-blown sandy peninsula was wrong on all counts. I was surprised at the diversity, from the protected coral reefs in Cabo Pulmo at the tip, massive whale migrations, pre-historic rock paintings of Sierra de San Francisco, UNESCO's Isla Espiritu Santo, the oasis desert town of Mulegé, the Bay of Sand Dunes at Balandra Beach, the southern historic and cultural capital of La Paz, the artists' colony of Todos Santos, the old fishing village of San Felipe with some of the world's biggest tides, and amazingly, the prestigious wine producing vineyards in the Valle de Guadalupe.

It was beginning to look like the perfect trip. The more facts I dug up about the place, the more fascinated I became, realizing there was going to be a lot more to explore than I'd imagined.

So with the best map I can get my hands on, the *Reise Know How* 1:650 000 scale edition of Baja California, I set about circling the places that look "interesting". I don't want to get tempted and look at pictures of the places or browse online. I want a total surprise, if nowadays that's at all possible. I'm guessing that's why the postcard has now gone out of fashion. People can no longer wait. Except for my mother, who always asks me to send her cards. She has a drawer full of them dating back from the '50s, which are like little edited stories of our family and friends' lives throughout the decades.

By the end of April, with the first cherry blossoms appearing on the trees and a week before I'm leaving, I've created a mouthwatering travel route, which should cover about 2,500 miles, taking in an incredible diversity of stopovers, which I didn't even think were imaginable or existed a few months ago. Even I've impressed myself!

So ironically, on Mexico's Cinco de Mayo celebration day, I turn the key in my flat and head out to the airport with a small backpack, suitcase, and a pair of flippers. In my backpack I remember to put in two important old envelopes containing reading matter for later on in the trip. I'm convinced they'll give me unique inspiration and strength if I need it along the way.

Walking into the Gatwick departure lounge, my phone vibrates in my jacket pocket. I've been texted. It's from Mr. Sexy, my guilty pleasure. "Hi what you up to sexy lady? I know where I'd like to be! x"

I smile, pondering whether I should answer back. I text back with one word "Flying x."

The flight over to Los Angeles in my tiny narrow "Low Fare" economy seat is fairly painless, except for my legs going numb a few times. I inquisitively peer through the little window. The route heads northwest skimming Iceland, over the incredible expanses of icy white landscapes of Greenland, then directly down through Canada, Montana, Idaho, Nevada, and landing punctually at the International LAX Airport at precisely 5:30PM local time. As usual, my heart mysteriously palpitates going through passport control anticipating any surprising interrogatory questions.

The only raised eyebrow that comes from the officer is when I reply to his, no doubt repetitive, question he asks everyone, "So ma'am, what are you doing in the US for three weeks?"

"Well sir, I'm leaving your country tomorrow. Hopefully I can get back in through Mexico when I'm flying out from here on the 26th."

He smiles and waves me through. At Customs I truthfully declare I haven't brought in any insects, snails, disease agents, whatever they are, or been in close proximity to livestock. Although I do feel I was in a bit of a cattle truck flying over. But I don't think they're including that.

While waiting for the luggage, I text my friend, Ginger, letting her know I've arrived and ask about plans to meet up for dinner. The quarters are put in to release the trolley, and the luggage swept off the carousel. I'm on a mission. I quickly head out of the entrance and jump onto a bus that takes me over to Bellanca Avenue to pick up the car. Oh God, we sure are in America! Everything's so efficient. To get the rental car, I have to process everything through a talking machine. I'm not having that. I go and queue up at the customer service counter to hopefully meet Tawny, the branch manager who helped in finding the alternative to the Mustang. I finally reach the desk with Tawny smiling from the other side. I know it's her as she's got her badge on.

"Hey, Tawny, you probably don't remember me, but I was that crazy girl in London panicking about having to change the Mustang for a car I could get into Mexico with!"

She smiles but quickly changes that to a serious look. "Hey, yea, good to see you. Now I have to draw your attention to a few things. Firstly, are you really sure this is the right sort of vehicle for the kind of trip you're planning to do? The car's low and may have issues with the rougher terrain you're gonna cross. I'd strongly advise you look into an all-terrain 4-wheel sports utility vehicle that'll have a higher suspension and thicker wheels."

I hadn't really thought about that, not being able to visualize or guess at this stage the extreme roads I was potentially going to have to navigate. The initial understanding I'd had in my mind was it was just one straight tarmacked road all the way down.

She continues, "And secondly, to legally drive into Mexico with one of our vehicles, you're gonna have to get and pay for

Mexican car insurance to confirm you can drive it. We can't process that here, so you're gonna have to go to the San Diego Airport, who'll do it all for you."

I gulp. How much is that going to cost? And an extra diversion with additional mileage and navigation I hadn't planned for tomorrow.

"That's gonna be about $35 a day, so about $700 for the entire duration."

I gulp again. That was very unexpected and will deeply dig into my budget.

"So getting back to this vehicle. I'm going to try and help. I'm seeing here if I can get you a deal on a more robust vehicle. Boy, I've heard some of those roads down there are crazy!" She scrolls down her screen and smiles.

"OK, this is good. We've got a small SUV Fiat 500X that's just come in. I'll do that for a couple of dollars extra per day. I promise you I'm not upselling you. I'm just wanting you to enjoy your trip and be safe out there. I'll walk you out to the parking lot so you can take a look, and then you can make up your mind."

We walk around the SUV, and I already feel it's the better option. We check if any previous damage needs to be recorded, and stupidly, like I know what I'm doing, I confidently kick a tyre like I do with my bike to check it's inflated. I get a quizzical stare back. The keys are handed to me. I climb up and into the driver's seat of the sparkly clean little black Fiat truck, more like a "Mini-Me" of the bigger versions, and look around me. There's no Sat Nav. Yes this will do just fine! Next to the other larger, more luxurious SUVs, it looks very small but feels right. I nod my head. This is a great option that I'm very happy with. Maps and hand-drawn directions are given to me to get to my first destination, the Travel Lodge on Sycamore Avenue at the airport and then to the Enterprise offices at San Diego Airport tomorrow morning.

I bung my bags into the back, put on my seat belt, and carefully release the automatic foot brake. It's been a while since I've driven, not owning a car back at home. Thank God, no parallel parking techniques here. Just in or out. My kind of driving. It lurches forward as I carefully head out of the carpark onto busy Westchester Parkway that hugs the airport, with the map on my lap. Trucks and cars are already speeding by with massive planes just overhead, either landing or taking off. The sun's slowly setting, and it's drizzling lightly. I can hear the sound of the rain on the road being splashed up and slightly obscuring the view on the windscreen. I lean forward slightly, looking for signs and rubbing the misted window. Ten minutes later, I stop outside the Travel Lodge, feeling happy I've already completed the first task without any mishaps and go to collect the key.

The choice to stay here was simple. It was by far the cheapest place I could find near the airport, with close proximity to the car rental place and ideally an easy departure tomorrow from Los Angeles to get straight out onto the highway, down the coast, and over into Mexico and to where I was to be staying. Hopefully, I'd reach my first destination by mid-afternoon.

I drive round to my room, parking almost directly outside the front door. That's America for you—pure convenience. I haul all my bags out again, leaving nothing inside the car for prying eyes to see and be potentially taken at this early part of the trip.

I walk up a few concrete steps, unlock the door, and enter a basic anonymous grey-toned travellers room. Three of its walls are external ones surrounded by the car park. Hopefully there won't be too much noise with cars arriving late and leaving early. Inside the dim room, I see the air conditioning machine spewing out freezing cold air from under the curtain-closed window, the beer filled fridge, and the obligatory over-sized TV hanging from the wall. Still with my boots on, I crash onto the bed. It looks directly through a door to a toilet.

Ginger texts me saying she's on her way in about an hour and will come and pick me up to take us over to Manhattan Beach for dinner and drinks. Great! That place certainly sounds more stylish than where I currently am. Enough time to splash water on my face, swig a beer from the fridge, comb my hair, and trawl through the TV's 100-plus channels.

Before long, there's a knock on the door, and out of precaution, maybe not paranoia at this stage, I look through the little spy hole. The smiling face of Ginger is on the other side. Embarrassed to show her the room, I quickly grab my bag and come out, locking the door behind me.

How wonderful to see her again after six months, when we'd last seen each other in London. So flying into LA tonight it made total sense and a was a no-brainer to meet up for a chinwag and put the world to rights. Ginger is one stylish chick, and she'd soon put her foot down, and we were cruising south along the coast to Manhattan Beach.

"Hey, Zoë, you're gonna love this place. It's an old boho haunt of mine where I used to live back in the '80s. Thought it would help set the scene for your trip. It's a real arty place with lots of great places to eat."

Already knowing my budget was tight, but always wanting to "go halves," I was hoping it wasn't going to be excessively expensive.

Quickly accelerating from a green light, Ginger continues, "But like everywhere in LA it's changed. And not for the better. I remember back then when I lived in an apartment at the top of the hill looking down the road to the beach. We'd skateboard down to the seafront. Dang, that was sooo much fun! No cars, no congestion, just cool people getting by, who thought this was a good distance out of central LA. Now it's all LA!"

We walk into the Rock'n Fish hip joint, ordering from the wall's "Special" menu, with good looking guys running around with drink laden trays. The taste of fresh grilled fish from the open kitchen and cool iced Margaritas is heaven.

Ginger asks curiously "So where's your first stop tomorrow night? Where will you be?"

I smile. "How can I explain? I've got to find a remote place up through the mountains south of Tecate. I've been invited by rancheros to stay with them at their farm. They breed horses, and I've been told there's going to be a tequila laden party there this weekend, with maybe a bit of cowboy riding thrown in. Apparently, it's so isolated and difficult to find they're going to meet me at some crossroads at 3PM sharp."

Her jaw drops. "And how the hell did you work that one out? You're amazing! You certainly don't do things halfway."

The day has been long, and back in London daybreak is already arriving. I'm genuinely happy but tired, knowing I've got a big and potentially complicated journey ahead of me early tomorrow morning. So after a second large cocktail and an evening full of laughs, we head back. But only after Ginger insists on paying and won't take "no" for an answer.

We hug each other goodbye, and on leaving, Ginger turns around smiling and winks. "Now remember! Only pick up the good looking hitchhikers!"

2

RANCHERO HOSPITALITY

If I'd followed all the rules, I'd never have gotten anywhere.

Marilyn Monroe

There's an annoying buzzing in my ear. I reach under the pillow to stop my phone's alarm from ringing. It's still dark. I'm glad I managed to have a good night's sleep. I switch on the coffee maker, and twenty minutes later, I've pulled on my jeans, drank a mug of coffee, and am hauling the luggage out to the truck.

I'd calculated there was only about 200 miles to drive. But I wanted to give myself ample time, as there seemed to be quite a bit to consider and fit in. Firstly, I had to navigate out of Los Angeles, hopefully before rush hour starts, then make a detour to San Diego airport to get the vehicle import and insurance paperwork issued, and then find my way to the Mexican border town of Tecate, with no idea on how long it will take to get through. Hopefully, I'll take a wander there and find a tasty authentic place for lunch. Then it would be off to find that mysterious meeting point. Just forty miles south of Tecate, I had to find a tiny track, which on the map looked to be in the middle of nowhere, and where Raúl at the farm had said we were to meet. He'd mentioned that, because of the mountains, phone reception might be poor so to just look out for a big orange truck at 1500 hours.

So as you can see, I had no idea how long it would all take. But I didn't want to rush. I turn the key and breathe deeply. I'm excited, maybe a bit nervous, but focused onto getting into Mexico without any problems. I look down at the map and trace the highlighted roads to take—405, 5, 8, and 94.

With it quickly getting lighter, I put my foot down and pull out, crossing the road to the gas station. I check the tank is full, stock up on bottles of water, some chocolate bars, and grab a warm bagel to eat. I've pretty much convinced myself that, as soon as I get out of sprawling Los Angeles, the roads will be quieter, and it'll just be a nice relaxing ride down along the coast to the border.

Not quite, and I should have known better. It's literally the beginning of rush hour. Already the road out from the hotel is manically busy, and before long I'm unsurprisingly stuck in the middle of five lanes of almost standstill commuter traffic. To make matters worse, it quickly darkens overhead and starts to pour down with rain with intermittent lightening flashing across the skies. This is something I hadn't expected in California in May. Always on the lookout for them, I'm not seeing any motorcycles out on the road. It's at that point, and for the first time, that I'm pleased to be where I am. I pass through Huntingdon Beach, and at San Clemente expect the traffic to have disappeared, or at least dissipated, but the massive road works and congestion continue right up until I see signs for San Diego. This is also exactly when the rain stops, and the sun begins to appear. This is more like it. I pull off the highway, park near the airport departures terminal just before 10AM, and walk out into warm sunshine.

Forty minutes later I'm $735 poorer but with an essential Mexican Insurance Identification card and a 24 hour toll free number for any accidents, theft, or breakdowns and not forgetting the $13 for the parking. It's one of those occasions you just need to forget about as soon as possible or it'll ruin things.

East of San Diego, I approach El Cajon and stop at the first gas station I see to fill up. Wow, almost seven gallons for just $19, or $2.79 a gallon. That's good compared to the astronomical prices in England now at £3.50 or about $5. But what interests me more is that everybody is already speaking Spanish. I'm happy to hear this other language. It's been a while since I've spoken it and now can just get by in being understood. I'm flattered when I get to the counter and the woman speaks Spanish to me. I smile and simply say, "Gracias." That'll do for the time being.

As I turn off the main highway and head down onto the narrower two-lane Route 94 heading to the border, the landscape dramatically changes from urban sprawl to country fields, rocky green thorn bush topped hills, and cloud covered mountains reaching far away into the distance. Unbelievably and without explanation, the roads have now become almost empty.

All of a sudden, in the middle of nowhere, a red stop light appears. There's no oncoming traffic and nobody to be seen in this isolated area, but I stop anyway. After waiting quite a while and with it still red, I proceed carefully and see over on my right a massive expanse of barriers surrounding a large building site. It looks like a strange windowless fortified red brick prison structure but with a glamorous pyramid-shaped front entrance. It looks like massive work is being undertaken, but the cranes, forklifts, and trucks are all silent. This is strange. There is no one around this building site. There are signs everywhere saying, "Warning. Do Not Enter!" I'm curious. Maybe wrongly, I pull over and cautiously get out. I walk towards the barriers, and still seeing no one, inquisitively peer through. On the wall of the building is a large panel: "Jamul Indian Village—A Kumeyaay Nation." But much more interestingly, on the other side is a massive red and yellow scripted sign: "Hollywood Casino."

All of a sudden, a guy from out of nowhere sees me and races over to the fence. "Get out of here! Get out of here now! Who are you? The Press?"

That shakes me, and I turn on my heels, locking the door of the car as I jump in. Not until I reached the ranch was I to hear more about the full extent of this controversial project. I quickly put my foot down and continue along the increasingly long, straight road that for the first time I see disappearing into the distance. From afar, the only other vehicle out on the road, a large ten-wheel white articulated truck approaches and quickly passes me honking its horn.

But out along the horizon I already see a scattering of tiny buildings on the hilltops. That must be Mexico. The land looks sparsely populated here; rough green grass fields come up to the roadside and the gorse-covered hills quickly approach me. I just don't know what to expect.

As I come ever closer to the mysterious cloud covered mountains and unknown place of Tecate, I'm imagining what the sixteenth century Spanish conquistadores were imagining they'd discover based on all the stories and myths they'd heard of Baja California.

It fascinates me.

Back then, Baja California was a land like no other place in the world, where the early explorers thought it was rich in gold, ruled by strong female Amazonian warriors, and governed by a queen. Calafia was the name of this legendary black Amazon warrior queen, associated with the mystical Island of California. The Island of California refers to a long held Spanish misconception, dating from that time, that California wasn't actually part of mainland North America but, rather, a large island separated from the continent by a strait, now known as the Gulf of California or the Sea of Cortes. One of the most cartographic errors in history, it was shown like this on many maps during the seventeenth and eighteenth centuries, despite evidence to the contrary from various explorers. The legend initially came to life with the idea that California was like the Garden of Eden or Atlantis.

The first known mention of this legend of the Island of California was the 1510 romance novel *Las Sergas de Esplandián* (*The Adventures of Esplandian*) by Spanish writer García Rodríguez de Montalvo:

> *It is known that on the right hand side of the Indies there is an island called California very close to the Terrestrial Paradise, and it's peopled by black women, without any men among them, for they live in the manner of Amazons.*

*They had beautiful robust bodies, spirited courage and
great strength. Their island was the most impregnable
in the world with its cliffs and headlands and rocky
coasts. Their weapons were all gold . . . because in all
the island there was no metal except gold. And there
ruled over that island of California a queen of majestic
proportions, more beautiful than all others, and in the
very vigour of her womanhood. She was not petite, nor
blond, nor golden-haired. She was large, and black as
the ace of clubs.*

*But the prejudice of colour did not then exist even
among the most brazen-faced or the most copper-
headed. For, as you will learn, she was reputed the most
beautiful of women; and it was she, O Californias!
who accomplished great deeds, she was valiant and
courageous and ardent with a brave heart, and had
ambitions to execute nobler ambitions than had been
performed by any other ruler—Queen Califia!*

This document helped to precipitate the Spanish hunt for
gold in North America. So in 1539, when conquistadores
arrived in the Baja California area after conquering the Mexico
mainland earlier that century, they believed they had reached
a mythical island of female warriors with supplies of gold. A
few years later, the explorer Cortes landed north of La Paz, still
searching but only discovering precious black pearls.

I shake myself back to the present and suddenly see a
green road sign: "Welcome to Tecate—an international trade
community." This is one of the forty-eight places along this
2,000 mile US and Mexican border where people can legally
enter. And I'm still the only one on the road! I reach over to my
bag and pull out my precious passport and vehicle documents.
It's midday. This could be a long wait, if it's anything like I'd
heard about Tijuana. Just as I'm approaching the official border
zone and leaving the US, I see two black American patrol cars
parked up on the roadside, no doubt seeing if there's anything

suspicious leaving. I arrive at the border and slowly drive through the passport control area where two Mexican guards just smile and wave me through. There is nobody here—no cars waiting or anyone checking entry papers, no customs control and no searching of cars' contents. Is everyone at church? I look around to see this isn't a joke, strangely in contrast to the strictest of entry procedures into the US, and just continue through. I've received no extended visitor visa or stamp on my passport.

I'm immediately transported into another world, entering an old frontier town with badly worn and rutted roads. I smile. I need to stop, pull out my new map, orientate myself on finding the right road out, and take a walk to stretch my legs and find a place to grab a bite to eat. I pull into a space in Calle Presidente Ortiz, making a note of where I'm parked so I don't get lost. This time it's easy, in front of an "Oro-Plata' gold and silver shop. Locking the door, an old man sitting on a chair outside the shop glances at my American number plate but nods his head in salute and gives me a small smile. That's nice. I smile back.

This place is quiet. I can see no visible tourists, and the townsfolk in the main square are just quietly walking their dogs or chatting with each other on the benches. I turn into a main thoroughfare and along this road once again smile to myself. My first encounter with graffiti or is it art? An entire wall has been painted in black and white of two men's faces staring with a shocked look at something far in the distance. With their little trimmed moustaches, dark gelled black hair, and scarves around their necks, they look like they're performing. An old reel of film is painted next to them, so maybe they're old classic actors from a bygone age.

On the other side of the road is a small white building with a massive marlin on its wooden slated roof. The red flashing light in the window says, "Abierto," so I wander over to see if it really is open. Crates containing bottles of Coca-Cola and water are stacked up outside, obscuring what looks like a fish shop or small eatery. I look up and see the sign: "Tacos & Mariscos." That'll do nicely.

I walk through the door of the Bella Sirena (Beautiful Mermaid) and see just a few tables, with the majority already taken by locals busily tucking in. That's reassuring. I sit at one next to a humming fridge and am greeted by a simple menu. Soon, I'm scooping my tacos into fresh, delicious avocado guacamole and then layering parsley, freshly chopped tomatoes, lettuce, and large cooked chilli peppers onto my succulent prawn tortilla, which is amply drizzled with cheese and sour cream. Not bad for a first meal "out on the road" and all for 77 pesos (about £2), and that's including a soft drink of my choice.

I return to the truck, noticing the old man still in his chair, and smile in a friendly way to him. Very quickly I've crossed the railway tracks onto Highway 3 south out of town and driven out into the countryside. Luckily, I've been given some directions by the ranch. But I'm here now, out on the roads in Mexico. I open my window to feel and smell everything new around me. It feels like all my senses have come to life and woken up.

Within thirty minutes I've passed through the town of Valle De Las Palmas, then through Teserazo and Vallecitos. Somewhere along the road, I see pink ornately painted gates with what appear to be like shrines or tombs behind them. I stop and get out. The gates are locked. Under the ornate cross at the top of them are the words *Tomas. Ruiz. Zunica. Pantheon Santo Tomas.* Peering through the gates, I notice pots of brightly coloured flowers adorning the tombs and small mausoleums. Whether the flowers are fresh or plastic I don't know, as I'm too far away.

Just fifteen minutes later, around a curvy section up a hill with the signs "Zona Arqueologica" appearing, I'm now descending back down again. I let out a sigh of relief as I see the turn onto the dirt track I need to take. This is where I've been told to wait. They must have thought I was a real explorer, as I'd even been given exact coordinates of their place—32° 09′ 26.82″N 116° 27′ 43.03″.

I'd been warned to be careful when crossing this narrow two-lane highway, as there was sometimes fast approaching traffic, and the best thing to do was to exit from the shoulder on my right side and then cross when clear. I wait there for a while next to a sign: "Ejido San Marcos." Tied between these two posts is an old potato sack with a red hand-painted arrow and the word *Rodeo* flapping in the wind under the cloudy sky. That tells me we've entered cowboy country. I quickly pull out and cross the road onto the dirt track and park up underneath a tree.

The engine's turned off, and I let out a deep sigh of satisfaction, but at the same time with a little trepidation of this unknown encounter. It's ten to three, just ten minutes before we're supposed to meet. I'm pretty chuffed with the timing, but there's no truck here yet. The place feels remote. There's nobody or anything here. But I'm curious and, even with only a few minutes, want to make the most of my time. I get out of the truck and walk towards a thatched hut with hundreds of empty beer and wine bottles stacked into masses of crates outside on the dusty ground. I peer through the barbed wire "wall" of the hut and see a counter, a few stools, and some sparsely filled shelves with glasses behind them. I look up. An old, tattered Mexican flag is proudly flying from the roof. Next to it is a massive old dilapidated and paint-peeled advertising billboard displaying one of the nation's beers, Pacifico.

I'm startled as a truck's horn blasts out. I turn around and see a massive orange truck approach and a guy jump out. This has to be the right person, surely! A smiling, stockily-built guy with a cream cowboy hat on approaches me with his hand held out, ready to shake mine.

"Buenos días. Are you Zoë? You must be!"

I nod. "And are you Raúl?"

He nods. We both smile. Then his smile drops, looking over at where I'm parked. With a strong but kindly Mexican accent, he continues, "Caroline, my wife, is waiting for us back at the ranch, which is in Las Bellotas Canyon, quite a way up this track, and which is gonna get a lot rougher. Your vehicle just ain't gonna make it."

Oh God. We're off to a good start.

"But hey, no es una problema! We can sort that! You follow me. Half way up, we'll just stop, and you can park it in one of my fields. It'll be safe out there for a few days. We can unload it, and you can then jump into my truck with me for the last part of getting down into our valley. No roads there!"

Talk about total trust. I just smile and enthusiastically agree to the plan.

It had been one of those bizarre things that had just happened planning the trip. Looking at the maps, I knew this was an interesting part of the peninsula, with mountains, livestock, horses, and ranches. What better way to get the initial feel and authenticity of Baja California than with its people and exploring this wild place on horseback. If only! But with further research, I came across a remote place that offered basic accommodation, quail hunting, and horse pack trips. It was just forty miles from the border, so a perfect first stop. I made contact, explaining what I was trying to do in uncovering some of the lesser known places. The reply was incredible. They would be delighted to invite me as their guest, if I was able to truthfully relate my time with them. I gratefully accepted, not knowing what to expect but knowing genuine hospitality had been offered at their home to a complete stranger. The famous Spanish words *Mi casa es su casa* (My house is your house) couldn't be more heartfelt.

I already felt that I was being welcomed to Baja with open arms.

We start both vehicles up, and I slowly follow Raúl through the rutted, bumpy road, which gradually starts to climb steeply until we're out onto open hillside, navigating around water drenched muddy holes on a small slippery track. I'm hoping already this won't go on for much longer, after uncontrollably sliding across the track yet again. The truck in front flashes its red emergency back lights and comes to a stop. So do I. Raúl walks over to a gate, lifts it up, swings it open, and waves me in. I drive slowly through a deeply grassed field, turn around to face outwards, and turn the engine off, letting out a sigh of relief. We both pull the luggage out, and I put my Stetson hat on. Now I feel at home.

I jump into the front, and with no seatbelts anywhere visible, we head on. The landscape of rolling hills and mountains open up, and we progressively continue climbing until it almost seems like we're on the top of one. And then we start to slowly and carefully proceed down what I can only describe as a very, very steep perilous (in my opinion) descent along a very narrow earth-covered track on the side of a mountain. We weave around it until, appearing in front of us and still a lot further down, is a green, fertile canyon with a solitary ranch building, stables, corrals, barns, and vegetable gardens surrounded by old oak trees. All around this are horses quietly grazing in fields.

It all looks like another world down there in the canyon. We finally come to a stop in front of a large wooden barn, and Raúl's four black and brown patched Australian farm dogs come running from out of it, wagging their tails and jumping up overjoyed to see their master back.

One of the jeaned and booted ranch hands approaches us, grabs the luggage, and we all walk to the farm house. The architecture is typical of the region; hand built, I'm told, from scratch, with beautiful shiny oak floors. There's a beautiful terraced veranda on the first floor that goes all the way around the building that must be a wonderful shady place to escape the heat. Outside the house is a beautiful area with cacti, olive trees, and a covered seating area looking over a small pool. Under some of the oak trees are saddles and bridles, already hung up on hooks.

A smiling lady walks out from the porch area. "Hey," she says with an American accent. "Welcome to La Bellota. I'm Caroline, the wife of Raúl. We're dying to hear about your trip here and what you plan to do. How was the journey over from Los Angeles?"

"Great, except for someone chasing me away from that casino being built just over the border."

A smile comes to their faces. "Yes, it's a bit of a news piece right now. The local residents just don't like the idea of this casino gaming venue being opened so close to where they live. It's created a bit of friction with the local community and the Indians, to say the least. Anyway, let me show you up to your room so you can get things sorted and maybe take a small siesta. We've got a few lady artists staying here over the weekend too, so should be fun. They're currently painting somewhere in the hills across those fields."

And with that, I'm shown up to the first floor into an oak floored room with two sets of bunk beds. I notice one has clothes on it already, so I opt for other one.

Caroline adds, "Make yourself at home. But remember, we don't have electricity here, and it gets dark quite early. There are oil lamps hanging in the bathroom over there and here in the bedroom. You can turn them up for more light or simply turn them off. Make sure to bring your torch down with you so you can find your way back up later. It also gets cold here at night, so there are spare blankets in that chest. Come down when you want a drink. We'll be next to the fire outside. The girls should be back soon too."

An hour later after a warm shower, I hear voices laughing and glasses clicking downstairs in the courtyard. I wander down to join the fun but with just a little trepidation about meeting new people. I have nothing to worry about. I'm greeted by smiling faces. Caroline interjects the merriment, "Hey guys, or rather, girls! This is Zoë, who's travelling on her own exploring Baja!"

She then rolls off all eight girls' names, which I almost immediately forget. Raúl approaches with a tray of drinks. "So Zoë, would you like one of our very special pineapple margaritas with only the best tequila?"

The girls put their thumbs up. A large thick tumbler is passed to me. I put my lips to the iced glass and savour the most exquisite drink ever—fresh, sweet pineapple juice over a smooth, rich tequila made from one hundred per cent pure agave, the plant native to the hot and arid regions of Mexico. This is good tequila. I'm told it's been left in oak barrels to mature, which gives it its wonderful deep golden brown colour. Its luxurious taste is nothing like the throat burning industrialized and processed tequilas I've tasted at the pubs back in the UK. It could be another drink altogether.

Raúl smiles and sees me enjoying the drink. "I can tell you a lot about tequila, and I'm sure you'll have tasted a lot more by the end of the weekend. But this is the real stuff. You know why they put salt rims on the glasses and you suck the lime with tequila drinks in North America? It's to hide the terrible flavour of the industrially-produced varieties, a lot of which are made from chemicals, sugarcane alcohol, and added colours—all just a big marketing ploy. The brands like José Cuervo are a lot to blame for this mass production. Be careful when you go and buy your tequila. Make sure it says on the bottle '100% agave.'"

Raúl starts poking at the large wood fire blazing out and upwards. With the chilly air setting in, we pull our chairs and the long bench closer around it. The sun has disappeared behind the mountain, bats are darting about, and there is now a strange cacophony of noises and sounds "out there" in the canyon and up in the hills. Across the dark sky, the stars start to quickly appear.

I'm curious to know who these girls are who've crossed the border to spend time painting here. The conversation flows easily. One's an acupuncturist, another one's a travel consultant, a couple of them are retired, and we even have our own psychic and astrologer! Amazingly, they all confess of having had a fear of crossing the border, which for some is the first time this weekend. They'd heard stories about the dangers of travelling into Mexico. But from how they've been welcomed and what they've seen so far here, they realize a lot of these stories are very untrue.

Raúl passionately interjects, "One of my aims here in the valley is to show and educate the Americans and other people who come and stay that Mexico isn't that bad. It's a beautiful place here where we live and so are our people in Baja. I take people not only around here to explore but on road trips down the coast to see the whales during their migrations. I just hope it will filter back."

The conversations before dinner, drinking that smooth tequila, jumping from one extreme topic to another that can only be described as wackily eclectic from one of the girls discussing about their three week retreat for colon irrigation— oh so Californian!—to instructions on how to best stuff back a sheep's uterus strongly recommending to use sugar on it to shrink it, to explaining about the wolf-free compound behind us. This is a place where each evening the sheep come back to on their own free will from up in the hills, to be protected from lynx and wolves.

It's then a hand bell is rung from outside the kitchen door, and we all quickly march in. The little apron-wearing Mexican lady in the kitchen is busy putting out freshly prepared plates of food on the counter. I look in bewilderment as some of these things I've never seen or eaten before. We have freshly cooked nopal cactus pads (or prickly pear), courgettes and peppers, green salad, Mexican black beans, tomato salsa, guacamole, and sublime cheese quesadillas made with chorizo de soya (soya mincemeat), and then sweet budin, which is a light caramel custard pudding. Everything is brought to the long wooden table we're all seated around. And it's all drank down with jugs of delicious and refreshing cantaloupe juice, "Agua de Melon." It all feels homely but very exotic.

By this stage my eyes are starting to close on their own. It's been an incredibly long day, and I can't quite believe how much extreme stuff has been packed in less than twenty-four hours.

Raúl notices and kindly says, "It's been a long day for you all. I know the girls are painting down by the river in the morning, and that may be a good time for me to ride out with Zoë to explore and show her a bit of the place. If we climb high enough, there are 360 degree views out to the valleys around us and into the wine country."

I smile appreciatively, not needing words to reply. Caroline chirps in, "So I guess we all need to retire."

I'm then prodded by Carole, the older lady I'm sharing the bunk room with, who smiles and puts something in my hand. "I thought you'd appreciate these. I snore quite loudly."

They're a set of earplugs!

3

FALLING EAGLES

The greatest reward & luxury of travel is to be able to experience everyday things as if for the first time, to be in a position in which almost nothing is so familiar it is taken for granted.

Bill Bryson

Before the sun has even risen, at 4:30 in the morning to be exact, I'm jarringly woken by cockerels crowing from the fields on one side from me and loud snoring from the other side. I lie there for a moment, re-orientating where I am exactly. It's been a cold night sometime during which I'd grabbed extra blankets from the top bunk. It's no use; I can't sleep. I reach down onto the floor, grabbing the torch, and then back under the blankets with my pad and pen start writing a few notes.

An hour later, with the sun starting to show itself, there's a loud chirping of birds just outside the window, and ten minutes later the horses are neighing, whinnying, and snorting out loudly. Heaven. The sounds of a ranch. I quietly get out of bed and curiously tip-toe to the window. Two men with their cowboy boots, straw hats, big buckled jeans, and ropes in their hands are ambling through the horse corral. The day obviously starts early here. I'm fascinated. Then at 5:50, I hear indistinct voices and cooking pans being shuffled around in the kitchen downstairs below us. The light is now filtering into the room. It's time to get up.

I walk out into the bright light and fresh re-born air of the morning and breathe in deeply, feeling it's a tonic cleansing my body. The sun is starting to curiously peek over the hill onto this place of still tranquillity and silence far from the distant cities. This time of the day is precious. I wander into the kitchen, and Caterina is already there brewing coffee over the wood burning stove. She nods with a smile; I do the same and pour myself a mug and wander back outside.

Before long, the place has become a lot more animated. Raúl and two of the ranch hands are carrying large pieces of firewood and logs to an outside cooking area and pit. A large fire is already being prepared and lit. They walk over and sit down next to me, pouring more coffee from the pot on the table.

"Morning, Zoë. Hope you're rested up. We need this fire to be good and ready. We're preparing something special for everyone tonight. One of our three month old lambs has just been slaughtered, skinned, and gutted this morning and will be cooked over this oak fire. It's gonna take a while to heat up, but when ready, we're gonna spread the carcass over a metal frame to slowly rotate over the fire for at least ten hours. You'll have never eaten anything or smelt anything so good. Muy rica! Our sheep, the ones that come down from the hills every night, are the short coat variety, good and hardy and bred just for their meat. We may see some of them up in the hills this morning."

A couple of the girls are walking towards us from the barn where they've been collecting their paints, brushes, and easels, ready for their morning outing. They sit down, and one of the ranch hands pours the coffee. Before long, everyone has joined us, and a hearty breakfast of freshly squeezed orange juice, oven baked muffins, fresh fruit jams, and huevos rancheros are kindly served up. "Ranchers Eggs" are perfect to start the day and I'm told a popular breakfast on rural farms. The basic dish is composed of fried eggs served upon lightly fried corn tortillas topped with a fresh tomato-chili sauce. Alongside it are refried beans, rice, and avocado slices. I wipe the juices up from the plate with a last piece of crusty bread.

I lean back, and it's then that I hear the clip-clopping of horses' hooves. I turn round and see two lovely bay American Quarter horses being led and tied up underneath one of the oak trees. The hands start tacking them up. Raúl looks over, "I heard you can ride OK, so we've brought in two who should provide a good pace this morning. I've also got these for you!"

He stands up and casually passes over the table, like it's nothing out of the normal, a pair of brown suede chaps. These are the real thing, massively wide and flared to also cover the horse's belly and decorated with silver-studded leather tassels down the sides of each leg.

"We're gonna be riding through rough terrain, so these will protect your legs and your jeans from being ripped."

All the girls start getting up, ready for their painting expedition. Walking away, Carole turns around, "We might see you. We're all going to be down by the river where you should pass before climbing up the hills. See you later."

I attach and tie the chaps around my legs and pull in the belt buckle around my waist. I put on my Stetson and a pair of leather gloves and wander over to the horses. No one is laughing at me for the way I look. I'm probably looking more normal to them now than when I'd first arrived. The horse I'm given roughly rubs my arm, as if to say, "Come on, let's get on with it."

Raúl puts a small bottle of water in the saddle bag thrown over the front of my saddle and asks, "So do you need help with a leg-up or want to use the steps over there to get on?"

I smile, grabbing the reins and mane, putting my left foot in the stirrup, and swinging into the saddle. He nods, also smiling, and walks over to his horse, untying the reins from around the tree. Both mounted, we step out, briskly leaving the ranch behind us and settle into an easy pace across the fields. Two of the dogs have happily followed us and are now running ahead, stopping and sniffing, running, stopping, and sniffing.

"So how does it feel back on a horse? Has it been a while? From what I can see, it's not the first time you've ridden a Quarter Horse Western-style with one hand. We're gonna be out until lunchtime, so hopefully will get to see plenty of stuff. In the afternoon, a few of the girls wanna go out, so you're more than welcome to join us for that ride too."

I smile and at this moment, not wishing to open up a big conversation, just nod and simply reply, "It feels great. Thanks." This horse is so sensitive. I'm just moving my right hand slightly forward with the reins loosely between two fingers, and he's picking up the pace. I swing my hand slightly to the left or right across his neck, and he immediately goes in that direction.

"Yep, that's how they best work with the cattle."

After a while, a large clump of trees in a little dip is seen, and Raúl points in that direction. "The girls are there where the small river is. Let's go and say hello."

Under the shadows of the trees, the eight girls are seated in chairs intently studying and painting the landscape around them. We pull up behind them and watch. Suddenly, Raúl catches my attention and quickly points upwards to the top of a tall tree without saying anything. It's there I see a very large bird's nest with an even larger bird, which immediately takes off and flies away. Everything, there and then, seems to go into overdrive.

Raúl shouts, "Madre mía! Oh my God, look! The Golden Eagle has accidently pushed one of the chicks out of the nest, and it's falling down through the tree!"

Without hesitation, he jumps off his horse, dropping the reins on the ground, and runs with the dogs chasing him to the base of the tree. He shoos the dogs away, knowing it would be their natural instinct to pick up the bird, or worse still, eat it. Everyone is standing up looking over. He walks slowly back to the horses with something now in both his hands. He reaches out for me to take it. I open my hands, and a soft little white bird is placed in them. I close my hands so there's no escape and feel it pecking my palm. Raúl quickly opens my saddle bag, as he'd forgotten his own that morning, takes the bird back, and carefully places it in the bag, closing the flap.

"In all the years I've lived here, I've never seen this before. We're gonna have to ride back to the ranch. The mother can't do anything now, and it would die out here on the ground. It can only be a week or so old. We'll see if we can get some help and advice. I know some guys who look after rescued birds of prey. That's our only hope."

So Raúl and I trot back to the ranch. The tiny white fluffy, yellow-beaked baby eagle is placed in a grass and moss lined cardboard box with a warm sock put closely next to it for, I guess, some kind of comfort, and the holed lid closed.

"I've just spoken with the guys at the sanctuary. They can't come over until late tomorrow or the day after. But they have given me just a bit of advice, particularly on how to feed it, which will probably be every few hours. Bits of raw chicken and water, which I'll need to put into a pipette to squeeze drops down its throat. I hope it works. There's not much more we can do now, so we'd better head out if we wanna make the most of the day."

We've soon cantered back over the fields, jumped over the small river, and climbed sure-footedly up into the open gorse covered barren hills where there's no fencing or boundaries, just open space. We continue at a leisurely walk, riding next to each other and with the dogs now out of sight far in the distance. The conversation now starts to flow more freely.

"So tell me again? Where did you say you'd picked up your Spanish? It's good. Your name too! "Cano"; that's from here!"

This is a loaded question. It's digging up the past, and I don't know how much detail I want to get into. But let's say I'd previously had significant ties with Mexico. My name is Mexican, although my maiden name was Matthews. But today, out here, I feel happy to tell some other parts of my story, which seem like a long time ago.

"Well, to start with, my father spoke some Spanish. He loved to travel and explore, and we were always finding Spanish grammar and story books at home. I then learned the language at school." I take a deep breath and plunge into the next sentence: "But I guess it's because I was once married to a Mexican. A Mexican Charro, to be exact."

I pause for a moment. Raúl's eyebrows rise up, and his eyes open wide for a second take on what he's just heard, not quite believing it.

I continue, "We'd met at an exhibition conference in Fort Lauderdale. He was living in the US, and I was still in

Paris. I was engaged to be married back in France and hadn't even wanted to go. But my French-Lebanese boss was taking holiday at the same time and delegated me to go. You could say I was blindly swept off my feet by this good looking Mexican. A year later, having moved from Paris to New York, where he lived, we got married at an authentic Charro wedding in Cuernavaca where, in those days,they could still carry guns. I remember my father and I arriving at an old white Catholic church in a horse-drawn carriage, escorted and surrounded by armed Charro horsemen. With large sombrero hats hiding their faces, the groom and his father were standing waiting outside the church with guns (loaded I was told) around their waists. I'm not exaggerating. It was then a crazy handful of years living over in the US, then back to Paris, and finally when we'd separated, I returned after a long absence to London.

"I haven't been back to Mexico since that time more than fifteen years ago, and I almost wanted this trip to exorcise my negative thoughts about that time of my life. I knew Baja was very different from the rest of Mexico, which helped, and had a beauty and history all of its own. I'd wanted to come here for a long time."

Raúl also carefully considers his reply. "Here in Baja you have to understand we are Rancheros. We are not Charros. You have to remember we're very different from them with our way of life. We couldn't be further in extremes. We are working cowboys on ranches. That is all we do. We live from the land. Charros, with their wide sombreros, heavily embroidered colourful jackets, and tightly cut trousers, are seen more nowadays as the richer classes and more as a hobby than a job. They ride good but participate at rodeos to show off their riding skills. Most have full time jobs doing other stuff. Yes, it's true. I know. Up until a few decades ago, you're right, Charros could carry guns. So let me tell you. Really everything from culture, etiquette, our mannerisms, clothing, traditions, and social status are very different."

I start to understand and nod my head in appreciation. I feel like a weight has been lifted off my shoulders.

"And you'll see later, we have another cowboy ranchero who's coming over from the village tonight to play the classical guitar. Very different and beautiful music. You will love it."

We continue on following the lines of the hills until we reach the top of one. The dogs join us, panting and flopping down for a rest. The warm breeze is blowing past us, and from this height we can see everything around us. Out into the distance the land flattens out into rich green vineyards or "wine country," which I'll be leaving for tomorrow.

"We are very proud of this land of ours. It is so rich, with so many unique birds and animals. You've already seen Golden Eagles, but there are condors, osprey, cougars, ocelots, prairie dogs, black bears, big horn sheep, jack rabbits, brown horned antelope . . . and lots, lots more . . . and not forgetting all the different sorts of snakes, lizards, and of course, scorpions. Hundreds of different birds live here too. And that's just on the land. And the sea around us; it is amazing! You can see schools of hammerheads, manta rays, or pods of dolphins. We have almost sixty varieties of sharks, and all the grey whales that come to our special isolated bays here to give birth during the migration season. I hope you see some of them on your travels."

We slowly turn around and descend back towards the Canyon. Over a ridge on another hillside we see a beautiful black horse, freely galloping and kicking its heels up. It abruptly stops, sees us, and with a shrill whinny, races off. Our horses prick their ears and look in its direction.

Raúl smiles. "That's our son's horse. He's a vet over the border. It only gets ridden when he's back, which isn't often. But he has said he'd ultimately like to do his job over this side. You see, he's got dual-nationality, with my wife being American, so not a problem. He feels he'd be helping a lot more here with the farmers. He'd certainly be helping his horse!"

He suddenly stops, turns the horse around on a dime, and crazily gallops down a steep ridge onto a small slope. He stands next to a tall green plant with a pyramid of white flowers at the top of it.

He shouts up, "This is also one of our native plants we have here and that you'll see a lot more of the further south you go. It's the foothill yucca. It has lots of other funny names, like the Chaparral Yucca, the Lord's Candle, and even Spanish Bayonet!"

He laughs and kicks his horse and gallops back up the hill. Before long, we're tying the horses up under the shaded oak trees. Approaching the house, I see the lamb is already slowly rotating above the fire, already emanating a wonderful smell. Later this evening it will be perfectly cooked. Walking into the cool kitchen, Raúl reaches up onto a high shelf and carefully brings down a bottle. "Now this is a special tequila. You can drink it on its own; it's that aged, good, and smooth!"

He pours us both a thumb-full into small glasses, and I take a sip. Oh my, that's good. Before long, we're all eating chicken tortillas and talking excitedly about the baby eagle and how it's going to survive. At that moment, Raúl walks back in with small pieces of raw chicken and a surgical pipette he explains he'll fill with water so the bird can be given something to drink. The box is put on the table and opened. We all stare in. Raúl takes a bit of chicken, dangling it in front of the chick's beak. The little bird immediately opens its mouth, grabs, and swallows it. He repeats this four or five times. We feel like clapping. The same is done with the pipette with water drops squeezed out. He closes the box and claps his hands.

"That's a good sign. OK. Let's get out of here for our afternoon ride back out in the hills."

Six of us leave, but the levels of experience are wide, so we're all just happy to leisurely and slowly ride, absorbing the landscapes and magnificent countryside around us.

Later that evening, licking our fingers and lips from the delicious meat feast and sipping cool beers, we return back to the burning fireplace and sit around it. Antonio, the ranchero who'd come over to play the guitar, had joined us for dinner and is now melodically and masterly playing wonderful tunes from past and present.

Once again, there's banter about everything and nothing, but particularly about our little joint adventure today in saving the fallen eagle.

Angela, one of the girls, says, "You know what? It's the first time I've seen an eagle, let alone stroke one!" Most of the other girls nod in agreement.

Caroline, who's sitting on the bench next to me, asks, "So, how about you, Zoë. Ever seen or touched another Golden Eagle?"

It's the second time in one day that my past jumps to the present. But this time I smile in fond memory. I can't help but laugh. "Well actually, yes!"

They all lean forward in curious anticipation, with one shouting out, "Come on, tell us the crazy story."

"Well, this is my other story," looking at Raúl, knowing he'd heard the first one of my connection with Mexico. "It was during my first job ever, working for a film rights company in Paris. Anne-Marie, my boss, had asked me to join her and go to the Cannes Film Festival to help show films we were distributing to overseas markets. One evening, a group of us from the film world were eating on one of the terraces along the seafront. I was young and naïve. It was the first time I felt I was with such important people. I even politely watched the etiquette to see how people ate their food. I will always remember we were served asparagus. I'd never eaten it before but quickly saw the French way. Picking the long stems up with my fingers, dipping the ends into the hollandaise sauce, and sexily raising it above my head and letting it drop into my mouth like everybody else was doing.

"At the end of the evening, Carlos Amador, a then well-known Mexican film producer, approaches me. He thanks me for the great work I'd done at the Festival and discreetly puts something into my hand, as if he didn't want anyone else to see his action. I'm intrigued but embarrassed that I'd been given unnecessary attention. I open my hand under the table and stare at a large Mexican gold fifty-peso coin, which even I knew must be worth a lot.

"On one side was the iconic Winged Victory—"The Angel of Independence"—with the years 1821-1947 and 37.5 Gr. Oro Puro stamped on it. So it's also an old coin. But what fascinates me is on the reverse side—Mexico's national coat of arms, featuring a golden eagle perched on a cactus with a snake in its beak. These pieces were in tribute to Mexico's year of independence from Spain in 1821. I trace my finger over the embossed eagle absorbing what I've been given. At that time it was probably worth a good few weeks salary. But I was starting to worry and imagining I was going to be bribed into doing something if I kept the secret. There's no other option. I have to come clean. With honesty, I tell Anne-Marie what I'd just been given, and to my surprise, with her typical French flair, she smiles and simply says, 'Make sure you keep it safe for a rainy day.'

"Over the years, I had kept it safe and always knew I had something to lean on in hard times. It reassured me. And that I did until I met my Charro boyfriend. He invited me to Mexico to visit his family, but I had no money, still earning very little in Paris. The only thing I had of any value was the gold coin. I offered to give him the fifty-peso coin to help towards the flight. I thought it had slipped through my fingers forever, but when we went our own ways, I bizarrely found it once again in an old box. I still have it, and I still feel the golden eagle will come to my rescue again if I need help."

There's a little gasp and a few sighs. Raúl prods the embers. Then the beautiful sound of the guitar begins again, drifting up into the night sky.

4

VALLE DE GUADALUPE

A person with increasing knowledge and sensory education may derive infinite enjoyment from wine.
Ernest Hemingway

Sitting quietly, looking at the mountains around me, with the sun just peeking out and touching their ridges, I'm in deep contemplation. My packed bags are by my side with one of the dogs lying next to them.

"Hey, what you thinking? You look a bit worried."

I'm jolted from my thoughts and look around. Raúl has two mugs of coffee.

"Just made them. You want one?"

I smile and take a mug from his hand. "For sure. Thanks. To be totally honest with you, I'm leaving here later I know, but I've got a bit of an issue I need to sort."

"I'm all ears. What is it?" And he sits down opposite.

"Well, coming in through Tecate they just waved me on, didn't stamp my passport, and I wasn't able to get that extended visa. I'm a bit worried that in a few days, travelling further into the country, I'll be illegal. The only thing I can think of doing is heading back to Tecate this morning to get the visa done, but that's extra time and mileage going the wrong way, which I could do without."

Raúl leans down to stroke one of the dogs lying by his chair. He scratches his own head like he's thinking of a plan. "Well, there is an option. And it's probably a better one. It's not just through the border towns you can get your passport stamped but also at the ports. Freight ships, boats, and yachts are always sailing in. I've gotta drive down to Ensenada this morning. I've promised to get some good bottles of tequila for the girls to take home with them when they leave after lunch.

Ensenada is a big port town. In fact, our daughter works with the cruise ships down there. You can come with me, and I'll take you to the immigration offices at the port and get it sorted there. Plus, it's a Sunday, so there shouldn't be too many people. Hopefully, we'll get it processed pretty quickly. You will also get to see my tequila shop, the best one anywhere! Then we'll drive back, and I can take you to your truck in the field. I reckon we'll have it all done by late morning. It's only about thirty-five miles each way."

I grin. Having a local person take me to the port, knowing exactly where to go, and potentially helping with any bureaucratic problems that may arise sounds pretty perfect. This is better than I could have imagined.

"Wow! That's something I didn't know or at least thought couldn't be done. I imagined it would have just been for people arriving there."

"No, no, no! The Port Authority deals with anyone coming from anywhere."

So after some fresh papaya and muffins, and saying goodbye to everyone, we jump into the truck and head south along Route 3.

The landscape weaves around twisty bends through arid hills until we get into a flatter, wider valley. As we continue, the fields appear increasingly more fertile. We pass the small village of Guadalupe.

"So where are you staying exactly tonight? Because this is the wine growing area, and it should be near this place."

"It's called 'Terra del Valle.' It's supposed to be a little bed and breakfast in the middle of the vineyards. I don't really have a full address." I pull out my notebook "It says, 'Ejido El Porvenir,' but I don't have much more."

"Well, we could take a little detour through the town and see if there's a turning or a sign. There are hundreds of vineyards here and all up small tracks. If we find something, at least you're then on the right route when you head back here on your own."

He quickly does a U-turn, and we slowly drive through this quiet little town. I immediately see picture road signs of grapes; bottles; glasses, knives, and forks; horses; bicycles; and hotels. A large "Valle de Guadalupe" sign is next to them.

All of a sudden there are signs everywhere up little narrow tracks to different vineyards. Approaching a crossroads, we see the possible direction on the right.

"I think it's here you'll need to turn. Make a note of what the house here with its green wall and palms trees looks like, so you won't forget where to turn."

I'm more grateful than he realizes. We turn back and continue south towards the coast. Before long, the area starts to become more and more built-up, with basic white-walled homes extending up the hillsides and along the road. We've reached the attractive town of Ensenada, just 100 km south of Tijuana and perched on the edge of the Bahía de Todos Santos. But I'm seeing no signs for the port. All of a sudden, Raúl indicates right and swerves down a small road, turns a corner, and drives alongside shipyards and stacks of containers. With no visible signs, I just wouldn't have known where we had to turn.

The truck stops outside a military looking building, which is the Centro Integral de Servicios. Again, I'd have had no idea this was the right place. We walk through mesh security gates, and up the pathway are five different signs—"Harbor Master," "Customs," "Bank," "Fishing Office," and "Immigration." No one else is here. There are no queues. We walk into an empty room with rows of chairs and three glass windowed counter offices around it.

Raúl points to the window at the far end: "Instituto Nacional de Migración. That's for the visas. They probably don't speak English, so just show your passport and ticket."

I walk over and notice a little bespectacled man obscurely seated behind a counter. He looks up from his newspaper. I smile politely, simply saying, "Estoy aquí veintiuno días."

He slides back a piece of paper to complete, and within ten minutes I have a 180-day tourist visa in exchange for 380 pesos.

Raúl smiles and puts his thumb up. "Bueno. I'm glad that worked out! Now let's go and see my friends at the tequila shop."

We head into town, driving along the main palm-lined ocean-front avenue and, before long, are parked up in a large retail area.

"Don't worry. We're not here for long. I just need to pick up my box of tequila."

I follow inside, passing a ten foot high bottle of tequila next to the front door. Good signage! Raúl walks directly to the counter and starts chatting with the shopkeeper, who lifts up a box from under the counter. But my mouth opens in disbelief. This shop really does just sell tequila, and there must be thousands upon thousands of different bottles of different shapes, sizes, varieties, colours, and costs. There are glass bottles in the shapes of skulls, life size rifles, and hand guns. I can't resist picking up the glass tequila gun and taking a shot at the guys at the counter. They laugh.

I continue curiously walking around the aisles mesmerized but feeling that since the weekend I might know just a bit more about tequila than when I'd arrived. I notice the *100% Agave* words and the rich oak colour of some of the bottles and see, without surprise, these are the most expensive. So we had, indeed, drank some of the best.

Raúl carries the box back to the truck, and we head back to the ranch. Finally turning off and back up the muddy hill, he stops by the field's gate where my truck's parked.

"Bueno, here we are. You drive safe now out on those roads on your own. Be careful and don't stop if you're flagged down by people who aren't officials. But really, you should be fine. Enjoy this wonderful place of ours."

I jump out, place my bags on the back seat, and carefully drive through the gate that Raúl is keeping open for me. I wave goodbye. What wonderful, kind, and hospitable people—a truly incredible, lucky, and unique introduction to Baja.

I'm now on my own again but feel good with less than twenty miles to drive and with the knowledge of which small road I need to turn off into to find the place I'm staying at tonight.

It's bizarre to be confidently re-tracing the route already taken earlier, in a region I'd never been to before. I easily reach the house with the green walls and turn right up a dusty, bumpy trail. Soon, I look around me and start seeing vast expanses of rich, green vineyards, as well as olive, orange, and grapefruit groves coming right up to the track. I'm really curious to visit at least one of these places and taste their wines.

I notice a small sign to turn left, which reassures me I'm headed in the right direction. A little further on, an impressive mud-walled, gated entrance with cacti on either side of it confirms I've reached my destination. With the windows open, I smell the land and the oranges and stretch my arm out to feel the warmth of the day. I drive up the stony track and arrive at a modest white-washed, one-storey house in the middle of all these vineyards. I walk up the cactus and palm lined pathway, where a man approaches me and holds out his hand to greet me.

"Hola. Welcome. You must be Señorita Cano. We only have you and one other room booked tonight."

He kindly takes my bags and leads me into a beautiful high-ceilinged room with mosquito nets hanging over the bed and a compulsory ceiling fan turning slowly round. Out at the back, through the bathroom door, is a shaded sandy area with a hammock. That'll be a nice place to have a little siesta later on.

He continues, "It might get a bit colder out later, so there are blankets in that cupboard, but it should be warm inside. Our house is constructed with straw bales between the plaster and bricks. They work as natural insulation, keeping the place warm, so we save energy naturally. There are bicycles outside if you want to explore a bit. And the Barón Balché Vineyard next to us is open late tonight, if you want to eat there. You can walk across our courtyard, crawl under the fence at the back, and walk across their vineyards to the farmhouse. Their food is delicioso! I can make a booking for you if you like. Does seven sound OK?"

I smile, thanking him, and close the door. I walk to the hammock outside and flop into it. It's perfect timing, just before midday. This whole area seems like a chilled, laidback place. With the blue sky above me, I push the hammock with my foot and lie back, looking at the vineyards in front of me. Out into the horizon farms, rock-strewn hills, and mountains go as far as the eye can see.

I sigh happily. I'm here in the Valle de Guadalupe, wine country, Mexico's most important wine producing region. This is a place I'd heard was buzzing, with some calling it the "new Napa Valley." There are restaurants here with international acclaim, stylish boutique hotels, and sprawling wineries, most with panoramic views. Just two decades ago you could count the wineries on both hands. Now there are more than 100 in this quiet, fourteen mile span of the valley, where most are hidden up similar dust tracks to where I am. It doesn't feel commercial or touristy here, but this is where at least seventy per cent of Mexico's wine comes from.

But this northern end of the Baja California peninsula is, in fact, one of the New World's oldest wine growing areas. Jesuit priests cultivated vines here in the eighteenth century, and the first commercial winery, Bodegas de Santo Tomás, opened in 1888.

But Mexico's wine reputation has been downplayed, given its history. Even earlier, in 1699, Spain banned Mexico from producing wine, because it simply posed a competitive threat to their own. Its dry, hot summers and cooler, damper winters, combined with porous soil and sea breezes, are the ideal combination for successful grape growing.

I swing back in the hammock and lazily look at the time. Time to eat . . . and drink! Reading up a bit on the place, I was keen to experience one of these eclectic, stylish wineries for myself. One was literally on my doorstep, just a few minutes from here, and was supposed to be one of the most exciting new additions to the valley, having just opened the year before in 2015.

I put some lippy on and drive up the hillside and through some big gates. An amazing glass and metal-framed, almost Guggenheim-style, structure is perched on the side of the hillside. This literally does look cutting edge. This is Decantos Winery. A terrace high up on the first floor surrounds it, and I can already see people eating and savouring the wines.

I walk up the large metal staircase and into a massive, contemporary area full of chatting, animated people. Rows and rows of wine bottles are stacked on shelves, and there are fridges behind and below the long glass bar, which is almost the entire length of this enormous space. Rows of large wooden barrels containing wines of different grape varieties and production years are being used to fill glasses of those just wine tasting. It's all very theatrical.

A waiter smiles and leads me to the outside terrace, where he shows me a table overlooking their valley filled with vines and the mountains reaching far out into the distance. I look around. There don't seem to be any tourists here in the traditional sense of the word, coming in large buses or clicking away with cameras or speaking foreign voices. Everyone seems to be Mexican. Although some of them may have come from afar, it looks mainly like families just coming out for a Sunday lunch. But I'm also feeling this place is more for the wealthier set based on the small things I notice. Kids are running around on the grass covered terrace below with iPhone selfie sticks. That already surprises me. Some men are asking their bejewelled women to pose in front of the valley views, so souvenir pictures can be taken. Everybody seems to be dressed in a very smart, casual way, like this is the place to be seen.

I browse the menu and, for the first time, see it's in US dollars. I order my first glass of wine, an incredibly robust and strong 2015 Chardonnay. The 60 pesos, or about £2.50, seems a lot compared to what I paid for an entire lunch at Tecate a few days ago, but this is in a league of its own. But like anything when travelling, it all needs to be averaged out. I look out at the captivating view with the wine in my hand and also feel special, absorbing the moment. The waiter returns with a tropical ceviche—a beautiful bowl of fresh fish with fruit, avocado, and cucumber, marinated in lemon and coconut cream and of course, even here, served with the obligatory tacos. Delicious, but $10! After a second (or was that a third?) delicious glass of wine, I'm very happy in more ways than one!

I walk back to my wheels and drive slowly and carefully down the bumpy track to Terra de Valle. I park up. There's still no one here. I let out a little giggle, probably due to the drink, and think it'll be a bit of fun to grab one of the bicycles stacked up under a tree to take a ride around. I set off, wobbling a bit, and soon notice there's only one gear. With a small incline to the track, after a couple of hundred yards, I'm exhausted and decide a siesta would be better exercise.

The hammock and late afternoon warm sunshine beckons. I reach down for the map and look at the route I've given myself to do the next day. Because of this, it's not going to be a late night. This will be one of the longest journeys I'm planning throughout the whole trip. I've got to get down to the border town of Guerrero Negro, between the northern and southern Baja California states. Tomorrow will also be the start of the Transpeninsular Highway route, which will take me through isolated deserts with nothing for miles around. I've calculated about 400 miles, so it's going to be an early start to make the most of the day and give me extra time for any potential mishaps.

Just before seven, the sun has set and it's getting dark, but I've managed to crawl under the fence and find myself walking over the rich soil of the Balché vineyards, with palm trees and flowering cacti plants dotted along the pathway. Large hand-painted signs are at the end of each row indicating the variety of grapes. I notice more than one I'd like to try.

Under a covered courtyard, I'm treated to sumptuous valley food this whole area is becoming ever more famous for. Baja chefs are also, without any doubt, doing their part to help forge the way for the Mexican wine world, cooking a style they call "Baja Med' for its heavy emphasis on fresh seafood coming from the nearby Pacific Ocean and Sea of Cortes.

Blackened, sweet octopus with mango salsa arrives and then mouth-watering lamb with fresh baby vegetables. At the end of the meal, the chef walks over, also with a glass of wine in his hand. I thank him for a wonderful meal and sipping my Merlot, he sits down.

"I'm glad you enjoyed our food. Mexico gets this reputation for being the Wild West. Tequila and mezcal are more synonymous with it, but we're all winning awards here, and the wineries can't keep up with the demand. The food goes hand in hand with the wine. There's such a richness here. I go hunting myself for the oysters, octopus, duck, and lamb!"

I nod sleepily, simply adding, "Claro." Of course, I'm not surprised; that's only normal here. I walk back under the clear dark sky, and through the vineyards hear music being played floating out into the night. This valley is still luckily a well-kept and very unspoilt secret to so many people.

5

DESERT MIRAGES

Not all those who wander are lost.

J. R. R. Tolkien

The morning ritual had started again. I lug the bags back to the four wheels and wander back up the pathway and into the kitchen to grab a cup of coffee. Nacho, who'd welcomed me yesterday, was already busy chopping up vegetables.

"Good morning, Señora Cano. How was your stay with us?"

I smile, thinking this time yesterday I was still in the lost canyon with the ranchers.

"It's been very interesting visiting this beautiful valley. The dinner at the winery last night, as you had said, was excellent. But it's a good thing I took my torch to find my way back through the vineyards in the dark!"

He leaves his vegetables and pours a mug of coffee for me, pushing a basket of bread and homemade jams my way.

"So, where are you going today? It's still early—only about 6:30."

I look down at my watch and nod. "Yes, but I have a long way to go. I'm hoping to get to Guerrero Negro by evening."

He looks impressed and curiously comes to sit down, obviously wanting to open the conversation.

"And have you ever been down that far before? Take lots of water and make sure the vehicle is always filled up. There are areas through the Parque Nacional del Desierto Central that will go on for a couple of hundred miles with nothing—just desert and cactus."

He pauses, "But be very careful! The highway is very narrow in many places, sometimes hardly wide enough for two trucks to pass even if they pull way over, slow down, and bring in their side mirrors. There are many blind corners with no safety barriers, and some vehicles drive very fast. Locos! So many accidents. Look out for long, giant freight trucks coming from the opposite direction. They will not stop."

Wow! I wasn't expecting that as an opener. I gulp the coffee down.

He smiles reassuringly, "But it's better now. The busy season has just finished, so there should be a lot fewer tourists with their massive RVs and all those cars. But this highway, Baja's Main Street, is a lifeline for us. Our trucks and buses must travel the road by day and night to take provisions and people to the villages and towns alongside it."

He gets up and goes to the counter. He generously fills a plastic shopping bag with oranges and grapefruit.

"Here. Take this for your trip. They're from my orchard."

I thank him for his spontaneous generosity and, saying goodbye, shake his hand with gratitude. Another kind person.

There's not a cloud in the sky as I bump along the muddy track back onto Route 3 south to Ensenada, where east of the city I'll finally get onto Route 1, otherwise known as the Transpeninsular Highway. But there's one last thing I want to do before navigating through that city and joining the highway. I remember Raúl telling us back at the ranch the story of the margarita cocktail and where the name came from. The famous bar, where supposedly it originated from, is on the seafront on my way through, so I'm going to make a pit stop and go and find it.

By 7:30, I'm parked up along the beach opposite a majestic white building—the Riviera Cultural Centre. I walk across the road to absorb its beauty, which looks like a mix of Spanish and Moorish-style architecture. But in another era it was a hotel, which at the time, dwarfed all other buildings in the picturesque fishing village. Back in 1930 it was Hotel Playa Ensenada, an elegant hotel and casino said to rival Monte Carlo. The Hollywood and international set were understandably attracted to it, and the opening act was apparently Bing Crosby! During the early 1930s it flourished, but when the US prohibition ended in 1933, American fun-seekers no longer needed to leave home and the hotel started to decline. But the nail in the coffin was when Mexico outlawed casino gambling in 1938, and the place had to close down. A few years later, in 1942, the hotel was re-opened as Riviera de Pacifico with Margarita Plant as one of the owners.

I walk through into the quiet bougainvillea lined and terra cotta tiled courtyard and find the famous Bar Andaluz. Raúl had told us that one evening Margarita was sitting at the bar and asked the bartender to prepare a drink based on tequila but to make it longer and more refreshing. So he mixed ice, limes, and Cointreau to the tequila and named it after her. Or that's how the story goes. This early in the day, the bar is closed, which is probably just as well, but I'm glad to see a small part of history has been saved!

Shortly, just around the corner and close to the tequila shop, I'm filling the truck to capacity. Another 15 litres for 203 pesos, or 13 pesos a litre. Sounds good to me! As advised, I also stock up on water and buy six one-litre bottles of water. I exit onto a busy road and immediately see signs for Highway 1 and soon merge into it. In my calculations this is a road I won't be leaving for quite a while today or even get very far from during the entire trip.

It has to be noted, though, at this stage in the journey, that due to the disappointment of not getting a motorcycle, I'm naively adamant to keep the window down and not put any AC on in order to at least get some natural air and feel and smell what's "outside" out on the road. So far it's been fine. I just smile that I'll probably have a very brown left arm!

I look down at the map on the seat next to me, registering that it's now straight all the way along the coast for about 150 miles until Rosario, where the road will start to head inland. But for the moment, I'm still in a congested suburban sprawl where cars are spontaneously crossing over the entire highway without signalling, buses stopping abruptly, and lots of erratic traffic lights. I need to keep my wits about me because it's probably in these bigger built-up areas where accidents are more likely to happen.

Reaching the next town of Rodolfo Sánchez Taboada, I start seeing ranges of mountains in front of me with spectacular dust rising out in the distance. The road has also narrowed to just two lanes, and on either side are parallel mud tracks with small, colourful shops and eateries with trucks parked up outside them. I notice a red, white, and blue barber's rotating pole along the roadside—a sign understood anywhere in the world.

As soon as I've passed through the small town, the road suddenly and unexpectedly quietens, and the traffic has almost disappeared. It's at this point that I realize most people probably don't have any reason to go any further, as there's now not a lot out here. I pass green, scrubby farmlands with fencing still separating the land from the road. It smoothly sweeps around wide corners with layers of hills and mountains sweeping the horizons. There is now virtually no traffic.

I grab one of the bottles, which has rolled close to my feet, and take a swig, resting my arm on the window, feeling the warm early morning breeze. This feels good. The road just continues smoothly along, sometimes taking in glimpses of wide blue ocean vistas.

About three hours into the journey, I'm approaching San Quentin but having only done about 120 miles. I haven't really got time to stop for long, except for filling up. But this is the "Clam Capital" of Baja, harvesting millions every year, which mostly end up north of the border. So on my way through I do try and see if there are any roadside vendors open to sample these delicious molluscs but, unfortunately, to no avail.

I continue out on the highway, absorbing every mile that goes under the wheels. Before long, the rough agricultural farmlands have been replaced by the first sighting of sandy, desert landscapes, but with the coastline still hugging tightly with views far out to sea. I stop on the side of the road to drink in the moment. I walk into the middle of the empty, straight road and look back along the solid yellow line that disappears out into the distance. I turn around in the opposite direction and see the same mirror image. This isn't what I'd call real desert but sandy, gorsy slopes and dunes that seem to go and slide down to the sea. It's all arid, dry, and hot. An old knobbly truck tyre has been thrown into this sandy barren landscape looking like, from the distance, a solitary sea turtle trying to escape back to the sea.

After just a few miles the landscape starts to once again vividly change. Massive clumps of yellow flowering cacti and other cacti of all shapes and sizes start to cover the roadsides and the surrounding hills around me. I'm feeling like this is a teaser for what I'm very soon going to see when I enter the protected desert after heading east from El Rosario.

Forty miles from "Clam Capital," I drop down a winding road that separates El Rosario from the Pacific. The frenzy of the busy towns I've driven through now seems to have disappeared. This is where many people, I've been told, feel that the real Baja begins. But it's just before I arrive that I come across the first army inspection checkpoint. An armed soldier waves me down to stop and tells me to get out. I show my passport, waiting for him to ask me to also empty out all my bags. But after just peering inside the car, he salutes and waves me on. But I know this won't be the last time.

There's a small bend in the road, and a small, dusty settlement appears, where it just looks like there are a few stores, modest hotels, bakeries, and places to eat. The next town of any significance, Guerrero Negro, is where I'm headed for tonight and is still another 220 miles away. Between here and there it's just desert. So it's here I'll need to again fill up and grab some food rations and water. I drive into the Pemex station at the town's entrance. Now I need to get a bite to eat. The choice is an easy one. Just down from the station is a little red brick building. Since 1930, even before the highway was built, travellers have been welcomed to Mama Espinoza's Place, where lobster burritos are one of the specialties.

Parking up just outside, I walk inside an eclectically decorated room full of old photos, maps, an old deer's head, and signed posters of famous off-roaders who've raced in the area. Crepe paper piñatas hang across the room from the ceiling. It feels like a quiet, simple travellers' rest spot. A couple are looking over a map at a table in the corner, and an American girl is chatting on a phone with a rucksack next to her. I take a seat opposite the bar and order prawn burritos served with rice and frijoles (beans)—simple but delicious. A painting of an old lady, Anita "Mama' Espinoza, who has become a legend among Baja travellers due to her hospitality and command of English, is hung behind the counter.

There's still more than halfway to go, so I'd better get going. I want to try and avoid driving in the dark. The road will now turn sharply inland and down into the very centre of the peninsula, cutting through the desert. I'd been warned that it's barren and godforsaken in its remoteness. Thank God I've sorted the emergency rescue and pick up service, but that's if I can even get phone reception out there.

I wind the window down again and, with the same hand, then touch my head that all will be alright and I won't break down or have an accident. The narrow asphalt road meanders around hills, then the land seems to start opening up a bit with ever wider vistas. Giant, tall cardon cactuses, like the ones you see in cartoons with the spiky multiple arms, start appearing on the dry rocky hillsides like military sentinels looking out to the horizon.

Carefully steering round yet another bend, I'm conscious of what I'd been warned about in the morning and hear those echoes in my head: "There may be no traffic but be careful and slow down! Anything could be round those corners!" And it's there, up a slight incline, that I see something with shock. A car has turned upside down on one lane, with a school bus next to it! I immediately slow down, seeing people standing by the roadside. They wave their hands up and down for me to slow down, look behind for no oncoming traffic, and then signal, waving me past. My heart has lost a beat or two. I thanked God I'd been careful going round that blind bend. Although not on two wheels, I already felt fully engaged with and even now vulnerable to these surroundings.

With the heat, monotony, isolation, and the long, long straight road that seems to go on forever, I feel slightly dazed that I'm starting to see mirages of those enormous giant cactuses maybe moving along the waves and sea of shimmering sand. Are they swaying? Are there masts of big ships out on that horizon? I shudder. Is that part of the same mirage that my father saw when he was in his own desert so many years ago during the war in Egypt? I shake myself out of this trance and notice that my foot has gone down, and I'm exceeding 90 mph! With the heat, this is dangerous. It's no good. I might have even drowsed. Maybe I was stupid not to shut the window and put the freezing AC on. I need to stop on the side of the road for a while, drink a lot of water, and stretch my legs. I'm thinking about my dad, about what he would have done. It was now I wanted to read one of those envelopes I'd brought with me from London. I think it would help me do this trip, become a stronger, braver person faced with the unknown, and draw inspiration from someone else who understood. It was a story my father had written just before he'd passed away, more than ten years ago. I'd asked him to write a little about his experience and memories in the North African desert all those years ago, which he'd rarely spoken about, and which I knew would soon be lost.

Parked on the side of the road, I sit back in the car with the door open and pull the envelope from out of my bag. I unfold the pages and am transported back into time . . .

> *At the instigation of my father, commissioned during the First World War and subsequently also in the Second, on January 15th 1935 I went down to Halton in Buckinghamshire to enlist in the RAF as an engineering apprentice, having previously passed the entrance exam from Bedford Modern School.*
>
> *I was 16 and the terms of engagement were three years apprenticeship, followed by 12 years in the Regular Air Force. Once there, there was no turning back. And boys were soon treated as men with sound discipline both at school (camp) and on the parade ground. Strangely we did not object to this new regime.*

We were given food and accommodation and 3/- (15p) a week for the first 2 years with plenty of sport. The third year pay was increased to 5/-. Remember, a similar amount was retained, so that each boy had the necessary for his fare home at leave time (Xmas, Easter and Summer). Boys whose home was in Scotland could afford the fare only once a year.

As soon as possible during the first year, each boy was taken up in an aeroplane to gain air experience, or to let him know he was now in the Air Force! Some reacted adversely, most enjoyed it; they were all open cockpit aircraft, goggles and heavy flying jackets of course. Being re-equipped with Bristol Blenheim twin engine bombers.

There were 400 boys in my Entry and subsequent entries of which there were two a year increased to around 1200 an intake. This was the time of the so called Expansion. My father knew like so many others war was imminent, and on September 3rd 1939 it was declared by Neville Chamberlain.

It was a Sunday morning when the sirens first sounded and our first action was to put on gas masks. Everyone was convinced the first assault would be GAS.

My apprenticeship eventually concluded. I was posted to my first Squadron 108 Bomber, equipped with Hawker Hind biplanes. This was the real Air Force! This was January 1938.

I stayed with 108 at Cranfield in Bedfordshire for about 6 months, when we moved to RAF Bassingbourn near Cambridge (my home was nearby).

By this time I had my first car—a 1929 Morris Minor fabric saloon for which I paid 9 guineas. Asking price *was 12 gns but I had a coupon from the Sunday Express for 3gns.*

My father took me to London where I collected the car from Raymond Way garage. It broke down before we got to Cambridge! But gave good service afterwards until war put paid to all motoring. I think I sold it for four pounds!

My next move was to 229 Squadron at Digby near Lincoln where we gave up the Blenheim for Hawker Hurricane fighters. This was January 1940, and the beginning of the most dreadful Winter. We had to go out at dawn to sweep the snow off the airfield aircraft in readiness for take-off.

Shortly 229 Sqdn moved to Wittering near Stamford. Henry Broadhurst (later Air Chief Marshall) was our CO then a F/LT then Sqdn Leader. The Battle of Britain was just beginning and again we moved down to the London area to Northolt, where we soon came under German bombing raids by day and by night. But that makes another story.

When the raids on London subsided, the Hun turned his attention to Merseyside. We made an overnight move to Liverpool to billet ourselves at Speke airfield. I will never forget the scene that greeted us as we got off the train. The whole of Liverpool town and docks were ablaze from end to end. I have to say the local people unlike the Londoners were ready to give in. Our stay in Speke only lasted two or three weeks (I can't remember exactly). One of our Sqdn pilots Sgt Arbuthnot, returning to Speke, sadly landed in the Mersey and did not survive.

As I remember there were several raids on Liverpool

during our stay, but I recall nothing of note, apart from the previous paragraph. On May 21st 1941, we embarked on the Christian Huygens troopship (a converted Dutch liner) en-route for we knew not where.

End of Part One

From Liverpool and the Clyde

The first three days at sea were rough, so much so, that almost every soul on board was horribly sea sick. My most worldly friend from Hereford will confirm this in colourful language. It was the first time in his life he'd been away from home! He would not see England again for four years.

We joined a convoy of about 25 or 30 ships in the Clyde and set a course across the North Atlantic—it was very rough! The German battleship Bismarck was hunting in this area and the aircraft carrier Hood was one of the first casualties. Each morning when we went on deck gaps in the convoy would indicate those unfortunate enough to have been picked off during the night. However we survived and one morning after some two or three weeks West Africa appeared off our starboard bow and we pulled into Freetown. Misfortune was ours the first night—a French destroyer rammed our ship whilst we were anchored puncturing a large hole in the bow on the water line.

Repairs by the Navy filling the hole with concrete took 3 weeks. On board ship on the Equator is not exactly summer holiday cruising! Eventually we departed Freetown, sailing down the West Coast of Africa till we docked at Durban. What a delight. No black out, a couple of trips ashore to be given hospitality by the white South Africans and a marvellous climate.

SUMMER CRUISE!
SELF ON TROOPSHIP TO EGYPT. 1941

Our delight was short lived. Our ship (the C.H) went on to India and Singapore where the majority were eventually interned as P.O.W.s by the Japanese.

Part of our ship's complement were embarked on the Aronda, a coal burning pre-war ship crewed by Lascars en-route for Aden where we dropped anchor for about 9 days. Coaling this boat by scores of natives had to be seen to be believed.

Finally refuelled, we left for Suez and there stepped ashore for the last time for 4 years!

Part Two

During the voyage to the Middle East we had had some opportunity to get acclimatised to the tropical sun. However the dry and dusty conditions in Egypt, and temperature, produced an almost insatiable thirst. Water was reasonably available for tea and washing.

Before long we left this first landfall and set up camp near Alexandria, this provided some fairly civilised excursions from camp. Alexandria is quite a nice town (seaside port) where the Navy had set up enormous defence guns, which when fired during air raids, could be heard for miles.

Our Squadron was now fully equipped with Hurricanes as a mobile self-contained unit, transport, cooks, the lot. Soon we set off with all our vehicles and paraphernalia Westwards to Libya and into Tripolitania and the Western Desert.

We soon formed little groups to share tents which remained until our departure from the Desert. Dust storms became a regular feature which could last as much as 3 days when to venture far from the tent made a return a dubious matter, visibility being virtually nil.

Our first camp in the W.D. was Sidi Haneish quite near to the sea and the bathing was good. From there we progressed across to Msas and Antelat. Our arrival in Libya at the latter was greeted by an attack by ME109s in which our W/Cdr Charles was shot down. As far as I know no other casualties.

After this raid our advance into Libya was halted; and we started the retreat eastwards back until we reached Gazala a forward landing ground a short distance from Benghazi. A couple of raids here hastened our departure once more. We firstly destroyed unflyable aircraft. I remember taking a saw and removing about 3ft from the airscrew blades of one Hurricane of ours to get it back to base!—greatly over revving, that pilot should have had a decoration but to the best of my knowledge never did. At this point we were about 1000 miles from the Suez Canal Zone, our final destination. Our landing ground and camp was established at Gianaclis some 20 or 30 miles from Ismalia, where we set up a Training Flight for foreign and British pilots.

The next two and a half years were relatively uneventful campaign wise, the Middle East conflict having moved on into Italy with its surrender.

The campaign in Europe began in earnest, of which I took no part, still being stationed in Egypt. Four years to the day from our departure for the Middle East we docked back in Liverpool, to take up duty in the peace time RAF.

FINIS

From a point of interest, the food we lived on was normal camp rations sufficient to appease hunger, and I think mostly canned.

When we got into the campaign area in the desert, food became a means of staying alive. Again tinned, 90% bully beef, mixed with crushed iron ration biscuits, to form a stew. Some vegetables, no fruit. Very occasionally wandering nomad Arabs would appear with a handful of eggs, this was indeed a treat!"

An Abridged Synopsis of My Life in the Royal Air Force 1935-1945, by William Alan Matthews

I sigh but also smile with total pride, but a little tear goes down my cheek. That truly was another time, a time when people were really brave but maybe still too hurt from the experiences, or maybe just proud, stoic, and humble to reveal and open up their stories to even their closest ones. He was only a boy and only twenty-one when he left England for another world. There were no immediate information channels to provide news from afar, only hand-written letters, and God forbid, none of the current phenomena of social media. Now stories, however important, only last seconds until the next news feed. Back then, most things were just kept quietly in people's memories. I put it back in my bag and start the engine. I'm off but will be careful.

Trucks have started appearing, which I'm starting to overtake, but I'm seeing more and more crosses set into the dry ground on the sides of these desert roads—more accidents, more unnecessary deaths.

After about another eighty miles on this remote road, that is forever long and straight, the cactuses have all but disappeared, with sand now smothering the increasingly flat land. Guerrero Negro is almost within spitting distance. But a few miles before I reach the border town, I'm once again signalled to stop at another military checkpoint. This time, two armed soldiers silently point to the boot with their rifles and ask I take my bags out. Oh God, I hope it's all OK, knowing it is, but still feeling guilty, or is it the nightmare that "someone" could have planted something in them?! I open the suitcase, bringing out flip flops, bras, and jeans. They nod. All seems to be in order. I quickly stuff everything back in again and make my way to where I'm staying, next to their military barracks, on the border line just before entering Guerrero Negro.

With the little I'd read, it kept reiterating that there just wasn't much here for the visitor. It is an isolated, dispiriting place, surrounded by vast saltpans and drab storage warehouses and is a place to probably just fill the tank and drive through. But that is like putting a "red rag to a bull" and makes me even more curious to find something interesting or slightly quirky here. Unfortunately, I'm not here from January to March, when it becomes home to one of Mexico's most extraordinary phenomenon—the congregation of masses of grey whales that come from the Artic to give birth to their calves in the lagoons of these warmer waters. That's really the only time people would come to stay. So let's see what else there is.

Approaching the army base, with its tall walls and turrets, I already notice three interesting things. Firstly, signs showed we had reached the border. We were now exactly on the 28th parallel line, which meant the border line between the two Baja States; Baja California (Norte) and Baja California Sur. So the clocks go forward an hour from Mountain to Pacific Time, which means losing an hour. Then I have to take a second look, as on this line is a gigantic contemporary steel 140-foot tall eagle monument sitting within the barracks. And without exaggerating, next to it the largest flag I've probably ever seen in my life. The flag of Mexico is flying high above the eagle, which in this barren, isolated place seems to make even more of an impact.

Directly opposite is a large concrete whale perched on a plinth in front of the Halfway Inn. Very convenient. I've arrived. But it's the style and look of the place which impresses but also surprises me. It bizarrely seems to be completely out of context in this austere isolated place. It could quite easily be lifted and placed in Miami's Art Deco Historic District or in Palm Springs. Against the radiant blue sky is this beautifully designed, one storey building with one bright yellow wall and another bright pink one with cactuses and palms on the grass in front. Bohemian and stylish right out of the '50s. Walking into the massively empty reception area with coloured glass wall panels, it's looking a bit rough around its edges, but considering it's the cheapest place I could find, I feel pretty good.

There are also still a couple of hours of daylight left to explore the place. I walk to the counter and hand my passport to an old man playing cards with a young girl. A key with a large wooden number is given to me. Again, this place is eerily empty with no one else here, except for a few desert camouflaged soldiers strolling around the reception area gazing at the maps posted on the walls.

With nothing to do here, I decide to head into town and drive the few miles down the empty, dusty road and turn down this one-street town, where just a few cars are driving past. I'm trying to imagine that this place is probably a whirlwind of activity in the wintertime, when people come to experience "contact" with the friendly whales that gather in Scammon's Lagoon, locally known as Laguna Ojo de Liebre (Eye of the Jack Rabbit Lagoon) and bringing in valuable income to the people here. The place is named after an old whaling ship wrecked in the lagoon back in 1858 called the *Black Warrior* (*Guerrero Negro*). The entrance to the lagoon was discovered by American whaler, Melville Scammon, just a year earlier, when these graceful mammals began to be slaughtered for their oil, whalebone, and meat.

Incredibly, just ten years later, the population of 30,000 whales became almost extinct. Whales only became officially protected here in 1972 when the Grey Whale Sanctuary was created, and now an estimated 1,500 are making this place their winter home.

But most of the money must surely come from the salt production. Since the 1950s, the town grew from nothing to now over 10,000 residents, mostly employed by the salt company. These salt flats are the largest natural outdoor salt facility in the world, with the vast salt pans covering 113 square miles around this little place of Guerrero Negro.

But bumping down the road, with sand sweeping across it, most places are shut. Although the whales have long left the lagoon, I did know it was an area rich in wildlife. I'd seen on the map in the hotel lobby a narrow, long spit of land projecting out to the sea with a lighthouse on its tip, just outside the town. This is what I want to try and find.

I notice a kid walking along the empty street. I don't know where I need to go so I stop and lean out of the window and with a friendly smile say, "Buenos Dias. Estoy buscando el Puerto Viejo."

He reshuffles the heavy bag he's carrying on his shoulder and points to the right. I know no better. All I can do is nod and believe him. I drive a couple of hundred metres and am struck by what I see in front of me. A narrow sandy strip of road disappears out into the distance with large truck wheel-marks embedded into the sand. And on each side of it are beautiful green, watery marshlands. I can't see the lighthouse but curiously drive up this quiet wild spit of land for at least a mile until I reach the tip, where the sea now surrounds it.

A few fishing boats are moored and tied up on the stony beach, and a few dilapidated storage buildings are standing silently in this bizarre remote place. And there, at this very tip, is an old white lighthouse, which doesn't seem to have shone out light in a long time. The sky is still a deep, rich blue, strongly contrasting against these austere white brick buildings. Another place with nobody. Suddenly, a myriad of birds fly by overhead, proving the place is alive.

I walk past an old fishing boat stacked with old ropes and bags of rubble in it. On the white wall behind it is a large painted message: "Cada Caricia dura un siglo," Octavio Paz. A picture of his face is stamped next to it. Paz was a Mexican poet who'd won a Nobel Prize in Literature, who some considered to be one of the most influential writers of the twentieth century and one of the greatest poets of all time. I try and translate it: "Every touch (or is that *stroke*?) lasts a century." I try and figure it out—maybe it's saying that a kind intention or action will last with us for a century. Then I see it was stamped in 2014, which I later find is 100 years since he was born, so it's celebrating his centenary. But why this symbolic message is here in one of the most remote of places is anyone's guess.

The sun starts to slowly set over the lagoon and wild marshes, so I turn back from this isolated place and down the sand track, with the water lapping up on either side. Almost leaving the town, I spot a pink-painted house and restaurant with a big whale sign and underneath it "Malarrimo." Perfect timing to eat, as there didn't seem to be too much happening back at my empty hotel. I walk into a room filled with terracotta potted plants, sea navigation maps plastered on the walls, and boating paraphernalia, including at least half a dozen large oars and buoys hung from the ceilings and dotted about the place. I'm glad I've stopped here, as the sign says it sources fish daily from the lagoons. The choice is easy. I order Bay Scallops in their open shells, then Shrimp Mojo de Ajo, with crispy local garlic and virgin olive oil.

Sitting back, I can't help but smile to myself at the leaflet I've been given about the place. It starts "Staff always Reddy to serve you" and ends with "Sorry, by Sanitary laws no pets are aloud in the rooms." With a beer now in one hand and looking up and around this quiet room, I'm so very pleased that I'd decided to stop at Guerrero Negro—a perfect, unique, one of a kind place.

6

Día de las Madres

I love to travel, but hate to arrive.

Albert Einstein

A soldier marches past me as I smile and enter a large, sparsely furnished room. Again, no one is here. Am I really the only person here for breakfast? The place really does feel like a transitory bolt hole. I can't help but notice just one very large long table, which has been decoratively laid, with fifteen chairs next to one another in a long line behind it. It strangely looks more like a table laid out for Jesus and his disciples in this austere setting.

At the other end of the room, all on its own, is a small empty, un-laid table with one chair. I guess that's for me. I wait in the still silence for someone to bring me coffee. Instead, three soldiers enter, one with a set of speakers and a microphone, and the other two with large black letters that they start hammering up onto the wall behind the long, solitary table. Soon it's spelt out: "DÍA DE LAS MADRES 10 May 2016."

I smile. That's right, I'd forgotten; it's the tenth of May and Mexico's national Mother's Day, a day of celebration. There must be a lunch being organized here later on. One of the soldiers looks out of the window. So do I. Opposite, in the cobbled, palm tree lined courtyard, is a beautiful hibiscus tree laden with bright red flowers. But it's the two tiny black and yellow humming birds which draw our attention with their agility and swiftness in hovering and feeding from one flower to the next. It's then I also look up and notice that the sky is covered in ever thickening grey clouds. It's 6:30 and time to leave and get on the road.

I return to my room to grab my bags. I'd forgotten to turn the TV off and hear snippets of news. CNN has the presidential election overload of Clinton v Trump. But we won't know the outcome of that for another eight months. That's definitely an interesting one! I flick to the national station, on which massive news is coming in. Mexico's kingpin drug lord, "El Chapo," has been cleared for extradition to the US. That's enough. I want to escape all that.

Outside, the wet, shining tiles show it's been raining overnight. I load the car and hear a loud chirping on the top of the fuchsia-pink wall. One of the desert camouflaged soldiers also looks up and marches over with a rifle slung over his shoulder.

"That's a baby sea osprey. He must be about six months old, as they're born around January time. He's calling out for his mother, who's gone out hunting. He's only just a bit smaller now than his parents."

Looking up, I see this beautiful bird with black wings and white feathered chest and head, who's also curiously peering down at us.

The soldier turns and points to a large, tall pole opposite. "You see that? These are built around the marshlands for them. They then make their nest at the very top and are safe from everything."

He salutes me and walks away. It's then that I start ominously rubbing my left eye. The eye is sore and itching. I'm starting to have a panic attack. Could the same thing be happening again out on the road? Just four years earlier, I'd had two eye ulcers on the same eye and almost gone blind. This had been due to being out on the road on my motorbike for so long. I'd been wearing contact lenses for extended periods of time and dirt had been collecting underneath them, rubbing the eye. But this time it's different. I'm wearing glasses now, due to that incident and damage, and haven't been subjected to the same conditions. I look in the car's mirror and see the scar on the iris is still there and the eye is going a bit red. God, I hope this isn't happening again. I rub it again and try and forget about it. Another potential problem out on the road, which will be difficult to resolve. It'll be OK. It's going to have to be.

I turn out onto Highway 1 on this cloudy, early morning, knowing it's a new day with new things to experience. But just a couple of miles down the road, more panic raises its ugly head. Out in front, the road has just simply been barricaded shut and cut off with piles of grit on it. There is no way through. There are no signs. There are no instructions on what to do. There is no other traffic. I look down at the map. There are no other roads.

Running parallel about ten feet below it and down a sandy slope is a muddy, rough track, which looks like it's just used for highway maintenance vehicles. It seems to go far out into the distance. Two options. I turn back to ask someone for advice or I drive along this track and see what happens. I opt for the latter. The wheels slide awkwardly down the slope and onto the slippery surface. I'll take it easy, knowing the vehicle isn't a heavy duty SUV. Then almost immediately, out in the distance I see a massive truck appear hurtling down the track spewing out dust, stones, and mud, creating in my mind a mini sand storm.

I quickly wind the window up just as dust almost obliterates my view as it passes. And almost immediately after that I encounter yet another "monster" truck, also roaring down the track with no intention of slowing down. The good thing about seeing these trucks on this dusty detour means they're coming from somewhere, which means I can hopefully get back onto the main road soon. But it's not for another two miles of driving through the dust and grime that I see a slope going back up onto the asphalt highway.

And with that the clouds also clear and the rising sun appears in an increasingly bright blue sky, allowing me to see rough gorse covered, sandy desert and cactus landscapes with the mountain ranges of the Sierra San Francisco out on my left.

As I drive further inland, the heat increases to twenty-seven degrees, but no doubt it'll probably get even hotter later on. The dry, sparse cactus lands of Desierto Vizcaíno open up until it's only that vista I can see out far, far beyond and around me. Out on this straight stretch, a solitary thatched roof hut appears with a large hand-painted sign leaning against it— "Café—Burritos—Machaca." A massive blue truck, as blue as the sky, is parked up next to it. Again, nobody in sight. A place to find a toilet and stretch my legs. Inexplicably, the pain in my eye disappears, which is good as I'm captivated by the scene and needing to take a closer look.

I curiously walk around to the back of the shack and discover what can only be called an apocalyptic scene. There are a set of rusty, sunburnt, dead looking hills with cacti painfully creeping up them, but in front is a scrapyard of litter, dead wood, burnt barrels, and a bizarrely raped Volkswagen camper van with no wheels, lights, or innards. It's as rusty as the hills, and how it got there is anybody's guess. All the shabby wood outbuildings are shut, and the driver from the truck is nowhere to be seen. No chance for a coffee. I'd also fancied trying the Machaca, a traditional dried meat similar to jerky and popular in the remoter areas, which is sometimes incorporated on a plate with eggs, peppers, and tortillas. Drying meat is one of the oldest forms of preservation here, and added with chilli it had been developed by the ranchers and cowboys in northern Mexico. Oh well, only in my dreams, but I do find a grubby toilet in one of the sheds. So I haven't stopped for nothing.

Just a few miles further down the road, I curiously stop again in this barren wilderness. A massive cactus is standing by the road but with an equally massive truck wheel thrown over and around one of its outreaching arms. Next to it are two wooden white crosses. I get out and walk towards them. Strewn around the crosses are remnants from a truck, including the large red front fender. "Descansa En Paz." Rest in Peace. Two poor people who lost their lives on 28/3/10 on this remote road but with the vehicle's skeleton also resting in peace alongside them. I shiver and walk back now starting to realize that this highway is much more than just a road. It's vital to life here and beyond.

Bizarrely, I quickly come across real life just down the road. Another patrol check point. I slow down, seeing two navy blue dressed federal policemen walking up towards me. One looks surprised to see me on my own and starts asking questions.

"¿Donde está su marido?" Where is your husband?

"Porque sola?" Why are you on your own?

I'm wondering what they'd think if I was on my bike. I tell a little white lie to dilute the situation and explain the "made-up" husband is back in England, and I'm here visiting to discover Baja California. I even show one of my promotional book cards to vouch for my authenticity. They nod and wave me through without searching the car.

With the patrol policemen hardly out of sight from my rear view mirror, I'm astonished to see a lone coyote run out over the road and disappear just as quickly into the scrubland. This must be a hard life out here for them. Then the horrible truth of the road. A dead coyote on the side of it and a bit further on another dead one. I'm recalling someone telling me that the trucks stopped for no one, let alone animals!

It's still relatively early as I approach the turning for the village of San Ignacio. Driving down the small road the world changes. Gone is the dust and arid landscapes. Here, the roadside is lined with lush green reeds around pools of fresh water and tall, luxuriant palm trees. And far out into the distance, behind the expanse of calm water, is what looks like a sleeping volcano.

The oasis of San Ignacio has long drawn people to its fertile valley. The local Indians at the time called the place *Kadakaaman*, a word in their cochimi language meaning "stream of reeds." Jesuit padres had been visiting the location for years before establishing a mission in 1728. This mission had a very important role in the regime's expansion, since the local soil and climate allowed early agricultural practices, which helped the founding of other religious settlements.

No more dithering. It's time for some sustenance. I park up in the small plaza, shaded by six giant laurel trees and where a handful of men are quietly gathered, looking like they're meeting to go someplace else. Brightly painted orange, yellow, cream, blue, and red one-storey brick colonial-looking buildings of small shops and cafés surround the square. Everything seems to be closed besides one mini bazaar shop selling everything from air fans, pots of artificial flowers, plastic life size swans, and suitcases, all out on display on the pavement. I walk into one empty café with the date 1923 above its door and sign language to the old lady drying glasses behind a counter for a cup of coffee. She nods. I sit back out on the shaded pavement, absorbing this quiet place where, once again, I'm the only person besides the old men who have now walked away.

I look across the square and absorb the simple beauty of the Misión San Ignacio de Kadakaaman. After leaving twenty pesos plus a tip for the good strong coffee, I decide to take a wander. This gorgeous white structure was built from volcanic lava blocks, dug up from the volcano I saw across the expanse of water when driving in—Volcán las Tres Vírgenes. Completed in 1786, it's said to be probably the prettiest example of colonial architecture in the whole of Baja California and one of the most successful missions, operating until 1840.

I reverently walk into the cool, simple building and immediately see a majestic, rich gold-panelled wall at the front with massive paintings and images of Christ, Mary, and Saints. I pray for a safe trip.

Leaving this beautiful oasis, I turn right and head back into the hot, unforgiving desert but very soon encountering something else to question. A solitary white building, in the middle of nowhere, stands proudly advertising itself as "3 Hermanos—Disco—Bar". I notice one of the obligatory "monsters" parked outside; maybe it's a place for truckers to let their hair down. But truly nothing and no one else is here.

The journey continues with the windows open and the warm breeze flowing in. I rub some suntan cream onto my left hand and arm. Slowly, out on the skyline, emerges an impressive volcano, and finally coming ever closer I realize it's actually one massive volcano with two smaller ones next to it. Thus the name *Tres Vírgenes*, with the largest reaching almost 2,000 metres in elevation.

The heat is, without surprise, quickly rising, but soon out of the corner of my eye, I notice a solitary golden eagle quietly following me high above on the hot thermal winds. The wings seem to just be floating on nothing. Is this another mirage? It feels that it's actually following me down this long road. I look again, and the majestic bird has disappeared.

Besides a couple of haulage trucks, I'm out here on my own and becoming ever more excited that very soon the first sightings of the east coast and the Sea of Cortez will appear. The large, cacti-filled plains and canyons with the mountains sweeping behind them continue to monopolise the views with the road climbing ever higher looking over it all.

All of a sudden, a few trucks appear parked up along the roadside with people mingling beside them. The well-known hand sign waving up and down to "slow down" is seen again. These are roadside labourers whose faces are totally covered and protected with scarves, except for their eyes looking curiously out at me. I wave to sort of say all in one go, "Hello, thank you, hope all's well," and the same is reciprocally done back to me. I smile and think I see their eyes smiling. The road continues to climb with the views becoming ever bigger and greater.

At the very top of the hilly road it flattens out, and it's here there's another unexpected police check post. I'm still curious on what they're trying to check or control. A smiling federal policeman in the habitual navy blue uniform, pistol around his waist, big silver-star badge, and a name plate pinned to his jacket indicating that he's called "Vite" (maybe that's a nickname for Vitorio?), walks towards me. His colleague, identically dressed but also wearing a baseball cap and with his hand on his gun holster, doesn't smile and walks away.

Vite almost puts his hand out to shake mine when he hears my bad accent.

"So where are you going, Señora?"

"Loreto."

"First time?"

"Yes. This place of yours here is so beautiful, and you're all so friendly"

He smiles, with his eyes almost closed, squinting from the sun. "Yes, it's true, but we don't meet many English or even Italians. They don't know Baja."

I also smile. "That's not such a bad thing."

There's no search and not many other questions. We simply shake hands, saying goodbye and wishing each other well.

From this moment on, I start to descend with the first views out to the "new sea." I'm expecting to see a lovely, little seaside town. I'm just a little disappointed. As I drop down to the coast, instead of a broad, sandy beach and a laid-back Mexican thatch-roofed village, I'm finding a rocky shoreline with lots of old smelting and mining equipment on the hillsides. This is, without doubt, an old mining town, which was established unbelievably by French miners in 1883. They created not only one of the world's major copper producing mines but a unique company town with a decidedly French flavour, which I would soon discover. It already had an intriguing feel.

Close to the main square I park up and take a little "stretch the legs" wander. Indeed, many of its buildings look

strikingly un-Mexican. I stroll down narrow street
of colourful wood-frame buildings with their flow
balconies and corrugated tin roofs that look more re
of French-Caribbean dwellings. It's like nothing else   ~~en
so far in Baja. These little dwellings were for the workers of the
mines, and large colonial residences lining the hill above were
for the managers. Everything about the place was company
built and company run by El Boleo Copper Company, from
the homes, the hotel, stores, and railroad. The name originated
from *Boleos*, the original copper ore discovered that appeared
as small, round blue and green ball shapes.

I wander past Iglesia de Santa Barbara, a fascinating pre-
fabricated iron church, which amazingly, is described as being
designed by none other than Gustave Eiffel of Eiffel Tower
fame and which was shipped from France. There's definitely
a very French flavour here. Some of the young children

playing in the streets seem to have features more European than Mexican, as I guess they must contain varying degrees of French blood.

I turn a corner and approach the large town plaza and see hundreds of chairs are being set up in rows of straight lines facing a highly decorated stage next to the church. Another "Mothers Day" spectacle, which will take place later on in the day. Walking to the back of the plaza I hear a kid's voice shouting out, "Fruta! Naranjas!" He's leaning next to an open-roofed truck laden with brightly coloured fruit and vegetables. Bags of oranges are hanging on the sides of the van, with large watermelons, potatoes, and tomatoes in boxes at the back. The kid, no more than twelve or thirteen, is next to a pair of giant, hanging scales and notices my interest. He points, in a serious business-like way, to the oranges. I nod. He puts half a dozen in a bag for me.

Across the way a long line of people are queuing outside a fading yellow, clapboard, tin-corrugated roofed building. This is the Panadería El Boleo: "World Famous Bread since 1901".

This old French bakery is known throughout the peninsula for its pastries and bread. Apparently, machinery was brought over from France in the 1880s, and a lot of it is still working. I'm curious. I walk past the line of people patiently waiting to buy their baguettes and peer through an open window. The waft of freshly baked bread is in the air. Wood-fired brick ovens are on full display behind the counter, as well as shelves of all sorts of fresh bread being carefully wrapped and passed over the counter. It all just feels like another place from where I've been to so far.

As I return to the now very dusty truck, I once again pass the "Eiffel Church" and see a handful of white doves fly past it and up over the pink spire into the blue sky—beautiful. Next to where I'm parked, I notice a small opening in a wall where inside shelves up to the ceiling are stacked with colourful gift boxes. A lady is carefully wrapping more boxes of all sizes on the counter with paper and ribbons. Obviously, these are gifts being prepared for mothers today.

I've been fascinated by this place and how it came to be. Maybe I'll have more time to stop off on my way back.

I pass an old Companía El Boleo steam train on display in the middle of a roundabout, but it soon becomes smaller and smaller in the rear view mirror, and I'm again out and away along the coastal road. Shortly after leaving Santa Rosalina, on the outskirts but in the rocky desert, I'm drawn to something a little disturbing. I slow down to get a better look. It's something you imagine just seeing in the movies. White, tall turrets are positioned on each corner of a high, fenced enclosure with guards looking out from them. This is the Santa Rosalina federal prison, and the security looks very tight, with lorries and police cars parked up alongside the high walls. Not a place I want to visit. I put my foot down and have quickly passed it. God knows what people have done to be in there.

Continuing south, it's not until I've reached and passed the river town of Mulegé that I'm able to fully start enjoying the beautiful coastal sea views. The pace feels slow, and that sea looks mighty inviting! It's hot, I'm a bit sweaty, and I want to finally just dip my feet into warm, fresh water. After a few turns down unsigned dirt tracks to beaches which look more like sites for dilapidated and nomadic caravans and shacks, I see a sign for Playa El Burro in the Bahía Conceptión. I bump down the sandy trail and am welcomed by still, blue waters lapping up to the beach, with mountains on the horizon and islands out to sea.

The sand is white and clean, and besides a few empty huts on the shoreline, one caravan, two cars, and two small boats pulled up onto the beach, it's deafeningly quiet and wild. I park up by one of the palm-roofed huts, kick my shoes off, dip my toes into the soft, caressing sand, and wander down to the water's edge. It's welcomingly warm, and I walk out through the shallows until the water's lapping up over my shorts. I sweep my hands through the water and put them through my hair. That's good. I slowly wade back up onto the beach feeling refreshed and re-energized.

Continuing south, Loreto appears, where I'll be staying overnight. I've done just over 250 miles and can now explore and hopefully find a place for late lunch. I open the gate to the little Iguana Inn on a small side road and park the car in the narrow driveway. A smiling lady with an American accent, who simply introduces herself as Julie, welcomes me and shows me to a room at the back of the small courtyard. Strange stone iguanas are dotted all around the place, including one in a stone, waterless fountain. It's basic, but for forty dollars is more than enough for such a short stay. Julie helpfully states we're just one block from the sea and there are a nice couple of bars along the walkway where all the ex-pats hang out and should be a good place for a drink or two. Hmmm, probably not. I'd prefer to walk another couple of blocks and get to the central plaza for food and drink. But at the moment, I'm just happy and curious to explore, so I do walk the one block and out onto the seafront promenade with its high rise condo developments and seafront shops and bars. It's the first time I feel a place is too modernized and spoilt by money and tourists. Walking a couple of hundred metres and seeing a few fat gringos drinking beers in a bar and leering out of the window, I turn back, wanting to find something a bit more authentic.

It doesn't take me long. I walk into the buzzy central plaza, with a band stand in the middle and children running up and down its circular stairs, and sit down at a table on the terrace of El Zopilote Brewery.

A bottle of Pacífico beer and a tuna salad are all I need to absorb this place. Like Santa Rosalia, a large stage is being prepared and masses of chairs already being positioned in lines. Definitely somewhere to come back to later on when it's all set up.

After another refreshing beer, I decide to promenade a little to find the old Mission Church of our Lady of Loreto (Misión de Nuestro Señora de Loreto). This is considered the head and mother of all the missions in the peninsula of Baja California. It was the very first Jesuit foundation, established in 1697, and it would become the first of a system that would colonize and settle, not only Baja California, but all the way up into northern California.

From the outside it looks somewhat austere, but this is probably due to it being heavily restored after centuries of earthquake damage. Quite a bit of history in one blink of an eye. Unfortunately, it's closed, so I walk back to the square and see something I'd like to investigate and "more up my street," as they say. It's the hotel Posada Las Flores Loreto. I wander into this old building, with its beautiful antique furniture and paintings generously depicting the rich heritage of the area. It's hot outside, and the shady, indoor courtyard is wonderful, but surely this place must have a swimming pool. I see signs up to the roof so wander up, and there, with a 360 degree view of the town, is an exquisite, transparent glass-floored pool, ready to jump into! I'm not a guest, but it should be easy to take a dip, as there's no one here.

Just as I'm slipping off my shorts, a waitress approaches me and asks me which room I'm in. I think quickly on my shoeless feet and state I was just looking at the view and will be down shortly. So, just cheekily dipping my toes in, I wander back down to the hive of activity in the square.

After a good siesta, I return to where hundreds of people have started to congregate to watch the show for the mothers of Loreto. I sit back down again at the back of the plaza with a beer at El Zopilóte and watch the world and its families come together.

By 7:45, with the show about to start, it's still a warm twenty-four degrees with a clear, starry sky—perfect for an

evening's outdoor entertainment. Everyone is getting excited, with families seated facing the stage and small children running crazily up and down and in between the rows of chairs. There's a wide, eclectic array of performances from the children including Hawaiian, flamenco, and rock and roll dancing, with even a bit of ballet thrown in.

And with that, everybody claps and cheers celebrating their favourite person—their mother.

7

ANGELS AND DEMONS

And above all, watch with glittering eyes the whole world around you because the greatest secrets are always hidden in the most unlikely places. Those who don't believe in magic will never find it.

Roald Dahl

I spread the map over the dusty bonnet in the shady iguana-lined courtyard and take a sip of coffee. I'm feeling a bit weak. My finger lands on the word *Loreto*, and I trace it down the red line to La Paz. I reckon that's got to be about 200 miles. It looks like I'll follow the coast for a while then head inland and continue due south. This is one part of the journey that I'd found little or no information about, so I was totally in the dark about what to expect. That's good. That doesn't worry me. That excites me.

The sun is just appearing over the roof as I hear the gate open, and in walks Julie with a shopping bag in one hand.

With her indecipherable American accent she smiles, "Hey Zoë. Good morning. You're up early. I've just been to get some milk and bread. It's a pity you're not here on Sunday. That's when we have a farmers' market with great local produce."

"Yea. I'm just getting ready to get on the road."

"So, did you enjoy your short stay here? You certainly picked the right day yesterday."

"Oh, Mothers Day! Quite a spectacle! And yes, as you mentioned, I did walk along the seafront but, to be totally truthful, was a little disappointed with all the new developments. It's still nice but not really for me. I was imagining it was just going to be a little fishing town. Fortunately, the spirit of the people during the evening's festivities made up for it."

She sighs. "I'm sorry to hear. To be truthful, I've been here for six years now, but I've recently put this place on the market. You're right. The developers are moving in, with another massive one just outside town being built by some Canadian group. These 'out of towners' just swan in at the weekends then leave again. I'm moving to Ecuador, where you can still find cheap and relatively quiet places. I'll probably set up something similar. But don't get me wrong. This place is still isolated enough to be three or four hours' drive to any bigger town, but I've had enough!"

I raise my eyebrows and fold the map. "Well thanks, Julie, for the hospitality. Hopefully, I'll also be in a new place later, looking out to sea in La Paz tonight. Good luck with things."

She puts her thumb up and, with that, kindly opens the gate for me to reverse out of. This is great. It's 6:30 and I'm stretching my wings to fly off again, even though I might be feeling a bit weak. Almost immediately, I'm out following the coastline with beautiful, clear blue skies welcoming the day. The roads are quiet, and I'm feeling happy and relaxed. Slowly, the still, flat Sea of Cortez changes with views out to sea of islands rearing their heads out of the water. It's too beautiful to continue. Even with the window open on this early morning, I need to really breathe in this landscape.

I see a roadside parking area a little further on and pull up. I turn the engine off and walk over to a low wall looking out to the sea, where yellow flowers are falling down a sandy cliff. The whole place looks mysterious and secret. The islands are black against the light horizon and seem to be totally bare of anything.

I turn to look out in the other direction and notice, at the far end of the wall, a large rock with a strange but colourful object standing on it. I walk curiously towards it and see a statuette of a saintly-looking woman surrounded by candles, crosses, and glasses filled with red plastic roses. But it's the beautiful painted colours of this lady which amaze me. She's covered in yellows, pinks, turquoise, and gold, which are all lit up against the bright blue sky.

This must be a travellers good luck saint. I'm fascinated to know the story and just a little frustrated that there's no "tourist info card" stuck below it. But, unintentionally, I'll find out a lot more about this lady the further I drive on. But for now, I naively appreciate her peaceful demeanour.

The straight, empty road with its double sun-drenched yellow line in the middle continues but with higher and higher jagged rocky mountains appearing on the horizon and large cactus starting to raise their heads once again up along the roadside slopes. It's at this point I glance out onto a sandy ridge and see a large black condor flapping its wings on the top of one of those huge spiky cactus, looking ready to take off. I quickly look back out onto the road, but when I gaze back, the black scavenger has disappeared.

Very soon, I've climbed up and around into the barren mountains on this narrow road. I suddenly hear something and looking into my rear view mirror notice a white truck quickly approaching me. I'm not a fast driver in conditions like this, and he isn't going to force me to put my foot down. But the bends are becoming more tortuous, I'm probably slowing down more, and this truck is now crazily and impatiently following me just a little too closely around the twists and turns. I almost feel it's going to touch my rear bumper at any moment. If I brake, there's no knowing what could happen. I put my hand on my head like "touching wood" that this crazy driver isn't going to try and overtake or fly over me.

Then it happens! The road descends, flattens out, and the truck honks its horn and crazily veers out to pass me. Phew! I'm glad that's over! And the landscape has opened up to a long, long road with agricultural lands of green tended fields of crops and fruit trees. Far away, outlining the entire horizon, I see what looks like a massive new range of mountains. But the nearer I approach, the more I feel they're maybe in reality nothing more than enormous smoke or dust clouds. But not even that! This feels strange and something I've never seen before. All of a sudden, I enter a world of cold misty clouds that envelope me with no visibility for more than a few metres. So, does that mean I'm still quite high up to be experiencing such a phenomenon?

I turn my headlights on, and with the moist drizzle running down the window, flick my wipers on to clean it away. And it's turned so cold that I'm literally rubbing my hands up and down my thighs. I wind the window up. So those mountains are actually clouds full of moisture that must help to nourish the land here. It's just 8AM, and I've already experienced about two different seasons and more than double that in landscapes!

It soon feels like I'm passing through the "sky of clouds" which then just as quickly opens up to sunny irrigated fields of corn and orange trees near the small agricultural outpost of Ciudad Insurgentes. Instead of the speed restriction signs along the roadside, they've now changed to precautionary images of cows and tractors! So I guess that's what I'm now going to see trying to overtake or run across the road.

At Ciudad Insurgentes, Highway 1 takes a sharp left turn, with the grey, arid dusty land and its orange groves continuing to follow me on either side until I reach the larger community of Ciudad Constitución. I immediately recognize its similarity to a place I visited more than a decade ago. It's an isolated, rural farming town very much like Ribeirao Preto in northern Brazil where I once worked promoting their agricultural shows. Now *there's* a story, which I may come back to later. Tractors here are as common as trucks ambling down this street, where both are also parked outside agricultural supplies stores along the roadside.

I'm dying for a coffee and maybe something to eat. My stomach feels a bit stronger now. I park up on the side of this palm tree lined, busy main road and wander to a little café. I hand a few pesos over for a milky coffee and a couple of pastries and sit outside on the pavement looking out to see what's happening. An old guy, probably knocking closer to 70 than 60 and a woman of probably the same age are industriously hand washing and cleaning cars parked up outside. That's one thing people are here and that's being industrious in finding ways to make money. Surely this must be a good way to make some money as there's never a lack of dirt or dust here.

The old guy sees a new face in town and excitedly points to my car raising his eyebrows like he's asking, "So, shall we do yours now?" I smile and shake my head. He quickly walks along the pavement asking the same of someone else. 161 pesos lighter but twelve litres of petrol heavier, I'm off again.

What I'm about to say has to be taken seriously. Leaving Ciudad Constitución, I continue on what I genuinely feel is the longest, straightest road I have ever been on. For seventy miles the road just disappears straight ahead of me into a watery, shimmering mirage with the same monotonous, gorsy flat land on either side. Nothing is different. Nothing changes. The blue sky just gets bigger and bigger above me, and if I wasn't continually looking at the yellow central line for direction, I'm convinced my focus would have shifted and taken me off the road! With nothing else out there, it is also easy to sleepily put the foot down even further into the floor. There's nowhere to stop for shade on this blistering morning. I just need to drink a lot of water. I'm telling myself I have to keep focused, and I've also got to slow down.

Still continuing almost in a daze and passing the "hole in the wall" place of Santa Rita, I vaguely register seeing flashing lights out in the distance. Suddenly, a bus appears parked on the side, and the driver standing next to it quickly signals with his hand for me to overtake. It's there, approaching the brow of a small incline, that I see a massive accident. Red road bollards have been put in the middle of the road. Federal police are also standing in the road next to their black trucks. An ambulance has just passed me, and the police wave me on to follow it. It all feels like it's just happened. There, on my right, is a massive bronze-fronted lorry and just behind it is another, even bigger monster truck facing the opposite direction but crashed and tipped onto one side. There is debris of glass and truck parts scattered everywhere. It must have been approaching the incline, saw the bronze truck approaching, and desperately tried to get out of its way.

Slowly passing them, I look back at the scene in the rear view mirror, seeing people inspecting the mess. How they're going to pull this monster back up is anyone's guess. My heart is once again palpitating, recognizing the unforeseen dangers out on this road, but maybe also the luck in it all. The distances and monotony are enormous, which is a recipe for disaster and which are, without doubt, the reasons for these horrendous accidents I'm seeing.

It would be good to make a stop somewhere very soon. Bizarrely, it's like my wish, and a lot more, is granted. Almost immediately, a little further on, a large parking area appears with a beautiful orange painted hexagonal looking place of worship with a gold cross on its roof. Bright red and pink bougainvillea decorate it and hang from the front, and a wooden bench is under the welcoming shade of a few palm trees. A surreal, white fishing boat is propped up behind it all. And very close to it is a beautiful but tiny aquamarine clapboard kiosk with its window invitingly open, looking like it's ready to sell drinks and maybe something to eat.

Over the hundreds of miles I was doing, the time I needed a safe place to rest most and take stock just appears! Someone has answered my prayers. I pull my baseball cap on to shield me from the piercing rays and walk towards this curious but impressive shrine. I quietly pass through the columns and see the same saintly woman I'd witnessed earlier along the coastline close to Mulegé. This time she's been painted on a wall of ceramic tiles with Christmas decorations of green and red baubles and ribbons hung around it and white candles stacked up and around her. People are obviously stopping here to pray, and I would imagine, asking for good luck out on their travels.

I wander to the tiny kiosk, not expecting to see anyone. I lean over the tall counter and happily see a tiny, smiling older lady slicing some chilli and looking up at me. She can see I'm curious, and at this stage I'm not afraid to ask what most people here would think is probably a silly question.

"Señora, who is this saintly lady? It's not the first time I've seen her today."

She smiles, puts down her knife, and wipes her hands on her apron. "That's Our Lady, the Virgin Mary, of Guadalupe, our patron saint of Mexico. Would you like to know more?"

I'm surprised and quietly nod my head. She walks outside and joins me walking back to the shrine. We sit on the bench underneath the palm trees.

"In 1531, Our Lady appeared to a poor, humble indigenous Aztec Indian called Juan Diego, who'd recently converted to the Catholic faith. She asks him to tell the bishop to build a church outside Mexico City so she can offer all her compassion, help, and protection to the people of Mexico.

The way in which she appeared and was dressed was very meaningful and reassuring to the Aztec Indians. She has brown skin like them. She was dressed in royal clothes that showed she was very important and perhaps a queen. She also had the symbol of the cross at her neck, which was the sign the Spaniards had on their ships and in the churches they built. She had a sash belt tied around her waist, which meant that she was with child, which was also the way the Aztec women dressed when they were pregnant. There was one special flower on her dress, among the many others, which was very significant. It only had four petals, and to the Aztecs, this was the symbol of God and was placed on her abdomen. The Aztecs immediately understood that this was the mother of God.

You see, the appearance of Our Lady of Guadalupe was very important to the history of our land. The Indians and the Spaniards were on the brink of war. The Aztec Indians' culture and religion was very different. They worshipped Gods and made many human sacrifices. The Spaniards were disgusted by this but were cruel too, treating them like animals and also sometimes killing them for no reason. A war would have destroyed so much.

But you see, Mary's appearance changed everything. It helped the Indians to embrace and understand Christianity, and it helped the Spaniards to treat the Indians with respect and as human beings. They also say that her appearance put an end to the worship of stone Gods and human sacrifice."

She walks over and lights a candle in a little glass pot. "So now perhaps you better understand. Look at how beautiful she is. The stars on Our Lady's dress shows she comes from heaven. She's standing on a moon, showing she's more powerful than the God of darkness, and rays of sunlight encircle her. People come here to stop and to pray that she provides safety out on the road."

She makes a sign of the cross across her chest and walks back to her little clapboard hut. I follow her. Although I don't need to, as a parting gesture I buy another bottle of water and a couple of packets of crisps from her and smile, thanking her and wishing her a good day. She does the same.

And just another fifteen to twenty miles further along, another impressive, bright pink shrine appears on the roadside with colourful plastic flowers in and around it and a large pink cross on the top. Like the other one, there's a small cabin painted in bright orange with a sorely tempting sign of "Burritos—Empanadas—Quesadillas—Carne—Heuvos—Café—Soda—Cigarros."

But like everywhere else, except for the last place, its shutters are closed, and no one is here to help with nourishment or to provide a story or two.

The song *Born to Be Wild* starts up as I put my foot down again, and the feeling of freedom and being out on the road is mighty good. It's now well past midday, with the heat cruelly increasing, and the sharp rays of the sun daggering down. Another mirage appears. With the sun shining directly onto the middle of the road, it creates studs of sparkling diamonds glittering in a long line out to the distance. Another bizarre vision.

The ever present giant cacti are now also silently marching along the ever long road with me. In a sort of trance, I feel like I'm dreaming, like I'm on some sort of acid trip. I'm asking myself what do they represent or look like? The strangest thoughts come to my mind. Kinky, prickly condoms? Cocks? One finger "up yours!"? Two finger victory sign? I drink more water and shake myself back to focusing on the hazy road.

Just forty to sixty miles from La Paz, the capital of Baja Sur, there are signs and visual evidence of giant road modernization projects here on Highway 1. With my enduring determination to keep the window down to have some resemblance of really travelling, dust from the construction works dramatically and unexpectedly blows through the window. It literally gets into my teeth, throat, and even in between my flip-flopped toes and feet. I wiggle my bum on the seat and can feel sand rubbing between my legs.

Strangely, I'm feeling a little saddened but at the same time happy I'm travelling here when I am. The old one lane highway with its unique character is visually changing to modernised non-descript dual carriageways. Sure, it will help with the traffic flow and safety, but I'm feeling here and now that the old historic "Transpeninsular Highway" is quickly changing and will never be quite the same again.

All of a sudden in the outskirts of La Paz, red traffic lights appear, and ever increasing amounts of traffic gather. I quickly look down at the map, an enlarged version I'd picked up in Loreto, and try and somehow find the road name *Independence*. There's no mention of it, or I just can't see it. The only solution in my mind is to stop at a gas station, fill up again, and kindly ask where this road where I'm staying is located. I do know it's in the centre of the old town, but how to get there is anyone's guess.

I cross another set of busy traffic lights and, with a last minute signal, turn sharply left into a busy repair garage and petrol station forecourt. As is the case here, a friendly young guy, almost a kid, promptly approaches and asks if he can fill the truck. I nod and look around. While he leaves the nozzle in to fill the tank, he walks to the window screen and kindly washes and wipes it clean. I walk around to him and show him the address, hopefully showing that I'm feeling totally lost and need some help and directions to get there. This place is a lot bigger than I'd imagined.

Ricardo smiles hearing my accent and follows me in to the till, waiting until I've paid. He turns to me and says without prompting that he'd be happy to help, and he'll simply jump into his truck, and all I need do is follow him. He mentions that some of the roads past the cathedral are one-way, and the road I need has to be approached from some other direction. Or something like that. I don't know what to say. I nod, asking if he's sure. He smiles and nods his head. Not what I expected!

He slowly turns left, and I follow. We descend down along the seafront, otherwise known as the Malecón, and are soon driving up a one-way street behind an old colonial-looking church in front of a large plaza, which I guess is La Paz's cathedral. One road across, he stops outside a beautiful white brick building. He simply puts his thumbs up. I wave and shout out, "¡Gracias!" and he disappears, no doubt back to the garage to help someone else.

Right outside this old building is a sign, "El Angel Azul"— The Blue Angel. We're here. I jump out and knock on the old, thick wooden door with its small grilled eye-hole. A smiling older lady opens it and politely shows me in. This is gorgeous. Walking into the cool interior, the white painted rooms of this peaceful inn are beautifully furnished and decorated, and lead out to a beautiful, shaded courtyard filled with green plants, flowering shrubs, and luxurious, reclining sunbeds. Incredibly, this fully restored building is part of La Paz's history, being over 140 years old and once the federal courthouse of the South Baja capital.

I'm courteously shown to a lovely room and thrilled I'll be here for three nights to rest and absorb what I know is going to be an interesting place. But now I need to eat. It's been too long since those two pastries back in the remote farmlands, which now seem like another world away. It's past three. I put my hat and sunglasses on and walk down the quiet street, and at the first junction already stop and smile! On the corner is a shop, but not just any shop. Outside it is a large phallic-shaped cactus, which also looks like it's doing the "one finger" sign. Bolted on the side of it is a large panel stating the shop is the "Love Boutique and Sex Shop." I smile, wondering more about the cactus and if it's pure coincidence that it has its provocative shape.

Walking the five blocks down to the seafront, I take a seat under a covered awning on the pavement outside "Ranchero Viejo" and hungrily order white fish tacos and fresh orange juice. The fish is moist and delicious, which I roll into the soft flour tortillas with fresh tomatoes and guacamole. Simple, but perfect. The view out across the road is also perfect; coconut leafed parasols on a wide expanse of white beach with some fishing boats and catamarans pushed up in front of blue ocean vistas.

Staying here for the next two days, I've promised myself to explore and learn more about La Paz and find the beautiful, remote beaches, which I know are just a short distance from here. I stroll slowly back and drop into a chair in the quiet courtyard, with no excuse not to take a little siesta.

A lot later in the warm evening, I return to the Malecón and step into a mouth-watering paradise of food heaven at the Bismarcito. For anyone who loves fish this is the place to be in La Paz. As the sun sets across the bay, large steamed chocolate clams, "Almeja Chocolate," are served, followed by "Pescado Zarandeado en Salsa Verde," local delicious grilled fish with chilli and garlic. And, of course, swilled down with a good white Mexican wine. The place is buzzing, with most tables full with laughing, friendly people.

I feel like I'm in heaven. But the thought has more meaning than normal. I rewind that thought from the past day's events and smile to myself, glad that I'm actually here. Being up in heaven with the angels was more of a possible reality a lot earlier on in the day. The only angel I'll have anything to do with tonight is the Blue Angel's bed!

8

THE PEARL OF THE SOUTH

The very air here is miraculous, and outlines of reality change with the moment. A dream hangs over the whole region, a brooding kind of hallucination.
John Steinbeck, *The Log from the Sea of Cortez*

The Blue Angel awakens me with the muted sound of chattering birds in the courtyard trees outside. Rays of light are entering the room, and I stretch out on the bed, feeling refreshed to take on the day.

The simple plan for the next few days will be to just wander and meander to better acquaint myself with this place and to discover the remote beaches east of La Paz. Sounds good. The feeling of total freedom with no set agenda will do me just fine.

It's still early, maybe 7:30ish, so what better to greet the day than to take a leisurely stroll a few blocks for breakfast.

The Mercado Madero, a daily market, is where I'd been told cheap food stalls served big plates of Mexican classics and "jugos" stalls made fresh juices. I fold the little map of La Paz into my shorts, stuff some peso notes in my pocket so as not to look like a tourist with the habitual backpack, and walk out onto the street, welcomed by unadulterated, pure blue skies.

They say everyone ends up in La Paz eventually, the state capital and largest city of Baja California Sur, with over 200,000 people. It's true that the outskirts seemed to be an ugly sprawl, but here in the old town centre it seems that it's managed to preserve a sleepy provincial atmosphere. And although I'd read, not quite believing it, that there's not much to see in the city itself, the surrounding beaches and the island of Espiritu Santo, with its rich marine life, should definitely be on the to-do list.

I pass the quiet main square on Cinco de Mayo, where the modest stone Catedral de Nuestra Señora de la Paz stands, turn left onto Calle Revolución, and start following a sweet old couple pushing a rickety shopping trolley, guessing they're also going to the market. I cross a road, where people are walking in and out of a bus station, and into a large market building. As I navigate this busy place, walking around people down and through the lines of market stalls, I'm looking out for the sign "Área de Comedor," where the food is. There's a bustle of activity. People are queuing at counters to buy fish, meat, vegetables, and fruit. "Pescaderio Lucy" has a lady in full concentration cutting and preparing piles of boneless fish fillets, two guys next door are cutting, slicing, and dicing even more fish behind glass counters, then there's the biggest, most jovial, smiling man at "Carnicería Guadalupana," in his blue overalls cutting and boning meat. Just looking at him would make you want to buy his meat!

I pass coffee bars and see well-groomed, dressed ladies sipping their first morning drink. One's sitting at the counter looking into a small hand mirror, putting her mascara on and pouting back at it. I'd forgotten, it's actually Thursday, so a working day for most. They must all be on their way to shops or offices.

The delicious smell of food being freshly cooked beckons me to where I'm greeted by at least fifteen little stalls busily preparing the first meal of the day. I sit on a bench with its red and white plastic-covered table, and soon piping hot huevos rancheros with steamy black beans, warm soft tortillas to wrap it all up in, and fresh orange juice are put in front of me with a big smile. This little place looks like a mecca for people just coming to grab good, simple, well-cooked and well-priced food. There are all sorts of people, from truck drivers, security guards, fat grandmothers, and cigarette smoking workmen. An old man walks in selling and stripping off rows of lottery tickets to people eager to dream of winning something. I feel comfortable here; no one is gawping at the stranger in town like I'm an alien. It all just feels right.

Behind one of the food stalls I notice a selection of beautiful, large, white abalone shells, which jolts my memory on what I'd read about La Paz and its pearls. It was searching for pearls that the Spanish conquistador Hernán Cortés came to La Paz, but he was unable to sustain the colony of Spanish settlers in 1535, so for the next 185 years the place was only visited by roaming pearl hunters, until a mission was built in 1720. La Paz was most noted for its black, actually greyish, pearls which had been harvested for almost 400 years. Until 1874, when diving suits were introduced, Indians, who were often naked, free-dived to bring up the shells and the prized pearls. But towards the end of the nineteenth century, the abalone shells, themselves, began to be harvested and shipped overseas, making the pearl almost secondary in importance.

Sadly, by 1941 the pearling industry had been wiped out completely due to over-harvesting and disease. But in that same year, John Steinbeck visited La Paz, basing his book *The Pearl* on his time there. He fell in love with the place:

> *... there is the genuine fascination of the city of La Paz. Everyone in the area knows of the greatness of La Paz. You can get anything in the world there they say. It is a huge place—beautiful out of all comparison ... A cloud of delight hangs over the distant city from the time when it was the great pearl centre of the world. The robes of the Spanish kings and the stoles of the bishops in Rome were stiff with the pearls from La Paz.*

I mop up the last of the eggs and beans, gratefully pay, and on the way out, buy bright yellow and orange mangoes, papaya, and bananas to stock up, as I'd heard the beaches had nothing in the way of provisions. I'll get water and more food if I can find a supermarket on the way back.

The rhythmic, timeless sound of music is coming from the bus station as I walk past. Seated under the shade of some trees, with buses all around them, two old rancheros with their Stetson hats, cowboy boots, and colourful shirts have stopped to take a rest from playing their old tatty accordions. A small, empty styrofoam cup is on the floor, silently asking for money in gratitude. One ranchero looks up at me. He's not pleading or desperate, but you can see in his dark, black eyes the sadness. There is pride. He does not want to blatantly ask—unlike you see so much of back in the UK. I dig into my pocket and throw all my coins in the cup, which isn't a lot. I only wish I was wealthier. He politely touches his hat in thanks, stubs his cigarette out with his foot, and starts playing the sad, melodic music again.

Wandering back, I ask a passerby for the nearest grocery store or supermarket and am pointed in the direction one block over from the cathedral square. I don't know if it's the same for everyone else, but I just love taking a shopping basket and strolling down the aisles of supermarkets in other countries to see the diversity and different products on display.

This place is no exception, and after buying some water, fresh bread, ham cut from a joint, cheese, and tomatoes, I walk back, passing the "sexy" cactus, and drop the food off in my room. It's still far too early to set off to lie on a beach, so I grab my hat to inquisitively explore the seafront malecón and maybe to the end, where the marinas are.

The tranquil malecón here in La Paz, with the waters lapping up to the beach, is said to be one of the prettiest in Mexico where views of the mountains can be seen across the bay. As I happily walk down to the sea, a pier juts out at the end of Avenida 16 de Septiembre. It's also known as the "Muelle de Reina," in honour of Queen Elizabeth II, who surprisingly came to visit the place in 1983. Every few yards are beautiful statues representing everything in connection with the sea—mermaids chasing dolphins, boat sails, shells, seals, hammerhead sharks, and even Jacques Cousteau with his diving suit and mask looking out to sea. One, in particular, draws my attention.

It's an old man looking out to sea. He's dressed in the sailor suit of a young boy, and his hat is a cutely folded paper boat, like the ones you'd have your parents make for you from newspapers when you were a kid. Around his waist he's wearing and holding another jumbo-sized paper boat. And he smiles. Below is a plaque in Spanish with some beautiful words:

> *The old man . . . and the sea?*
> *I have a paper boat . . .*
> *It's made from a page*
> *On which I have written my dreams.*
> *It has neither anchors, nor mooring ropes.*
> *I want to sail in it,*
> *on the seven seas; in the eighth,*
> *where I know, I will run aground in the port of my desires.*
> *. . . has someone ever seen the light shining from his lighthouse*
>
> Guillermo Gómez Macías

Continuing alongside the beach, I'm impressed to see that this really is a clean place with very little litter. That's probably thanks to the fact that there're also seal and sea turtle shaped trash cans every few yards. I reach the end of the walkway and find the Marina Cortez, where expensive looking sailboats and yachts are moored up. A few cafés are dotted around it, but all look closed, so I turn back and jump down onto the beach, take off my flip-flops, and wade through the warm sea splashing it up.

Now's probably a good time to grab my towel, swimming suit, mask and snorkel, food, and drink and go find those beaches!

I'm shortly navigating and driving through the narrow streets until I hit the sea and turn right, driving alongside it out of the city. This side of town, on the east, is quiet with very little traffic and seems a lot less populated. There are particularly two beaches I want to find—Playa Balandara and Playa El Tecolote. But they're about twenty-five kilometres away, and before that I'll be passing a couple of other beaches hugging this beautiful coastline. The first one I see is Playa El Tresoro, about thirteen kilometres out of town, with what looks like a couple of restaurants and kayak rental places. A little further is Pichilingue, home to the La Paz ferry services, which take you to mainland Mexico. But I continue around the coast until I see a simple, non-descript sign for "Playa." This must be it.

I drive down through a small, windy, sandy road with mangroves and big brown rocky hills surrounding the area. I descend slowly, and out in front is a beautiful horseshoe-shaped beach and bay with a tiny outlet to the open sea. This is Playa Balandra, famous for its shallow waters and safety from the rest of the sea. There are maybe just four jeeps parked up in this isolated, silent place. It looks perfect and just what I'm looking for. But before too hastily settling down here, I'm sorely tempted to go suss out the other beach, just three kilometres further up the coast at the tip of this small peninsula shoreline.

I turn back and am soon bumping down another sandy track leading down to the better known and more frequented Playa El Tecolate where at the weekends and peak season there's a real party atmosphere with its beach lined drink and food shacks. But as I approach, the place is empty. Wandering down to the white beach, it's the views across to Isla Espiritu Santo, that hosts a large sea lion colony and multitudes of sea life, which is the real stunner. The area is protected and was declared part of a Biosphere Reserve by UNESCO in the mid '90s. The surrounding reefs are home to parrotfish and angelfish, while many other species pass nearby, including sharks, rays, turtles, dolphins and whales. Birds include brown pelicans, great blue herons, snowy egrets, turkey vultures, and hummingbirds. Any sort of poetic description of the view will simply not justify this mouth-opening display of natural beauty—layers of colours—snow white sand melting into turquoise emerald waters and azure blue skies with fluffy wispy clouds with the hazy mysterious dark island emerging out onto the horizon.

A solitary man, with his boat at the edge of the water, points over to the island. I kindly shake my head that today I won't be requiring his services to get over there, even if there is an opportunity to see the wild seals. But as I look around, I'm indeed starting to notice a little more hive of activity, with men starting to carry stacked chairs out from the shacks and open up the bar areas. A couple of them look curiously over to me, and I'm suspecting before long they'll be wanting me to pay for the plastic lounger I'm casually lying on. Balandra is much more basic and to my liking today. I'll head back and pitch up there.

Finally with today's essentials under a shaded beach palapa, I walk through the warm, soft sand and into the tepid shallow waters where I simply fall back into it and quietly float under the rich blue sky. I feel tickling around my feet and see a shoal of tiny fish race past me and through my legs. Besides noticing a couple walking a dog some distance up along the beach, there are only just a handful of other people swimming further out to sea.

It's then I notice a bigger than average couple hauling stuff down the beach. One has a kayak and the other an inflated lilo bed. They've also got stuff packed on their backs like they're on a serious escape expedition. The guy nonchalantly jumps into the boat and starts quickly paddling away to the other side of the bay, where it looks like access to the rocky beach can only be reached from the water. His lady friend somehow stoically follows by lying front forward and paddling hard with her hands and with her legs up in the air, stopping every so often to catch her breath. Before long they've both almost disappeared out of view looking like no more than two dots moving around on the opposite beach.

The afternoon fades away quickly, which is often the case when you're enjoying yourself. But I'm happy because I can come back again tomorrow!

It feels like Groundhog Day. I'm back at Balandra Beach the next morning under the same palapa and with the same colourful, bright sea and skies around me. Even the same people are here; on my right are the two gay couples under their palm tree umbrella and on the other side the totally covered older woman wearing trousers, scarf, wide-brimmed hat and a cape.

I slide once again into the warm, clear inviting waters and soak up the simple but extreme beauty around me. With the tickly little fish once again swimming to me, I can understand why Jacques Cousteau called this area "The Aquarium of the World." It's definitely worth the effort to go that extra mile and not always compromise with the easier options closer to home. But by mid-afternoon, I'm getting myself sorted to leave the beach and get back to La Paz. There's still a few things I want to do. Unfortunately, due to a bit of sunburn, I need to keep one piece of clothing off—no rubbing bra straps for at least a day.

Disastrously, I miss the turn to get me back along the beachfront malecón and instead detour all around the congested city and end up driving in from the other side of town from where I'd originally arrived—another precious hour lost. That's not good, but at least I found my way back without the help of the garage attendant.

I can't wait to get the sweat and sea salt off me. But walking into my room I see an ominous notice on the door: "Dear Guests. Today the government started to fix some water issues we have here in La Paz. For that reason, we are NOT getting water for the next 3 days from the city. Here at The Angel we do have a cistern but we kindly ask you to save water; to take short showers and flush the toilet only for bigger business! Thanks a lot!" It's a good job I'm leaving tomorrow.

After a problem free, cool but short shower and change of clothes, I wander back to the seafront, and it's only walking down Avenida Independencia that I witness the most hilarious and bizarre commotion. Along the side walk, six burly men are carrying a wingless life-size two-seater airplane up four steep, stony pavement steps and manoeuvring it through the door of a building. Even the wheels and propeller are still on it. I have to do a second take and put my curiosity hat on, having come to no conclusion on what this is all about. One of the panting guys comes to sit on the pavement.

I smile, "What was that all about?"

He also smiles, rubbing his sweaty forehead with the back of his hand, "Friends of ours. It's going to be an accessory for a new restaurant opening here soon."

Well, alright, that's pretty obvious—not! I thank him for the clarification and wish him the best of luck.

It's about time for a drink, so I walk into the legendary Hotel Perla, built in an art nouveau style, which when opened in 1940, was considered the first modern hotel in the state of Baja California Sur. When Steinbeck visited La Paz at the time, he was partially prophetic in his reaction:

> On the water's edge of La Paz a new hotel was going up, and it looked very expensive. Probably the airplanes will bring weekenders from Los Angeles before long, and the beautiful, poor bedraggled old town will bloom with a Floridian ugliness.

I walk through into the reception area and up a flight of stairs, where the bar and roof terrace are. But sadly, despite the modern renovations, it looks a little past its date from its crazy party days, and besides a few people seated quietly in shaded alcoves, it's empty; I decide I'd prefer my beer elsewhere. The open-air restaurant on the ground floor of Hotel Perla is still known as the town's gathering place and thankfully feels more vibrant. I'm currently finishing an excellent mystery thriller book, *Murder in La Paz* by Murdoch Hughes, that I'd picked up from one of The Angel's book shelves. I'd decided it would maybe help to better absorb this place of La Paz while I was here, and it didn't disappoint. I sit down on the pavement terrace with a chilled beer and curiously watch the world go by.

Besides packing and eating later, there is just one last place, which I'd seen off the Cathedral Square and which seemed worth going back to. I tip the waiter and get up to leave.

Walking around to the side of the hotel, I once again have to stop to absorb what I'm seeing. It's not a particularly pleasant site and leaves a lump in my throat in its extremes. Besides this luxurious hotel, under the Salon Madre Perla's red canvas awning, is an ornately painted white, metal bench. Lying on it is a barefooted man with dirty feet, trousers, and shirt. His eyes are closed, and his arms are crossed over his chest. He looks like he badly needs some rest. His feet are propped up on an old, black wooden box, similar to ones I'd seen before, which I'm imagining means he's a shoe cleaner, a job which probably doesn't pay much. Ironically, I do notice a pair of shoes under the bench. But they're old, split, dusty, and look like they'd be very uncomfortable to wear. I doubt if this guy has much money for a new pair.

But it's directly opposite, outside a bar, just a few feet away that shocks me most. Six well-dressed business guys are casually sitting on stools, drinking back their beers like they haven't a care in the world and totally ignoring anything around them. Almost right next to them is this person, who probably can't imagine sitting at a bar like that. Such close extremes. I raise my eyebrows in pain and breathe deeply, fighting back the emotion, and continue walking.

On the other side of the plaza from the cathedral is the nineteenth century Casa de Gobierno, which has been converted into the Centro de Artes Populares. Walking back from the supermarket, I'd noticed they were featuring a photographic exhibition of the rancheros of this region and their history. Entry is free as I walk into this old atmospheric place with beautiful black and white photographs of the Southern Baja rancheros' life. I'm saddened to read that there is clearly a risk they are in danger, due to irreversible urbanization and the younger generations leaving the country for the cities. *The Real Dictionary of the Spanish Language* defines *rancho* as "Location outside town, where several families or individuals are housed." Over the centuries the descendants of the missions' soldiers and people working at them settled in the mountain regions (the Sierra) and tried to make a living using natural resources. They created gardens, where in the shade of fruit trees and date palms, vegetables were grown and fruit preserves and cheese were made for extra income. And from breeding cattle, workshops were built to make the leather into clothing and footwear. I'm just wondering how long this lifestyle of the Southern Baja cowboys can last.

I walk up the road through the blistering heat and strangely see a mural graffiti of a skeleton riding a motorcycle. It's not the first time I've thought about how I would have coped on two wheels out here and along the lost desert roads. My throat dries thinking about those accidents, and I touch my head again that I'm safe and out of danger.

Back in the quiet sanctuary of The Blue Angel, the "honesty" bar invites me to pour a shot of old brown tequila into a glass. I write on the pad what I've taken. Sitting outside, looking up at the sky in the courtyard, the stars pop out one by one, and my only job now will be to decide where I'll be following them for a five-star meal in this beautiful place.

9

WINDOW TO
ANOTHER WORLD

*The sea, once it casts its spell, holds one in its net of
wonder forever.*

Jacques Yves Cousteau

The cathedral bells in the twin towers ring out, calling the
first worshippers of the day, as I sit outside the tranquil Plaza
Jardin Velasco with my first coffee of the day and reading the
local *El Sudcaliforniano* newspaper.

Packed and ready to go, I just want to take a little wander
to breathe in the special atmosphere of La Paz one last time.
This main square is quiet, besides a few pigeons flying down
from the trees to peck at the ground. I lean back and flick
through Saturday's pages of news with all its extra sections.
Just like anywhere in the world, there are pull outs for the usual
weekend: Travel, Property, Jobs, Finance, and . . . then I stop

and gasp: "Policiaca," a full-size colour paper for exclusively covering police activities; drug cartel incidents, deaths, killings, shootings, armed robberies, and road accidents. The front page has graphic pictures of armed drug enforcement officers marching people away and a number of cars with bullet holes through the windows.

It makes me think that there's obviously enough crime, violence, and corruption in this area for it to warrant its own paper. It's the first time I'd seen this sort of massive coverage and am a little surprised, as I'd noticed so little police presence here and also nothing in other towns. But like anywhere, a lot must be gang-related and in the outskirts of these towns.

I politely return the papers inside and walk back to The Angel. To be perfectly honest, the coffee hadn't been too good, so I decide to make breakfast before I leave. I'd left some fruit in the main kitchen, which we were told we could use to make meals, so I go about slicing a massive, juicy papaya and bananas, squeezing lime juice all over them—delicious. Someone has put fresh coffee on, and I pour myself a mug and walk out to the shady terrace. I see the little upside-down glass bottles have been refilled with the sugar and water nectar for the humming birds. This has been a magical place, and I've been very lucky to have found it. I'd imagine in the busy season it would be hard to get a room, another reason I'm happy I'd planned ahead.

I look down at today's folded section of the road map and feel good for two reasons about what I see. I'm finally going to get off the Transpeninsular Highway and travel down the minor road 286 out across to the east coast and to a little place on the Sea of Cortez called La Ventana. I'd chosen this place for its isolation and sparse information. Another good thing in its favour is it's only about forty-five miles away, so with any luck, I'll easily be there by lunchtime. Yes, that's good. The idea of looking out to sea in a remote place with a nice plate of food has got to bring a smile.

The whole place is quieter today, and before I'm even out of the city, I've quickly exited Highway 1 and jumped onto Route 286, which should take me most of the way. The sprawling suburbs and outlying districts have soon disappeared, and now it's once again just me and the road. The window's open and the warm, hot air teasingly stroking and blowing over my skin and face. I have no need to put my foot down or rush. I have, as they say, "all the time in the world." The empty, sand-lined road with scrubland on either side just rolls out in one straight line to the distance. About five miles on, I look into the rear view mirror and see the long road disappear directly through the town and into the sea on the horizon—quite a beautiful sight.

But I'm certainly not only looking through rose-tinted glasses. The further I head out along this isolated road, the more rubbish I see thrown out onto the side, with piles of bottles and cans indiscriminately cluttering the place. And without exaggeration, the majority of the white concrete road posts have been knocked or run down, probably due to excessive speeding or drinking. At some point along the way, I curiously get out and walk to one of these knocked down posts on the edge of the road. Large truck tyre prints in the sand look like they've recently swerved onto the sandy, rocky track, hitting the post and then jumping back onto the road. It all feels a bit like the Wild West here.

And with that, continuing on, comes more crosses on the side of the road pointing out the true gravity and danger of the place. And it's not just trucks you need to look out for. After just a few miles, a solitary, white ox appears, slowly crossing the road in front and then, just like that, decides to stop on the oncoming side of the road without a care in the world. The idea of what could happen with an oncoming truck or, God forbid, a bike is too gory to linger on.

The same arid, barren landscape with the spikey gorse bushes continues without respite. I wonder if many people actually live out here. It's then a strange sight appears, and

I can't help but stop, which may also answer that previous question. Out here, on its own, the body of a massive, old rusty camper home, but without the driving cabin, engine, and wheels, is floating high above the sandy ground on four steel girder poles. Everything is being used to keep it joisted up, including wood poles, a massive steel frame, which was maybe once a bed, and even an old chair! It all looks just a bit precarious. An old sun-bleached curtain is flapping from outside a small window, with a big hand-written symbol on the glass window next to it: "$". I'm imagining that means it's for sale. Who on earth would want to buy this piece of old rubbish, and how would they even move it?

But the more I look, the more I feel someone might actually be living in it. There's even a hole in the side of it with electric socket connections. But again, no one to explain anything. Not even a phone number to call if you decided to buy it! A friendly flea-bitten mongrel appears from under the shaded underbelly of it, but it's too hot for it to do any more than slowly wag a limp tail and slump back down again out of the sun.

I also want to get back into the shade of the truck, even if it is roasting in there. Shortly, and once again, I'm seeing signs that massive road construction "enhancement" work is underway to broaden the highways. Arrows direct me onto a sandy, gravely parallel road that is visibly the new section, which will easily double the original width very shortly. It feels like this area is also on the cusp of big change.

Very soon, a van quickly approaches from behind, and I let out a giggle. A white FedEx van signals and rushes past me, just like you'd see in a TV commercial. Even in the remotest places I'm guessing stuff has to arrive, and there's always someone that needs something urgently. Trucks up in front are creating dust clouds, which force me to close the window. It's stiflingly hot, and my hands are sticking to the wheel. I turn the AC button on, which is still stiff, as I've hardly used it, and a sharp cold breeze blows through. Ahhh, that's actually quite nice for once. Again, my mind stops to try and imagine how my ride would have been like on a loaded bike with no AC or ventilation. I prefer not to!

Shortly, there's a thankful sign on the left indicating directions up a narrow road to La Ventana, a small fishing village on the shores of the bay of La Ventana. It winds and twists up sandy, hilly slopes, with wild windswept views out to sea. This is looking good. It appears to be pretty remote. The tiny community of La Ventana appears, with just a couple of shops and beach homes dispersed throughout the sandy and hilly terrain. I'd been told to continue through, make a turn up another bumpy, even smaller track, and continue along the shoreline towards El Sergente and the lighthouse.

And there, descending slowly down a sandy, pebble-lined road disappearing down to the sea, and in between cacti and palms, are a handful of white-domed ceramic encrusted buildings. The nearer I approach, the more they're reminiscent of Greek orthodox churches or the Trulli conical roofed homes in Bari, southern Italy.

The wheels come to a sliding halt beside one of them, and I step out into warm silence, besides the chirping of birds hidden in leafy palm trees. Someone must have heard me break the silence, as a smiling guy wanders out to greet me.

"Buenos días. Welcome to Ventana. I'm Antonio. You must be Señora Cano, as you're the only person arriving today. Let me show you the way down to where you'll be staying."

It's unbelievable. I've found yet another beautiful place, which is again empty. We walk down some white, stone steps onto a wide, sandy open terrace with a hammock swinging dreamily between two tall palm trees and which drops immediately down to a massive white beach. He turns around and slides open a large glass door and walks inside. I follow closely behind to see an idyllic room with a bed facing out to sea.

"Now, as you probably know, it's quiet here at the moment, so I'm more than happy to upgrade you to the best suite here. It's bigger. Come and take a look!"

We walk around a little bush and next door to the only other room here on the seafront terrace. I'm flattered. But kindly decline, as the room is too big for me, with a kitchen and lounge area. Sometimes the simple things are better.

By now we're on first names, and Antonio asks, "So Zoë, have you eaten along the way, or would you like lunch? We can make something for you in about an hour out on the terrace above."

I genuinely smile with appreciation, "That would be perfect."

"Leave it to us. We have no menu. We just make everything from the best local food. You wait and see!" He wanders away.

I kick my flip-flops off and crash onto the bed, looking directly out to the palm trees and sea. But it's the swinging, shaded hammock, with shells hanging from its tassels, out on the terrace which beckons me. Far out on the calm sea, I notice a small, green fishing boat and brown mountains out in the distance. The beautiful beach is totally empty. This is too tempting. I wrap a sarong around my waist and, walking barefoot, go down the few steps onto a beach path leading down to a gate. There are two giant surfboards decoratively standing up on either side, but the gate is locked. So I squeeze between one of the surfboards and the gate, and my feet immediately sink into warm soft sand. The soft ripples and small waves come lapping up to the shore, and birds similar to sandpipers are running in and out of the water along the shoreline.

Time is slipping away as quickly as the sand going through my toes, as I see a waving hand from the thatched roof terrace beckoning me that food is ready. It's here that I see the beachfront house blends so well with the landscape that it almost looks like one of the enormous sand dunes next to it. I climb up the red and white bougainvillea-lined steps into a palm thatched room with tables and chairs. At the far end I hear a woman's voice humming away quietly to herself. I walk towards an open door into a kitchen with a lady busily chopping onions and tomatoes. Whatever it is smells good. The kitchen is ornately decorated with a beautiful fish-tiled round table, where everything is being prepared. Here in Mexico, the heart of the house is often the kitchen, where love and care is given to the food.

I smile, "Hola y buenos días."

She timidly smiles back, quickly looks down, and continues with her chopping. I can see everything she's preparing is being added to a plate of pulled chicken strips and avocado slices. She asks me in Spanish whether I'd like to eat here inside or outside on the sandy terrace downstairs. I nod for the latter.

Within ten minutes I'm devouring the most exquisite chicken enchilladas with sour cream drizzled over them, guacamole, and the freshest salad of crispy lettuce, cucumber, tomatoes, and peppers that tastes like the vegetables have just been pulled out of the garden. Compared to last night's city meal, it's like chalk and cheese in flavour. This is real home food made from the heart and is delicious.

I'd also been kindly given a wonderful, refreshing jug of cooled, iced juice. With its light-green colour, it was to die for and like nothing I'd ever tasted before. I just had to find out what it was.

I walk back into the kitchen with the empty plate, and the smiling, shy lady is clearing everything up. She turns around and seems shocked that I've brought the plate back in and smiles, waving a finger as if to say, "You needn't have done that!"

I place it in the sink and try and ask in basic Spanish what I'm curious to know. "Thank you. Your lunch was amazing, but the drink was like nothing I've ever tasted before. What was it?"

She smiles, appreciating the interest, "Thank you, Señora."

I interject before she can continue, "No, please call me Zoë."

She smiles again, and it seems that she starts to relax a little. "OK. And I'm Carla. I do all the cooking here from homemade recipes. Here's what you need to do."

She walks over to the fridge and pulls out one big cucumber. And so here's the secret recipe, and it's ideal as a healthy summer drink.

CARLA'S CUCUMBER DRINK—"AGUA DE PEPINO"

Chill a litre jug to put the juice in.

Peel the skin along a large cucumber, alternating to leave un-peeled strips in between.

Wash the cucumber clean with water and cut the ends off. Chop the cucumber up and liquidize with about a quarter litre of water. Sieve it.

Add 1 to 2 tablespoons of castor sugar. Check the taste, and you can add more water.

At the very end, Carla's secret is to add the juice of 1 lime. Pour into the chilled jug and add ice.

If not drunk immediately, it'll last in the fridge for 1- 2 days.

Finally having had a small siesta in the hammock, I idly wander back down to the quiet beach and plunge into the refreshing, sandy-floored sea. Sublime. There are many beaches and places in exotic places I'd visited around the world, but this has to rank up at the top. There's a very good feel to this place and I want to find out more. Maybe Antonio will be around later to have a chat. The afternoon slides by, and soon the sun is setting directly behind the mountains out across the Sea of Cortez, turning them a rich, golden brown. Black-looking storks appear and fly low over and then out across the water.

Fully refreshed from a "hectic" afternoon doing not a lot, I walk back up the pink bougainvillea staircase and walk towards a table on the outdoor terrace looking out to sea. A couple have appeared out of nowhere and are quietly eating at a table close by. I nod and they nod back. I sit down and look out at the ever-darkening sky to see bats crazily swooping and racing back and forth. Doves are nestled in the trees close by, and large, orange-yellow-headed chaffinches sit perched in the palm trees. But this isn't the last of the show, as pelicans appear overhead and swoop down into the sea for their own dinner.

A delicious prawn and avocado ceviche cocktail with tacos and fresh guacamole is devoured. And then Jurel, a grilled yellowtail fish, caught within eye sight from here, with a delicious ratatouille of asparagus, cauliflower, carrots, peppers, and tomatoes equally disappears. It's all topped off by Pastel de Sonoria, a soft, spicy carrot cake with a smooth custard of Philadelphia cream and icing sugar over it. And without forgetting a mouth-watering jug of fresh, orange-melon juice. I'm in Seventh Heaven!

As I'm wiping the last cake morsels off the plate, Antonio walks in and, after a chat with the departing couple, wanders over.

"So how are you liking the place? I hope everything's OK."

I smile, and he sees I'm happy.

"I can't start to say what a great time I've already had, and I'm excited to explore the beach and coast tomorrow with a good walk and my snorkelling gear. Have you a few minutes? I've got just a bit to ask."

He takes a seat opposite. "Sure, I'm not heading home back to the village for a while. What would you like to know?"

"Well, I guess first of all, where's the best place to see fish and snorkel? Is there any accessible reef nearby? And what about those mountains over there? I've been trying to figure if that's mainland or an island."

At that precise moment, a giant, and I'm not exaggerating, giant wasp lands on the table.

Antonio leaps up, leaning back to get out of the way. "Careful now! Leave it to fly off—those can even kill scorpions!"

He sits cautiously back down. "So, where were we? Oh yes. Well, I can answer all those questions, which means your day might be a busy one tomorrow!" he says smiling.

"Those mountains you see across the bay, well, it's actually the Jacques Cousteau Island, or better known here as Isla Cerralvo. It's twenty-nine kilometres long, and the steepest bluff is over 600 metres. They changed its name in 2009, as Cousteau had led many expeditions in the area, but a lot of the locals aren't too happy, as we hadn't been consulted. So most of us here have kept its original name and always refer to it as Cerralvo. In our peak season, the water visibility there is very good—up to thirty metres—making it good for big game fishing. There's masses of marine life due to the current, so you'll see out there marlin, swordfish, sailfish, and golden grouper.

"Closer to the shore, where you can easily snorkel without swimming out too far or using scuba gear, is a reef only a couple of hundred metres from here on your left. Look out for a set of dunes and a gateway between them. The reef is directly opposite, about thirty metres out to sea.

"And if you want to take a much longer walk, then you have to get to El Sargente, before the lighthouse. That's where the hot springs are, a little bay with a few umbrellas. The beach is called that, as hot springs come down from the mountains there. If you want to find the hot spring, you have to dig a little into the sea bottom. The best time to do that is when the tide is low and the water is flat. Tomorrow might be good, as the ocean is quiet at this time of the year. If you want to make your life easier and don't want to walk that far, you can always use one of the kayaks stacked in the beach hut as you walk through the gate. Just remember the sea current. It's harder to kayak upwards, left out of the beach, but much faster coming down, so be careful."

By now, we're both drinking bottles of beer, and I'm trying to absorb everything he's saying.

He continues, "I don't know if you'd heard, but La Ventana goes crazy from mid-October to mid-April. It's known as the best place in Baja California for kiteboarding, and people come from all over the place, with international competitions. We've heard it's as good as Tarifa in Spain. There's warm water and consistent wind here to suit everybody, from beginners to experts. The north wind here is better and much more reliable than other Baja locations due to the Venturi "pinching" effect created by Cerralvo Island and the thermal suction from the rising hot air from the desert peninsula to the south. Another reason for you to come back!"

I look out to sea and strangely see fog coming up through the water, pointing in that direction.

"Yes, I know what you're going to ask. We've got fog or sea smoke here because cold air is moving over the warmer water, which condenses it similar to steam produced over a hot bath. So you see, for a small place, we have a lot going on!

"And one last thing. There's something special going on in the sky tonight, which doesn't happen often! Make sure to look up at the moon, and you'll see Jupiter has moved right next to it, on the left. It's massive and very bright, and you can't miss it. After tomorrow, they'll have moved away from each other.

I yawn, putting my hand over my mouth, and excuse myself, wandering back down to the sandy terrace to sit back for a while under the night sky. With all artificial light now turned off, I'm almost blinded by the bright light of the moon and Jupiter. Only here!

10

SEA STORMS AND SCORPIONS

You only live once, but if you do it right, once is enough.
Mae West

What better feeling to wake up to, the sound of crashing waves, early morning sunshine pouring onto the tip of the bed, and the smell of freshly brewed coffee? Joy of joys, that's what my senses got this morning and all in one blast!

I pull the sliding door open and barefooted step through onto the sandy footpath to follow the wonderful smell emanating from upstairs. The day is starting bright, with maybe a few clouds further out to sea, but the chaffinches are contentedly chirping away and darting from one bougainvillea branch to another. I don't bother immediately sitting down but walk directly into the kitchen to say hello.

With a red pinafore and baseball cap, Carla looks up from grating cheese in a bowl and smiles warmly to me. The tomatoes, peppers, and garlic are already chopped and a frying pan is warming up on the hob. "Morning Zoë. Are you ready for breakfast? It should just be another five minutes."

I smile and eagerly nod. She continues, "I'm making you my special Baja huevos rancheros. I hope you like them."

"Wonderful. To be honest, I've eaten them a few times already in Baja, but I was always curious to know exactly how they were made. Do you mind if I take a look?"

Carla looks flattered and casually continues. I like what I see and think that maybe something similar can be done back at home. As the finishing touches are added, I walk back to the terrace and look out to sea. As they say, the greatest compliment to any chef is an empty plate, and as I wipe it clean I see a smile coming from the kitchen.

CARLA'S HUEVOS RANCHEROS (GOOD FOR 2 PEOPLE)

1. First make the "salsa" (sauce). Sauté half a chopped onion in a little oil on medium heat. Once clear, add a tin of tomatoes (or 1-2 large fresh chopped vine-ripened tomatoes when in season) and juices. Add a little diced green chilli, about half a big red pepper seeded and cut into pieces. You can add more if you like and some chipotle chilli powder or garlic powder or even regular chilli powder. Simmer for about 10 minutes while you're doing the rest.

2. Warm the plates in the oven.

3. Prepare the corn tortillas (4). Heat a teaspoon of olive oil in a large frying pan. Heat the tortillas, one by one, maybe a minute each side until they're heated through, softened, and there are pockets of air bubbles inside them. Remove them and stack on one of the plates in the oven to keep warm.

4. Fry the eggs. Add salt and pepper. Using the same

pan, add a bit of butter and on a medium heat cook them for 3-4 minutes for runny yolks and until the whites are crisp on the edges.

5. Assemble and serve. Spoon a little of the sauce onto the warm plate. Top with a tortilla, then a fried egg, top with more sauce. Sprinkle grated cheese (mozzarella is good) over it and chopped coriander (cilantro). A good dollop of refried beans (frijoles) spread over the tortillas before adding the eggs and salsa makes it even better! Sliced avocado on the side of the plate is good too. You can serve 1 or 2 eggs and tortillas per plate depending on how hungry you are!

Carla smiles at my more than empty plate and surprisingly opens up, "That makes me very happy. I woke up very early this morning."

I look surprised. "I thought you lived here!"

She raises her eyebrows. "No, no, no!" You were on your own here last night. I live about thirty kilometres away and drive here every day. My husband also works and helps here with maintenance and gardening. We both need to work."

Carla shyly pulls out a photograph of a young boy from her purse like she wants to share something. "This is our son. He is often ill and has very bad asthma. It's expensive to cure."

Another stranger who has opened up to tell me something important about their lives. Again, I feel humbled. I spontaneously walk over and give her a hug. She goes on to quickly tell me something about food later on in the evening, which I don't quite understand, but says lunch will be served at whatever time I want. I pour another coffee from the pot and return to sit looking out to sea.

Since we've been chatting and trying to understand each other, the clouds out at sea have gathered and darkened and are ominously and quickly approaching overhead, blocking out the sun. The sky is blackening, and rain is starting to fall. Up here, I'm feeling like I'm on the deck of a ship, with the wooden boards beneath me, looking helplessly out to sea and waiting for a storm to arrive.

My mind once again and uncontrollably jumps back in time, remembering when I had, indeed, been on the deck of a boat and had felt for the very first time in my life the uncontrollable fear that perhaps I was going to die.

It was August 1999, and I'd naively volunteered, without any previous sailing experience, to help crew a boat to cross the English Channel to witness the total eclipse of the sun. France was going to be the only place to see it in totality when the moon completely crossed the sun's path to obscure it. It was going to be the first total eclipse in the area since 1927, so everyone in the UK was talking about it. I'd known Scott, the skipper, for a while, and with two other crew members, Sharon and Ozzey, we'd set off on his little thirty foot sailing boat. Before leaving we'd had the customary tour of the life-saving equipment of life jackets, harnesses, flares, radio, and even a horn. Little did I realise just how important all this equipment would be later on in the trip.

After consultation with the charts, forecast, and tide tables, we quickly left the signs of land and started navigating the Channel and crossing the giant shipping lanes. We were like a sitting duck and in the line of fire of those enormous unstoppable vessels. Passing Boulogne-sur-Mer, rumours abounded that the wind was predicted to pick up quite dramatically. We turned our stern to the wind, and the boat sped off at six knots. As the day wore on, our progress was good, and we were all in good spirits. The wind did pick up, but as we were running with the waves, we hardly noticed that they too had picked up in speed. We were effectively water skiing down them. The boat occasionally slewed from one side to the other as we got to the bottom of each wave.

A yacht some distance away was sailing north into the wind and bounced from one wave to the next with spray flying continuously up and over the crew. On several occasions their whole vessel appeared to come out of the water heading skywards then splashed down with a horrendous crash. The sky was now overcast, with a storm approaching and it getting darker. We were now racing at more than eight knots, with waves getting ever higher and throwing us all around. We were in ever increasing desperation to find a safe harbour. We tried to radio the port of Le Treport to see if there was any room for us to get in.

No response. This was getting dangerous, with the boat now racing on both sails. With the strong wind, the waves were getting even higher, ten feet or more, and throwing us all around. We literally hung on for grim life!

Life belts on and clipped to the sides, the sky continued to get darker, and things were beginning to get a bit too serious. The charts said we should see a lighthouse in front on the chalk hills, five miles ahead, but nothing. In the almost complete darkness, the tide seemed to turn and was now flowing against us, feeling like we were being battered in a cauldron of waves by the ferocious winds.

For the first time in my life, I thought that was the end. I felt that the sea would consume us at any moment. There was nothing I could do or say. I was totally helpless and at the mercy of nature.

The sails became entangled, and someone had to go up front to release them before we entered the harbour. With Sharon's harness securely clipped on, the boat was pointed into the ferocious winds. It was deafening. The waves, what could be seen of them, seemed as high as mountains. Sharon, up front, disappeared completely from our gaze at the arrival of each large wave. As the boat re-emerged from the watery grave so also did Sharon, still wedged in fighting furiously to release the jammed mechanism. Finally, the water drenched her so completely her life jacket exploded out of its red container, taking on a life of its own, rather like a blow up doll and forming a firm hold around her neck. This forced her to look no other way but up and therefore she was no longer able to see what she was doing. She was forced to return to the relative safety of the cockpit, but the engine throttle got knocked by accident to full speed making the oncoming effect of the waves even more thrillingly frightening!

Thus we had gone from reasonable control in tough conditions to absolute chaos in less than half an hour. With the engine now on and the sails flapping about in total disarray, we motored towards the harbour lights. But this wasn't the end. The large harbour offered very little in way of protection from the rough seas, and the battering waves seemed just as bad. We were informed over the VHF radio that the little marina just behind it was full, and our only option was to continue motoring around and to "dry up" as the tide fell. Not good news, as the water wouldn't drop for five hours. There was no point to anchor as there was significant danger that the boat would drag and be knocked into the harbour wall. I don't know how we did it, but we continued motoring around until two hours later the radio came to life and said we could now actually enter the marina. They must have been feeling sorry for us.

Just to say how weather patterns can change so quickly, the next morning, the day of the eclipse, the sky was clear of clouds and the wind had dropped almost totally. We calmly sailed out into the sea and started to witness the moon slowly covering the sun. There was little change to the intensity of light until five or ten minutes before the event. Sea birds started flying for the land, and it was getting colder. The light was noticeably changing. There were various hues of blues on the horizon that I had never seen before and verging on deep purple as the moment arrived.

The white of the boat took on a waxy appearance, and our shadows became fuzzy. It became colder, and the sky went dark. Stars started to appear, and the sun, through protective glasses, could be seen as a corona with knobs of fiery light sticking out from the covering disc of the moon. After just two minutes, the light re-appeared so dramatically quickly that it was as if someone had turned on a light switch. We were safe and had a reason to celebrate. The champagne was opened, and the oysters brought out from the cool box. We'd become members of "The Full Eclipse Club"!

I shudder slightly from the memory and look out to sea, hearing the thunder becoming increasingly distant and the bolts of lightning now almost non-existent. It's now just lightly raining, with the sun slowly beginning to appear from behind the clouds.

The decision is made to go and find that coral reef Antonio had talked about yesterday. I swing the net bag with the flippers, mask, and snorkel over my shoulder and walk barefooted out along the straight, wide beach. Not another person is in sight. Ironically, at times like this, you question whether it's safe out there on your own. Why wouldn't it be? I look out for the gate, which should give some indication on where the reef is, but somehow I don't see it.

Walking ever further up the silent beach, a small fishing community appears with boats pulled up onto the sand and their nets spread out. Surely, it can't be further than this. I'll go on just a bit more. And there, round a sandy dune, I see a short distance away a group of camper vans pitched up on the beach with some kids playing close to the shoreline. This is probably the place, but it has to be said that Antonio had exaggerated just slightly on the distance. It'll be good to take a swim. Particularly as my naked feet had taken a bit of a battering along the way from some of the pebbles and shells.

But even before I can sit down on the sand and pull my flippers on, I hear loud barking, and to my horror, see a big pit bull dog, with even bigger teeth, tearing across the beach towards me! Oh God, I'm already not the greatest lover of dogs, and this one's looking like he's guarding his bit of beach! Just as quickly, I see the kids come racing after the dog and grab it by the rough of its neck, just as I feel it was going to grab me! They smile almost apologetically. I smile back, thinking ironically, this is probably a good opportunity to ask about the mysterious reef.

So with animated hand gestures and pointing with my snorkel, as I don't know much of the vocabulary to explain, I try and act out that I'm looking for fish. They understandably scratch their heads then shake them. So this doesn't seem right. Then they smile, eagerly nodding like they understand and put four fingers up in the air, and looking at their watches, for me to understand it's four hours later I need to come back. Maybe the tide will be shallower for better visibility. I nod and put my thumbs up in thanks, giving the impression I understand everything and walk back. But I'm not going to be defeated. I am going to find that damn coral reef and see some fish!

As I was to later learn, I'd actually arrived at the thermal hot springs, and it was not until the end of the afternoon that the tides would turn, making it shallower to dig into the sand and feel the warm waters flowing into the sea. I'd simply walked too far.

Having easily walked at least a couple of miles, swam out to sea to optimistically find the hidden reef, it has to be said that a little later on the tasty fish lunch goes down a treat. So having had a quick chat with Carla, on my second outing I feel I'm more organized and have a better plan. I pull a heavy kayak down the sloping beach and into the sea. With the waves pounding against it, I crawl in and paddle off. This is more like it. I stop and rest for a while, putting my feet up along the boat, and lean back. This is lovely. The ripples bounce the boat up and down a little bit, and then just a bit further up, I see the gate between the dunes, knowing the reef should be here under the kayak. I peer and squint down through the water and see the coral reefs with fish of all sizes swimming in, over, and around it. This is more like it.

The yellow kayak is hoisted up onto the beach, and this time I successfully pull the flippers on and swim out to marvel at the colourful beauty of the sea life underneath the surface. By the time I get back, the afternoon has almost disappeared. And by early evening, I feel a beer wouldn't go amiss, and surely it must also be time for dinner. But it strangely feels very quiet, like no one is here.

With the last rays of light fast disappearing, I wander upstairs into an eerily quiet and darkened room, where bizarrely, just quiet music is coming from hidden speakers. I sit at my table and politely wait. Nothing. I start tapping my fingers on it with just a little bit of impatience. Still nothing and still no one. I get up and walk to the kitchen. The lights are off, and all the tops have been cleared. It looks like nothing has been prepared. Surely this isn't right. It looks like they've all gone home and forgotten me.

So what would you do in a situation like this? I'm hungry after all that kayaking and walking, so I guess I've got to be self-sufficient and take a look to see what there is. I tip-toe to the fridge and inquisitively open it to see what's inside. Like a pillaging pirate looking into a sea chest, I take a plastic box out and see it's the lovely chilli chicken I'd had the day before, some tomatoes, half a massive avocado, and a whole papaya. That's about all there is. I also see a large slice of the carrot cake and nick that too. I put it all on a plate but somehow can't find any utensils. I walk back to the terrace and the setting sun. Just one more thing—something to drink. I walk behind the bar at the end of the room and grab a bottle of wine from the fridge. That'll do nicely.

With only my sharp pocket knife, I stab at the meat and start hungrily eating. I slice into the juicy papaya, and eating with my hands only, and with no twenty-first century eating manners, the juice runs down my mouth. I wipe it away with my arm. It feels like pure decadence. I'm in what I feel is a five-star place yet doing exactly what I want! It's surreal. I'm imagining that this is how someone like Sir Richard Branson would be if he found himself on his own on Necker Island and had to pillage the kitchen. Or maybe it's Robinson Crusoe living in luxury. I take a gulp of wine from the bottle and smile. This is probably the best meal of the trip. Simple, but naughty!

The only problem is there are no lights on, and I'm unable to find their switches or any matches to light the candles on the table. And obviously my torch is downstairs in my room. But I do see the lighthouse flashing from across the waters from Cousteau's Island and am hearing a lively R&B track playing from the sound system. I beat my feet in rhythm to it on the wall. I'm living the dream.

But seriously, I ask myself would anyone have done what I've just done. Or would they have gone and found someone to scream and complain to? I prefer to just take in the breeze and acknowledge how lucky I am to be so totally free. With no lights, I'm also pretty proud of myself for having found everything before it got too dark. I return the half-empty bottle to the fridge and switch the music system off. Calm, night silence now, with only the repetitive sound of waves crashing up onto the beach.

Totally chilled, but in the semi-darkness, I walk into the bathroom to clean my teeth. God, I jump back in fright. A large scorpion, with its tail up ready to sting and inject its venom, is in the sink. Unlike a spider, I'm not going to be able to pick this up. I carefully lower a glass over it and slide it up onto the basin top. That should do the trick until tomorrow morning, when it can be released. With the sheets tightly up and under my chin, I'm just hoping there aren't more scorpions crawling up or over the bed tonight.

11

RED LIPSTICK AND CHIHUAHUAS

If you're in trouble, or hurt or need, go to the poor people. They're the only ones that'll help—the only ones.
John Steinbeck

An uncontrollable giggle is let out, remembering last night's antics, as Antonio walks over with my breakfast of huevos à la Mexicana. He quizzically looks at me but places the plate on the table.

"Buenos dias, Zoë. Hope you enjoy! The bright colours of the scrambled eggs, red tomatoes, white onion, and the green jalapeños look like the colours of our Mexican flag, don't you think? But why are you laughing?"

"I had quite an adventure last night. No one was here. So I helped myself to some food in the fridge. I didn't know what else to do."

He looks surprised, "Don't you remember us saying that we close on Sunday nights but that there are places open in the village? I'm so sorry. I hope you found something."

I smile in a kind way, digging into the eggs. "It was great. It really wasn't a problem. In fact, it was quite enjoyable until I found the scorpion!"

He sighs with relief, possibly thinking I was going to make a complaint. "So, how was yesterday? Did you explore a bit?"

"It was great, besides a near miss with a dog at the hot springs. I think I got there when the tide was too high, so I couldn't relax in them, but I did find your reef."

"Yes, sorry you couldn't experience the 'hot tub.' It's soon the start of our summer here in La Ventana, which brings calmer and warmer water with higher visibility for the reefs and fish. So this is the best time for spear fishing."

My eyes widen, "And what's that all about? Never heard of it."

"Well, it's as it says. In the summer there are giant fish migrating through here to catch, and guys go out scuba diving with compressed gas-powered guns to strike the fish. Most of this is what they call extreme spear fishing, for large fish, mainly like the wahoo, ruster fish, yellow tail king fish, Humber jack, dorado, yellow fin tuna, and marlin. Spear fishing is an ancient method of fishing, which used to be done free-diving here with long spears. But everyone is careful here today to just catch what is needed. There are giant fish out there and people come from all over the world."

Not really my thing, but I nod. He continues, "That small rain storm yesterday was quite unexpected. But there's been a lot worse here over the years!"

After I've finished my coffee, he follows me out to help carry the bags to the truck.

"In September 2006, we had a really bad hurricane come over this area. La Ventana was caught in the eye of Hurricane John, and thousands in the area had to be evacuated. But I got stuck here! I couldn't escape. I'd waited too late to leave.

I had to find a place to hide and shelter away from the storm. It can be deadly. So I used your room here. I pushed the big mattress against the window to stop flying glass coming in and lay under the bed frame. I heard it come over. The noise was so frightening. On the East Cape here they say the winds were as strong as 120 mph.

"There was a lot of serious damage to property here along the coast. About half the power poles had been broken. The highway toward La Paz and Los Cabos was closed by flash flood arroyos—you know, steep-sided gullies got flooded with fast flowing water from the storm. Looking out now to sea, you cannot imagine what it was like. It was terrible."

He takes my bags and beckons me to follow him. "Come over here and take a look at what it did."

We climb the steps and approach six enormous, tall saguaro cacti, each at least thirty feet tall. On one side is a smooth, healthy, waxy green trunk with its nasty two inch spines poking out. But on the other side the trunks look almost dead, with a brown grey colour and totally stripped of their ferociously sharp spines. Very strange.

"You see? That was with the speed of the hurricane's wind. It blew the sand at huge forces across the land, which battered and destroyed the cactus on this side. A lot of others were completely destroyed, and we're amazed these survived! But this land of ours has had to learn to survive, as hurricanes are a common occurrence here."

At the civilized time of mid-morning, goodbyes are exchanged, and I drive up and out of the sandy track, closing the gate behind me, and through the sleepy village of La Ventana, whose atmosphere will be very different in six months when the wind surfers will be back in town. I follow the sun ahead in the east for a couple of miles until I rejoin Route 286. Then at El Alcambrado I drive onto the even more isolated Carreterra San Antonio-San Juan de los Planes, which heading due south, should hopefully re-connect me to the Transpeninsular Highway.

Now, if there was a beautiful road out there, this has got to be one of them. It's long and straight out to the mountainous horizon with the sky reaching cacti on either side and with its black, smooth, clean surface resembling a snake who'd only shed its skin for a new one yesterday. There's no signs of farms, dwellings, or livestock here. The total emptiness is something I will never take for granted or become complacent with. It's also sorely tempting to just jam the foot down, but speed signs warn the traveller to not exceed sixty miles per hour! Seeing a few crashed into and wrecked concrete, roadside bollards, I dutifully respect the notices—more or less.

In the middle of this nowhereness, with the sun blindingly bright in front of me, I screw my eyes up tight to focus on seeing a solitary scruffy hobo walking out in front with a rucksack on his back. He doesn't bother to look at the approaching vehicle but simply continues out into this godforsaken heat. Shall I? Shan't I? Again, on a bike, this wouldn't have even come into the equation. I want to, but the gut instinct says no, and I guiltily pass him, feeling I could have helped. But I'm already justifying it by thinking I shouldn't either be stupid, as someone seeing a woman travelling on her own may just sway it to their advantage. That was my excuse anyway.

But I also remember all those other times when I'd picked up curiously fascinating people elsewhere in the world with their own little stories. Travelling around Cuba back in the mid '90s when Castro was still in power, was a prime case to better know the people and hear directly what was happening in their country. At that time, there were only unreliable and jammed public buses, trucks, lorries, and antiquated trains to ferry people around. Hundreds of people would walk along the roads to ask for short or long haul lifts. I picked up fishermen going back to see their families on the other side of the island, farmers going to market, a lady and her children needing to get to school, and a teacher who kindly wouldn't get out until she'd directed me into the right part of a bustling unknown town. I was grateful to all of them, and it enhanced my journey and knowledge of the place.

So I'm still feeling just a bit guilty when a few miles down the road I see a fat madre with her small kid and carrying a large water barrel. I can make up for it. I slow down and lean out of the window. She understandably and cautiously looks at this stranger as if to say, "What are you doing?" and that it's maybe me who's going to create the problem. But I persevere, and without her asking, offer them a lift.

She smiles. "¡No gracias, estamos aquí!"

I can't help but smile too, as she's saying they've got to where they need to be and don't want to go any further. Oh well, I'm sure there'll be other people out on the road I can offer my taxi services to. At the junction of San Antonio, lined by shaded trees, after checking the map, I jump back onto the relentlessly hot and arid Highway 1. My hot arm leaning out of the window tells me to grab my water bottle and take a slurp. Turning right would take me back to La Paz, and heading left to where I'm going will ultimately go all the way around the cape and back up the peninsula. Just a bit further along, nothing has changed, as the road's verges are once more homes to accident memorials. If it's appropriate to say, one in particular is actually very beautiful—a little blue and white house with candles inside and terracotta pots of coloured plastic flowers standing next to it.

The unexpected and surprising sight of green, sloped hills and palm trees start appearing as I enter San Bartolo, a recognised little desert oasis in the mountainous gulley, where colourful wooden thatched shops and a café or two line the road for the thirsty traveller. I curiously drive down one of the muddy tracks and notice a little stream of water flowing through the trees at the bottom of it, with a few cattle drinking from it. Amazing! And it doesn't stop with surprises here in this "off the radar" remote place. Just on the outskirts, a spectacularly large Virgin of Guadalupe is painted on the entire height of the rocky cliff face directly onto the road. There's nowhere to stop on this dangerous bend, so I just put my foot down and continue on.

Immediately, the dry desert highway landscape appears again. A few miles on, close to Las Palmas and under the heat of the sun, a young woman is walking slowly on her own with a big bag slung over her shoulder. She's not hitchhiking but looking down as she walks along the side of the stony road. She doesn't appear like she's got much more than two pennies to rub together. I pull over without hesitation and call out.

"Senora! Can I help? Would you like a ride?"

She looks up and over her shoulder, as though I'm talking to somebody else. I nod my head and smile to indicate it is her I'm speaking to. She cautiously approaches me, not quite believing her luck, nods, and walks around to get in. I lean over to open the passenger door, and she quietly sits next to me with her hands in her lap, again looking down. I'm saddened by the way she looks, and I gently smile, putting on a little bit of quiet music. I notice the beginning of a small apologetic smile coming across her face, and I can see for some reason she's battling with some thoughts.

I break the silence. "Where would you like to go to?"

I'm expecting her to say maybe a mile or two further down. She points with a finger directly down the road and mentions something about Los Barriles. I've no idea where that is, so ask her to tell me when we get there. I can see she's uncomfortable, so after more silence, I casually tell her what I'm doing here in Baja California; travelling on my own, writing stories, and trying to learn more about this beautiful place.

Her old, soulful sad eyes open in disbelief. Somehow, a key has unlocked her silence, "Los Barriles is where the gringos live. I'm looking for work, house cleaning. It's very difficult. There's no work here, so I'm trying there."

I nod in non-judgmental silence, and unexpectedly, she continues, "Where you picked me up there's a caravan and camping site where I am with my children. They are four and six years old. My husband was badly abusing me when we lived in Cabo San Lucas, so I had no choice but to run away. With nothing. I have no car so have to walk the thirteen kilometres to Los Barriles. I've walked there several times, and nobody ever wants to pick me up. This is the first time." She looks back down at her hands.

I'm shocked and saddened by what I hear and can't even begin to imagine what hell she must have endured and is still living through. We continue on respecting each other's silence. In a while she points to a turn in the road, indicating she wants to get out. I slow down and stop. And then she says something which flabbergasts me with her sincere generosity.

Her beautiful face looks to me, "Zoë, I know you're going to strange places that you don't know. You must be careful. Would you like my cell phone number in case you need any help?"

I'm speechless. Somebody with nothing is offering everything they have to a total stranger. I'm again humbled. My eyes well up and there's a lump in my throat and I only wish I could offer something as valuable in return. It's pathetic, but I give her all the change in my pocket, which I know isn't a lot. She accepts, I lean over, and we hug each other. She climbs out and crosses the road. By the time I look around she has disappeared. That's a time I would have prayed to a Virgin of Guadalupe out on the roadside for someone else's well-being and happiness.

I'm soon passing over a vast, water estuary where I turn off onto Carreterra La Riboa, a beautiful road with green mango orchards and rich fertile soil. As ever, at this time of the day, it's getting hotter and hotter and almost thirty degrees. With the ever increasing sweat under my arms and butt, and putting my foot ever down, I'm feeling I'm surreally trying to drive away to escape this merciless heat. It's no good. It's keeping up with me!

Once again, I'm asking myself what actual real enjoyment I would have had riding here on a bike. For a start, I wouldn't have been able to help and give people lifts and hear their stories. How would I have coped with this heat?

This is yet another barren lifeless road but with its surprisingly clean asphalt feels like it was only newly paved and re-born yesterday. It feels like it's preparation for something—maybe a change—and I'm starting to feel this place also feels a little wealthier. Maybe this is due to signs and hoardings appearing intermittently by "Quality Realty" for "Lots of Land and Homes for Sale." The barren land looks like it's being advertised as a tempting area for people to invest in, close to the wealthiest part of the peninsula in the very south, with Cabo San Lucas and those protected seas. But for now it appears that it's just at the very beginning of any kind of development, and I can't see anything physical built out here yet, besides the ever present roadside memorials and crosses. In contrast, I'd wanted to come here knowing it was probably still one of the most protected ocean sites and reefs in Mexico.

All of a sudden the normal road abruptly peters out to a sandy, rocky trackway. Next to a big open gateway is a massive hoarding with a photograph of shoals of fish swimming in the sea. Underneath it the simple words say "Bienvenidos— Welcome to Cabo Pulmo National Park"—A UNESCO and Conservation Site. Picture symbols explain that divers need to keep two metres above the coral, there's whale watching, exploration around the shoreline needs permission, no coral or shells are to be taken, no exotic species can be introduced and outside beach fires are not allowed.

I slowly enter the reserve again, unaware of what to expect and only with the knowledge I have a little beachside cabana for a couple of nights and not to expect much else. I'm imagining the curving track with the dust blowing out behind into the distance will shortly come down to the beach. But it spectacularly goes on for another ten kilometres through the sandy landscape and through a little settlement with even a school and mini provision store. The views of the turquoise blue sea out in the distance are teasingly getting ever closer.

I carry on, continuously avoiding and steering round large deep potholes, and finally enter a tiny settlement consisting of a few palm thatched houses offering accommodation and diving expeditions and a little café tempting travellers with fresh seafood. But it's all quiet, and everywhere is looking shuttered up and closed for the season. At the very end of the track I drive into a large sandy parking area with a solitary, two-storey palm roofed, blue building plonked in the middle of it. Signage explains that it's the "PADI School & Diving— Cabo Pulmo. Eco-Tourism." And we're right on the very line of the Tropic of Cancer! Ninety miles from starting this morning, and I've arrived.

I slip my flip-flops back on again and wander over to the little office, where just outside diving jackets are hanging up drying with rows of diving tanks lined up next to them. This looks like a serious place, which of course it is.

A tanned girl with so many leather wristbands on they almost reach her elbow is drinking a bottle of cola with her feet casually up on the table. Seeing me, she quickly puts them down. With a kind of Scandinavian accent, she smiles, "Hi, how you doing? What can I do to help?"

I simply provide my name, and in return, she looks at her written list on a pad and hands me a key with directions to drive down the even sandier smaller track and turn right where cabin six can be found. So I follow her instructions and make my way down a little bougainvillea lined, sandy lane with homes on either side, some larger than others but all with what you'd describe as having a casual, simple, naturally built beach feel.

I stop at a little wooden gate and smile to see a turquoise hand-painted sign nailed to it "6—Shark Shack". Through it and up a plant lined pathway is a round, green painted and palm roofed "shack." There's the obligatory hammock hanging above the sandy floored yard under some palm trees. I unlock the door and enter a round room with a bed covered in mosquito netting, a fan already turning around from the top of the coned thatched ceiling, a little kitchen area, and even a small sofa under one of the pink muslin covered windows. Very simple, not exactly cheap, but it'll do me nicely. I'll have plenty of time to explore tomorrow or later on, but right now I can't think of anything better but to wander down to the beach and find that café I'd been told about by the bracelet girl.

The pathway outside leads me to a strange little half-built "doorway" through a brick wall, which makes me feel I'm passing into another world. I enter a surprisingly large area with boats parked up on trailers with diving school and boat repair outfits dotted around under palm covered buildings.

The sea and beach are just here, and walking towards the water I can't help but gasp at its wild beauty. This is Cabo Pulmo, created as an official National Marine Park in 1995, on the east coast, sixty miles from Cabo San Lucas. Before the establishment of the park, the area had become heavily over fished, but after its creation and with marine policing, sea life has increased four-fold, due mainly to the healthy, untouched condition of the reef. Incredibly, this place has the oldest of only three coral reefs on the west coast of North America and is the northernmost coral reef in the eastern Pacific. Here the reef is estimated to be 20,000 years old!

In his book, *The Log from the Sea of Cortez*, John Steinbeck describes the Cabo Pulmo Reef:

> *The complexity of the life pattern on Pulmo Reef was even greater than at Cabo San Lucas. Clinging to the coral, growing on it, burrowing into it, was a teeming fauna. Every piece of the soft material broken off, skittered and pulsed with life, little crabs and worms and snails. One small piece of coral might conceal 30 or 40 species, and the colors on the reef were electric.*

Up a few steps from the beach I find a little solitary café. It's another simple place, and the menu is short. The smell emanating from the small, open kitchen behind the counter is wonderful. Within ten minutes I'm drinking from a bottle of Modelo beer and squeezing lime juice over a plate of delicate, succulent, fried calamari. The waves are lapping up onto the beach, and there's now a greatly appreciated warm refreshing breeze coming in from the sea. This is a pretty good way to be introduced to this place!

I yearn to swim out to sea and see it all, but I was also very conscious of my budget, having seen the expensive prices posted on the huts for dives out to the reefs. Although I am PADI qualified, from passing it ten years prior in Jordan's Dead Sea and have dived in other places like Cuba, Cozumel on Mexico's Gulf side, and Cuba, I'd need a refresher dive or two to get up to speed and feel safe. That was all an extra cost and something I felt I could do without. The flippers and snorkel would do me just fine for the next day.

The water beckons, and I walk out onto the beach and submerse myself in the warm, protected sea. Besides a few boats full of divers motoring out to the reefs, the place feels sleepy and a long way from anywhere. And just ninety miles down from where I'd come from this morning, it feels and looks so totally different. Ironically, if that's even possible, it feels a bit more developed, but that's probably the wrong word to use. Let's say just a few more people, and that's not such a bad thing.

Beached out and after an obligatory hammock swinging siesta, the sun is quickly setting as I wander back through the brick wall to the little café, where the distant roaring of the waves can be heard somewhere out in the endless dark. Walking up the steps I check in my bag that I've brought my torch and see that the place now has a completely different vibe. I'd brought Bill Brysons *Notes from a Small Island* with its brown, weather beaten pages to keep me company at the table, but it's not really needed. It seems like it's going to be more of a people watching evening.

I order a Cuba Libra (all I need now is a cigar), a plate of gambas with rice, and sit back and relax, looking out into the room feeling comfortable with Bill's book in my hand. It all feels quite unintentionally theatrical with the coming and goings of an eclectic set of people I hadn't before set eyes on. A couple come and sit down at the table next to me, giving the customary polite smiles. The bronzed lady with a bright red, swishing dress pulls something out of a bag from her shoulder. It's a cute little three-legged chocolate and white Chihuahua, Mexico's iconic national breed of dog. Surprisingly, they pull a third chair up and place the tiny dog on it, with its head just peering over the table. As I take a sip to drink, it turns imploringly up to me like it wouldn't say no to some of the rum. Or at least that's what I'm thinking.

As I devour the prawns, there are families with well-behaved children seated at long tables chatting away and older couples looking at each silently across their plates of fish. But what fascinates me most is, without exaggerating, every woman (besides me, of course) has blonde peroxide hair, bright red lipstick and is looking like they're dressed to the nines in this very basic place. Why? Where are they going afterwards, or is this the destination to be at! They'd be more suited in Manchester night clubs or the Costa del

Sol's Magaluf. But it does feel maybe just an incy-wincy bit of an exclusive playground for some of them, which is totally out of context on what I was expecting.

Where are the surfers and Jacques Cousteau explorers? Tucking into my prawns, my eyes don't stop subtly but naturally divert to other people across the room. Maybe I first got the habit of people watching when I lived in Paris. For a small espresso at a café, and without being harassed to leave, it was the cheapest form of entertainment. It would be amazing what you'd see and hear! With no surprise now, another two blonde ladies arrive and sit at the table next to me. We nod our heads in acknowledgement, and I strain to decipher what language they're speaking. Although their hair colour is not natural, coming directly out of a bottle, they look totally Latin, with fine chiselled features, large rings on their fingers, and brightly coloured clothes. I smile as I see one of them add even more red lipstick to the proceedings.

The three-legged Chihuahua leans its head to one side, looking curiously up to me with its saucer brown eyes and decides to give out a big, wide yawn, nestling down into the seat. I'm not going to do the same but feel tired too and put my hand up for the bill.

12

LIVIN' IT UP AT THE HOTEL CALIFORNIA

Twenty years from now, you will be more disappointed by the things you didn't do than by the ones you did do. So throw off the bowlines, sail away from the safe harbour. Catch the trade winds in your sails. Explore. Dream. Discover.

Mark Twain

They'd told me no one would be up so early, so I push the key through the diving school office letterbox with a paper note scrunched around it simply thanking them for the last two days' stay. On the door above is an interesting note— "Indications out in the Pacific show there is a 20% likelihood of a hurricane—950 miles SSW of Baja and moving W Northward. Update information—www.eebmike.com". I look inquisitively up at the sky and see a quick moving, gathering of grey and black clouds, but the likelihood of the storm passing here must surely be low. But it had only been yesterday out on the beach that I'd heard that due to the warm water and other weather conditions out at sea this forecast was surprisingly unusual at this time of the year. The hurricane season normally started much later, in August and September.

I take one last look at the beautiful Sea of Cortez, as later in the day I'll be back over along the Pacific coastline, and turn out onto the long, rubbly sand track for the 140 mile drive over to historic Todos Santos. Whatever's happening out at sea is certainly making the weather here just a little bizarre. Strange, massive, dark, puffed up clouds almost covering the sky are drifting at low altitude above the still silent desert. They're creating strange, bright gold and ghostly shadowy colours in the bushy vegetation and on the sandy earth. The shadows are long, and the colours look like they've been turned up to a higher definition of clarity. The base of the blackening clouds look as though they're teasingly brushing the tips of the tall cacti.

But as I've come to see in Baja, things can change just as quickly. By the time I've navigated and bumped back along to the estuary and the intersection onto Highway 1, the sky has brightened up. It's still burdened with heavy, dense white clouds, but at least they now seem to be floating a lot higher up in the sky and dissipating out into the distance. That's probably a good sign.

My mind is pretty empty on this reborn day just relishing the newness of the place when out of nowhere a truck passes me in the opposite direction, honking and blasting his horn at me. What that means, I have no idea. But instinctively, I slow down, and that's good, because just up ahead towards a bend is a large, slow moving procession of at least fifteen floppy necked cows ambling across the road. There are no ranchero cowboys herding them. They're just going out for their morning stroll. I cautiously look down the bank to see there aren't more floppy necks who might just quickly appear and jump out in front, but seeing nothing with the road now clear, I carefully continue on. Another good lesson in appreciating this wild road isn't used just by vehicles.

Just a few miles further, along a rather non-descript and uninteresting barren stretch of land, I just have to stop. All I see is a small roadside sign, but which declares "Tropico de

Cancer". I'm 23.26 north of the equator, and it's the most northerly circle of latitude on the earth at which the sun can be directly overhead. This happens in June, just a month later, when the northern hemisphere is tilted toward the sun to its maximum extent. There's no ceremony here, with gift shops or big statues. It's just a fact out here.

The landscape slowly becomes dramatically more beautiful, and out in the distance I catch a glimpse of unexpected towering mountains rising up in the Sierra de La Laguna National Park, with the Picacho de La Laguna reaching a height of more than 7,000 ft. Baja California, I'm further witnessing, is a contradictory land of desert, sea, and mountains. With the Sea of Cortez just a few miles east from here, and the Pacific Ocean over in the west, these granite mountains rise from the dry tropical forest below them and the sandy shores close by. The whole region seems to be a mix of rugged mountains, steep valleys and canyons, and vast dry plains. It's incredible to think that in such close proximity are the party towns of Cabo San Lucas on the tip of the peninsula, where most people just go for the beaches and fishing and don't even step a foot outside it.

My stomach is rumbling with hunger, and I thought leaving so early, around 6:30, I'd be able to get some form of breakfast on the road. But so far there's been nothing out here. Maybe I'll find somewhere the closer I get to the main, wealthier hubs of San José del Cabo and Cabo San Lucas.

Very quickly the wild, remote land is disappearing and being replaced by small towns, then the international airport of Los Cabos, with the speed of life uncontrollably picking up once again. The road merges into a busy, dual carriageway with anonymous exits out to the beachside resorts. I'd already told myself that I had no interest whatsoever to visit San José del Cabo or Cabo San Lucas, as for me they were too built up, commercial, and not what I needed to see. That could be left for others. Time was too precious. I needed the simpler, less materialistic experience, even if it did mean waiting longer for breakfast.

The more I saw of this area driving through, with its masses of newly built high rise condos and holiday resorts sitting side by side to each other and the tidily pruned golf courses along this majestic coast, the happier I felt getting further away from it. It had always fascinated me that we "escape" to go on holiday to be away from everything and everyone, but these resorts create the opposite in maximizing the space and people into one small area.

So with Baja California finally running out of land where the Pacific and Sea of Cortez come together on the tip of this most exclusive parcel of land, I make my way north along Highway 19, running straight up the Pacific coast for Todos Santos. And still not a bagel or cup of coffee in sight! But it also feels ironically saddening, turning away from the mass congestions and construction from the tip of the cape, as I'm also already mentally getting ready for the return leg of the trip northbound. Although I still had more mileage to do than I'd already done, I sadly sighed with the fact that I was "returning" and not "going away."

Very quickly, the road gains its remote label again, and iconic coastal views are seen of the pounding ocean out into the distance. It's mid-morning, the sky has turned blue again, and any threatening clouds have now completely vanished. A number of unmarked dirt tracks lead for a mile or so down to wild beaches, some of which I drive down naively hoping to find a relaxing beachfront café. But each time there's nothing; just closed and boarded up beach homes with their empty beaches and nobody around.

But I did know of one place before I reached my destination which had sounded interesting. Just eight miles out of Todos Santos is El Pescadero, a small dusty village close to some of the best surf breaks and beaches on the coast. My prayers are answered as I drive through the quiet village street, and on the wind-blown sandy side of the road I notice a red brick building with inviting, shade umbrellas outside and a coffee cup embossed into the wall announcing "Cafelix Coffee & Kitchen".

Strangely, this spontaneous stop out on the road was going to be more significant than I could have imagined. I quietly sit at a table drinking a rich, fresh coffee with yoghurt, fruit, and croissant. Out of context, I know, but incredibly good.

Dipping the croissant into the coffee, I can't help but look over at the only other occupied table. It's almost the first time on the trip I've heard English being spoken by people other than Mexicans. To say these two guys are good looking is an understatement. They're gorgeous—tall, dark, handsome, with just the right amount of tattoos down their bronzed arms and stylishly well- dressed, but in an unpretentious, cool, casual way. It's reassuring to know that men like that do exist out there! Unfortunately for me, they've only got eyes for each other as they lean closer towards one other over the table.

But one of them catches my eye and smiles. I reciprocate.

"Hey there! How are you? We saw you driving in. Where you headed?"

The flow of conversation with these guys, Garry and Joseph, is easy. They're down for a week from Los Angeles to do some bird watching in a remote place somewhere up in the hills overlooking the sea, just outside Todos Santos.

"I've swallowed the bullet on cost and am staying at the Hotel California for a few nights."

They sit back in surprise, and Garry continues, looking me up and down, "Honey, I can't imagine you staying there as an indie traveller. Not for me to say, but you might just find it a bit touristy and "out there on the map." We're staying at Los Colibris. It's out of this world. And it's an amazing place for bird watching, being high up in the hills overlooking a natural lake by the sea. The birds fly down to our swimming pool to drink!"

His face turns slightly more serious, "But there's a lot of controversial stuff happening in and around this area, which we don't like. There's a professor back at Stanford University who frighteningly predicts Baja will not exist as it is by 2025. More and more people are coming here and developing the fragile land, which keeps all the wildlife and fauna alive. You'll see if you come up to Los Colibris. The lake below is tidal and should be half seawater and half from the natural waters flowing from its incoming river. But people are greedy here. All around it new homes are being built and the water taken away for them. It's destroying things."

He takes a sip of coffee and passionately continues, "As conservationists and naturalists, we're very concerned that the rapid development of Todos Santos is being done with little or no oversight of the natural resources critical to the existence of unique and endemic plants and animals in the area. It's sometimes all to do with politics and power. We've sadly seen the marsh below Los Colibris suffering from a die off of the precious marsh plants that the local Belding's yellowthroat bird, living exclusively here, needs for survival. It will no doubt become extinct. It'll be yet another species gone from our planet. And, yes, the lack of fresh water coming into the marsh, which combines with the salt water that also fills it when the storms break through the beach, is sadly ongoing and irreversible. It's the combination of these waters that keeps everything alive there. The dead, brown marsh plants which we've seen are a sign that the salinity of the place has changed and can no longer support life. When we look down at the development around it, it's easy to see and speculate that the fresh water is being diverted and channelled to humans and the expensive housing and new hotel development. The lake will dry out, and these rare birds will also die."

He passionately bangs his hand on the table with a frustrated look. "Who permits this development and the water use? And we want to know who represents the natural resources of the area. It's all so fragile. When we think about incredible Baja, we also have to think about its political landscape and how it is, but which also ultimately predicts what its physical landscape looks like. If you venture out and decide to come up to Los Colibris we'll tell you more. Terre Peninsular is a conservation organisation based north of Todos Santos, and they've got interesting stories on greed and wealth in other conservation areas of the peninsula."

I hungrily absorb this fascinating but shocking information and feel more and more curious to check this place out for myself and jettison the third night at the Hotel California and make my way over to the hills.

Joseph continues along the same thread, "So as you see, Zoë, there's a lot happening here that a lot of people don't know about. You've travelled a lot, and this is a place that'll open your eyes to the changes going on here. Remember, like we said, we've also all been to Cuba at about the same time, ten years ago, when there was no influence or greed from the outside world. It all changes and not for the better. I'm, you could say, a well-known jeweller and in with the fashion industry back in LA. I know what happened in Havana just a few months ago in March. Kurt Geiger was doing a fashion show. I was told by direct sources that local Cubans were asked to be extras for the cat walk extravaganza to make it 'real!' How can people and things be so used and manipulated? It's vulgar, and the place will get ruined."

Both guys have given me more than enough food for thought, and after one last coffee, we get up and give each other a "traveller's good luck and pleased to have met you" hug. But not before Joseph adds, "And don't forget, try and get *La Muerte de Artemio Cruz* by Carlos Fuentes. I'm reading it at the moment. Written back in 1962, it is considered to be a milestone in the Latin American boom of literature back then. And don't forget to check our little place if you decide to come and stay. Give them a call or email them. There should be availability, and their rooms are to die for! We'll be there for another couple of days!" He smiles looking knowingly down at my wrist "And those lovely purple amethyst stones on your bracelet, well you know they're good luck for travelling so what more could you want!"

I'm curious and adrenalin pumped to be arriving at this old, historic town rich in culture, stories, and art. I've been out on the road now for almost two weeks and want a sanctuary and new resting place from the desert.

> *On a dark desert highway, cool wind in my hair*
> *Warm smell of colitis, rising up from the air*
> *Up ahead in the distance, I saw a shimmering light*
> *My head grew heavy and my sight grew dim*
> *I had to stop for the night.*
>
> —Eagles

The journey continues slowly down Highway 1, which magically turns into a small, silent street with old colonial buildings on either side. I stop opposite a five-arched terracotta palm-fronted hotel. I'm here at the Hotel California, the original place that has always been hyped as where the Eagles had the inspiration to create the song. Most know it's a myth and fantasy, but the place feels pretty special, and my appetite is whetted with curiosity to see and learn more about it.

But first I need to sort a few things. I breathe in and walk confidently up to the reception desk. I'm already juggling in my head what the best thing is to say, as there's now no reimbursement from the booking I'd made for the three nights. A simple email from my phone confirmed that I had a room for the third night at Los Colibris Casitas, where the boys were staying. It's strange that no sooner have I arrived, that I'm planning my escape route out.

A young, sharply dressed guy behind an exotic wood-lined and exotic, flower laden counter looks up and smiles professionally.

I also put on my professional smile. "Morning. I'm Señora Cano. I'm here with a booking." He looks down, nods, and I continue, "However, I'm an investigative journalist and have been asked to cover another story in two days elsewhere so will only need the room for two nights."

Let's see what that does. He awkwardly rubs his pen between thumb and forefinger then questioningly looks at his older colleague next to him, who immediately shakes his head.

"I'm sorry Señora, but you booked a while back, and you can't cancel now. It's too late."

I'm not going to accept this. This place looks pretty quiet, in fact it looks pretty empty, like once again, I'm the only guest!

I continue unperturbed, "This really is important. I'm also going to be reviewing the hotel, and I have no choice but to leave in two days. May I speak to your manager?"

After pacing up and down for about five minutes, I see the manager walk over and put his hand out. "Señora Cano. Welcome. It's not a problem. We're happy to have you here. We can always make an exception to the rule. We hope you enjoy your time with us."

And with that, I'm swiftly escorted up through the lush salmon pink and lipstick-red bougainvillea lined terraces to the second floor, down a dark, black shadowed corridor, and ironically to another Room Six. The large room, a stylish mix of Mexican and Moorish décor, looks out onto the terrace and street below. The shops opposite, on the other side of the road, which I'm detecting are for the tourists, look closed and still haven't woken up.

This is perfect. It's heavenly quiet in this tropical paradise of an oasis and feels like a sanctuary from the dusty hot world just outside. All I need do now is find the pool and relax. Past dark, azure blue, white, and terracotta painted walls covered with large colourful pieces of contemporary art, majestic wrought iron candle stands, palm trees, and luxuriant green plants, I'm led enticingly to two solitary padded chaise lounges next to a blue, mosaic-lined pool. Next to the pool is an old red brick wall with the pale yellow mission church soaring up behind it and chiming its bells. Besides birds chirping in the trees, that is the only noise I can hear.

I step down into the ripple-free round pool and, floating on the warm water, look up at the piercingly blue sky and the date palms and banana trees above on the terraces, waving slightly with the breeze. I close my eyes, with the warm sun gently absorbing into me, knowing this is one of the greatest feelings of happiness and peace. The undisturbed tranquillity continues as I tuck into a lunch of chicken salad with pecans, avocado, dates, lettuce, and goat cheese. Then once again, I calmly close my eyes to absorb the rich decadence of this place solely for me.

But very shortly this thought and feeling is totally ambushed and destroyed. Little was I to know how "well-trodden" this place is on the tourist map.

Coughing, laughing, loud voices, and the click of cameras hijack the scene. A group of about ten people, led by a member of the hotel staff, is led through the poolside where they come to an abrupt stop to view the scene, including me! Their cameras are clicking away in every direction. Oh my God, this is so touristy. I'm for a split second feeling like a famous person having their picture taken or maybe more like a zoo animal unable to escape this orchestrated and unwanted scene. I've had enough for a while. I pull on my shorts and get up to leave for a little wander.

On the other side of the brick wall, walking up the street I find the palm-fringed Plaza Todos Santos and the beautiful pale yellow and white Misión de Nuestra Señora del Pilar de la Paz, founded in 1723. A few other people are meandering past cafés and a few shops. Walking past an elegant looking theatre and a quirky sun monument based on the Aztec calendar, it's quiet, and everyone seems to have disappeared for the ritual afternoon siesta.

I feel it's time for me to have one by the pool, and hopefully, the photo-snappers have disappeared. But, not for the first time on the trip, my stomach is feeling a bit queasy. I walk quickly by the pool to find the toilets but frustratingly find them locked. So embarrassingly, I walk to reception, asking for the toilets to be quickly opened with apologies given to me saying they're always locked when the tourists come visiting the place.

I sit back by the pool in peace, but not for long. Comical mayhem starts to ensue. Firstly, an overall clad man appears out of nowhere with hoses, spraying the entire pavement area around the pool, and then another two men appear with long ladders, noisily carrying them up onto the terrace to do roof repairs. At the same time as all of this, more smiling men appear carrying large dustbins and going back and forth and in and out of the red-bricked, wall door at the back of the pool. All are curiously looking at me each time they go past.

By late afternoon, I've had enough of this circus. But it's then I pleasingly hear a beautiful, echoing woman's voice singing from inside the mission from the other side of the wall. Then a small black-attired woman waddles past me and through the garden gate to, no doubt, join the evening mass. She leaves the gate open, revealing a dirty work site of heaped rubble and sand, which looks totally out of context with the beauty here on the other side.

I have to smile. I'm finding it quite funny. I know it's not peak season and work has to be done, but I've honestly never seen so many hotel staff go past one area all at the same time all afternoon. It feels busier than Clapham Junction! Very aptly, music comes wafting out of nowhere from behind speakers in the hotel shrubs shouting the Rolling Stones lyrics of *It's Only Rock 'n' Roll*, which I have to smile and agree to.

It's not until a lot later in the evening that I wander over and sit on a stool in this dark, bohemian, silent bar where two groovy young-looking bartenders have probably spent their entire evening polishing glasses and just wanting to serve someone.

I point to one of the tequila bottles behind the counter, and from then on for the next couple of hours, the conversation seems to roll.

"¡Bienvenido! How would you like the tequila? We can make it into any sort of fresh fruit margarita—strawberries, classic lime, mango—or surely not on its own!"

I nod and in the dark pull the bottle towards me to take a better look at it that I'll be drinking good stuff. "Thanks, but I want to drink 100% tequila. This one isn't!"

They stand back and look at each other slightly surprised that a punter possibly knows a bit. Victor, a cool dude with massive, big black glasses and a little moustache that looks like it's his first one, smiles, nods his head, and walks back to the shelf stacked with bottles. Without exaggerating, he then proceeds to carry over at least half a dozen bottles. Only four are a hundred per cent. I point at the Don Julio bottle, and a couple of very generous measures are poured out for a classic margarita. I sit back and nod pleasingly. That's damn good.

Victor looks impressed and curiously asks, "Glad that's good, but it's pretty unusual people ask much about the tequila. How come you know?"

I smile. "Sorry, but on my travels here, I've already had some better than average tequila, starting with some friends near Tecate who educated me a bit about it. They were the ones who told me about being careful to make sure what I drank was always 100% agave. You must know, but if it's not 100% then there's added things and industrial chemicals put in it by the big producers."

They raise their eyebrows, now curiously inspecting some of the bottles' labels for themselves. Surely it's not true that they don't know this. It's almost comical that I feel I'm educating the bartenders at the Hotel California about the nuances of tequila!

With just the three of us at the bar, the conversation flows probably easier than normal. Victor winks and brings yet another bottle onto the bar. But this bizarrely shaped bottle, with honey-coloured drink inside, looks very different, and certainly isn't tequila.

"So, you're looking to experience different things here in Todos. This is the first I can tell you about. It's Guayacara Damiana liquor. Here, take a quick taste."

He pours a shot into a small glass and sniffs into the bottle before screwing the cap back on. It tastes sweet, with a herbal twang.

He smiles. "Damiana plants grow here in Baja California, and the leaves and stems are used to make it. They say it's good for you know what! Aphrodisiac for men! It was the indigenous Guayacara Indians who used it in religious ceremonies—good for women too. That's why this bottle is shaped like a naked pregnant woman or goddess!"

My eyes roll back in surprise at his story, and I take another swig. Not bad. With the bottles lined up along the bar, I choose another one hundred per center for another margarita. The full, chilled glass is pushed across the bar to me, and after a sip, I can't help but ask, "So I'm curious about this place. It's Hotel California, right? But nothing to do with The Eagles? Even though I can hear their music playing here in the background."

With a finger, Victor pushes his glasses up his nose, smiles, and pulls a stool up behind the bar, like this is going to be an interesting session. He takes the remote control and also slightly turns the background noise of the TV down, where up until now, we'd also been intermittently watching the live football game between America and Monterrey.

"Sure. I can tell you more. It was about sixty years ago. Building of this place began in 1947, and it was finished three years later, in 1950. The owner was a good man called Mr. Wong. He was born in China, but he wanted the locals to believe he was a Mexican man, so he changed his name to Antonio Tabasco. He then became known as Señor Antonio Wong Tabasco or "Chino" Tabasco.

"'Chino' lived in this sixteen-room hotel with his wife and seven daughters. He helped with agriculture in the area in exchange for gold. He had a general store, a restaurant, and also a bar. For the first time ever seen in Todos Santos, he brought ice from La Paz and was serving the only cold beer in town. 'Chino' also opened the first gas station in town. He sure was a guy ahead of his times.

"But when he died, the hotel got sold, and its name changed for a short while, but then that guy sold it to some Americans, who changed the name back. For a while in the '90s it was boarded up and for sale again. It was empty for about four years. Then a Canadian couple, John and Debbie, arrived in 2001 and bought it, but a lot of work had to be done. It was very run down. The rooms were made much bigger, and it now has just eleven rooms, with the restaurant here next door. We've got a shop where the gas station used to be. Yes, for sure, hundreds of tourists come here looking for the legend and connection to the song. But what they find here is perhaps just the inspiration of an interesting tale."

I nod and continue to listen to things I've never heard before.

"Now, if you want a real tale to shock you, you'll somehow need to find the grave of La Ahoracadita or the "hanged girl" in a remote place just outside the town. It's not easy to find. You'll need to stop and ask people when you get to the area, as it's hidden up a small farm track. There aren't any signs."

My eyes open. "Sorry, what's that about?"

"Well, you can find more information about the story in our Cultural Centre up the road from here. Those who know the story say that a pregnant woman named Matilde died mysteriously. She was found hanging from a tree in an open field. We think it was the mother-in-law who did it. According to the last living relatives, she performs miracles for those who pray for her and give her gifts. They've even made a film about the story! The Ahoracadito Tomba is north out of town, opposite Calle Puesta del Sol. Go past the Multiservicios Brisas on Camino a la Playitas and then start asking for directions."

I'm strangely, if not morbidly, interested to maybe take a recce tomorrow. It's the first time I'd heard about it. "I might go and find the place tomorrow. Hopefully, it's safe to get there?"

"Sure. But as I said, you're gonna have to persist in asking. And you know, too, that there are plenty of witches here! Black and white, practicing ones! This place is very special. People are always looking for their dreams. Talking about dreams, my grandfather, who's passed away, used to be a "gambesino," a gold prospector, in the '50s and '60s. But I'm not sure how much he actually found."

The football game has finished, and Victor turns the TV off in the silent bar. I finish the last of the tequila margarita and push the empty glass back across the bar to them.

"Thanks, guys, for a great evening. I'm sure tomorrow is going to be an interesting one. I'll report back here tomorrow night."

They smile, and turning the lights off, we all walk out of the bar. Kicking my shoes off across the room, I crash out onto the bed, disappearing into soft, cool white linen and pillows, which feel like marshmallows. It feels like heaven as I peacefully go to sleep in the quiet of the night.

13

GHOSTS ON THE ROAD

The big lesson in life, baby, is never be scared of anyone or anything.

Frank Sinatra

No! No! Surely this can't be happening, as I'm abruptly woken from a peaceful slumber in the middle of the night! Out in the street, and far beyond, I hear incessant barking and howling of dogs, with more and more joining in. I slam the pillow over my head, but it's no use. The more I listen to them, the more I get the impression they're weirdly communicating with each other throughout this otherwise totally silent town. And I thought my neighbour back home with her dogs was bad—there's no comparison! I toss and turn. Does this happen every night? I sigh deeply. We'll have to see.

I must have somehow dozed off, but after just a few more hours of shut eye, the rumble of the monster trucks on this narrow, residential part of the Transpeninsular Highway directly below my bedroom, abruptly judders me awake.

With the rays of light, I walk over to the window and twist the wooden blinds slightly open to peek out onto the street. Besides an old man slowly sweeping the pavement with a broom, the place looks still asleep. Or is it? Walking up the street is a handful of people who look like hikers with sturdy walking boots and small rucksacks on their backs. They stop in front, on the other side of the road, and curiously look up and across to the hotel. That's my cue to also get up and do a bit of exploring.

The day's already looking good, with clear cloudless skies. I wander past the silent bar, grinning to see the eclectic stack of tequila bottles still on it, and head to the little café next door for breakfast. The tantalizing smells of fresh food being prepared behind the counter are soon brought to the table. Huevos a la Mexicano is my pick of the day. Delicious scrambled eggs with fresh tomato, serrano chilli pepper, coriander, and onions served with dark red, spicy chorizo, black beans, and tortillas.

Wiping the plate clean, I unfold the basic free map I'd been given and trace my finger north out of Todos Santos to try and find the approximate place where the boys had explained I'd find the grave "somewhere hidden up an unmarked kind of track." I find the supermarket they'd mentioned a couple of miles out of town, so I'll start with that. There's also a spanner sign next to it, so that must be a garage, which should also be a good place to ask for local directions. Are they going to think this gringo is weird?

I drive slowly out of the carpark behind the hotel and onto the empty main street of Juarez, turning left up onto Topete and out of the historic district. The road twists through fertile expanses of palm trees and continues through a poorer, outlying district with small bar-grilled stores dotted along the street between green mango trees. Temporary looking electric poles have multitudes of cables strewn and hanging from one building to another, some of which look only half built and possibly never will be finished. I'd heard some time ago that if buildings weren't totally finished then they wouldn't be liable to be totally taxed. But that was on mainland Mexico a long time ago and may be a myth.

Driving slowly through the place, absorbing the atmosphere, I catch sight of yet another unfinished building with cables coming out of its concrete foundations and walls. Below, with the sign "Tortillas de Harina," a lady is walking out of it with a wicker shopping basket with food for the day. But up on the very top of this flat roof a large black and white mongrel has somehow got up there and is proudly barking out loud that he's the boss around here.

I continue on through the ever increasing, barren terrain, with its sparse prickly shrubs and cacti resembling a stubbly unshaved chin. The roads on the left are leading some distance away down to the sea, while a few rugged paths on the other side are seemingly leading nowhere into the desert. On passing a schoolbus full of uniformed children, I unfortunately see the supermarket and garage are closed. Now what had the boys said? It was close to Calle Los Mangos or Calle Puesta del Sol? As expected, this isn't going to be easy to find, but I do know it must be within a hundred metre stretch of this road.

So I drive up and down it, only noticing shacks and litter. I'm tempted to hijack it all and drive down Calle los Mangos, where I'd been told was the protected beach, where between November and May the sea turtles dug their sand nests to lay their thousands of eggs. When hatched, they'd all return back to sea until the next year. But they'd now all left. The beach would be empty.

Passing that very lane, I notice opposite a laundromat with a little café next door. I pull over and walk to it. There are stacks of clothes drying on washing lines in the small sunny yard and garden around the building, but no one to speak to. So I stroll into the café. An apron attired gentleman walks out of the kitchen smiling and introduces himself without question as Alberto.

"Morning, Señora, I saw that car going past a few times. You look lost. How can I help you?"

I gratefully smile, but without believing I'll get a sensible reply, simply say, "¿La Ahorcadita?"

He nods in an un-shocked way and points with a finger "Yes, she's just opposite, up that desert track. You'll go past a few casitas, and it's behind the white house on the other side of the brick wall." He salutes me and wishes me a good day.

And true to his word, I rattle up the sandy track, and behind a half-built wall is a black, rectangular, railed tomb with a headstone. I get out under the hot sun and walk quietly towards it and am shocked in what I see. Stacked up and around it are gifts of dolls of all kinds—some which haven't even left their boxes—toys, babies' clothes, angel statues, plastic flowers, and beaded cross necklaces hanging everywhere. The land is barren, and everything is dead around here, even the cacti. But strangely, around the grave are four healthy, large green trees.

This remote empty place feels a little unsettling, and I'm sensing a tingling sensation on the back of my hands, so I decide I don't need to be here for too much longer. I can probably obtain more information at the Cultural Centre.

I respectfully turn from the grave, and everything turns strange. Out of nowhere, walking towards me is a limping man, truthfully looking a bit crazy with his erratic gestures. My act of immediately jumping into the car is stopped by his strange question as he approaches ever closer to me.

"Do you live here?"

I don't really know how to answer. I don't want to get him angry thinking I'm possibly trespassing on someone else's land, so with car keys ready in hand, I pacifyingly reply, "No. But it's sad, isn't it?"

He looks at me and simply laughs out loud. And with that reaction, and with my heart palpitating just slightly, I go to open the door. But again, I'm strangely approached—this time by a large dog, which silently stops and looks up at me. It weirdly has one white eye. Quite a bizarre experience. I go to leave, and the old man follows me down the track.

Back without any mishaps, in downtown Todos Santos I'm now even more curious to investigate a little more. I enter the Cultural Centre on Juarez, part of a red brick primary school built in 1931. Inside the entrance are impressive, beautiful hand-painted murals from the era, depicting the lifestyle of the region. In little side rooms are collections of local handicrafts; local art, including an original Frida Kahlo surrounded by parrots and smoking her habitual cigarette; and old black and white photographs of local people and their stories. There's even the story about Mr. Wong, who left China in 1910 to eventually run the Hotel California. But hidden in a shady recess, I notice two old, framed newspaper clippings.

As legends would have it, about 200 years ago, the story of La Ahorcadita began. Living a simple life on the rancho, a young woman called Matilde Martinez became with child under mysterious circumstances—or so her mother-in-law stated. This woman thought it was due to sinister forces and that the girl had to be freed from evil, so struck her down with a metate, a flat stone used for grinding grain. In order to cover up the dirty deed, the body was wrapped in cow hide, was taken to an olive tree outside the pueblo, and made to look like she'd hung herself. And out of nowhere grew four trees around the tomb, which people say symbolize her months of pregnancy. No one really knows what the true story is, but it's said people come from all over to pray for her and her unborn child.

I walk out and wander a little aimlessly around the narrow streets. A few art galleries are open, and I can't resist walking into a few. Surprisingly, without knowing it, I strike up a conversation with one of the area's most renowned artists. Gabo is sitting quietly in his studio in front of his beautiful large canvases, which are all astronomically out of my price range. He's an interesting guy who produces complex, contemporary work inspired by Baja Sur and has exhibited all over the world.

I'm feeling it's time to head back for a quiet afternoon siesta by the poolside, but only if the workmen aren't out there again. I enter the shadowy entrance to the hotel, where there's a surprising bustling scene of raucous voices and busy activity. There are five giggling girls, with long coiffed hair and made-up to the nines with body-hugging black dresses. One is leaning over the balcony upstairs for what looks like a photoshoot by a dashing, young photographer, who's smiling and looking like he's in his element.

But these animated girls look pretty young, as one also bends over to tie her shoe laces, showing long, flowered boxing shorts and socks. And it's certainly too early to be going out for the evening. A few suited boys, tightly seated next to each other on a couch, look timidly at the scene. What are they doing here? Then from a car at the front, steps out a beautifully bejewelled sixth girl wearing a long, flowing, sparkling red dress with layers and layers of underskirts, making her look quite spectacular, but if not a little rotund. She also giggles, twizzling around, and walks in to join her friends. She's certainly not a bride with that colour and looks more like a teenager. Maybe this is Mexico's teen prom equivalent?

I walk through the crowd of kids to collect my key and questioningly look at Pedro behind the counter.

He nods, like he can read what I want to know. "This is Sophia's fifteenth birthday today or 'Fiesta de Quince Años,' which celebrates the transition from childhood to a young woman. It's a strong tradition here and celebrated in different ways all over Latin America. Here in Mexico they first go to mass and then celebrate with good food, music, and dancing with friends and family. It will go on until quite late today."

Back at the pool, I'm pleased to see the frenzy from yesterday has died down, and poolside rest from a fairly sleepless night is gratefully taken in readiness for a few margaritas in the bar later on. I open Bill Bryson's book and get immersed with the cold, dreary landscapes back home. This brings me down to earth and reminds me I haven't been in contact with my mother since I left. She lives on her own and had asked I send some postcards. Maybe a bit of Facetime to tell her I'm OK, to show her we can talk and see each other from the other side of the world, and maybe "walk her around" the Hotel California. This should be interesting to see if connection can be made.

It's good to see her friendly face, and after briefly exchanging formalities, the conversation automatically goes to the state of the weather and what's going on back home.

"So, how's the weather in Hereford, Mum?"

"Oh, you know what it's like! I don't know. It's looking like it's going to rain again."

I notice that she's wearing a woolly jumper and a shawl, so it can't be that warm, although it is mid-May.

"So what have you been up to Mum?"

"Oh, this and that. Oh yes, well I can tell you that the hedge has been dramatically clipped, and the garden shed has finally been demolished, and dad's old knick-knacks were taken off by some roaming gypsies when they came to collect the wood."

She swivels her iPad, with me now only seeing her hand on it and some sky, to show me out of the kitchen window the work done. In return, I show the toilet here to reassure her we're not crouching over holes. After about twenty minutes, I see her looking at her watch, and with profuse apologies she quickly says the conversation has to end, as there's another important event happening soon—Coronation Street!

Later that evening, I'm perched up at the bar, showing pictures to the boys of La Ahorcadita. I'm surprised they'd never been there and seem quite taken by the story of what happened.

"So, what do you suggest is good to eat? I'm pretty hungry."

"There's no question. You've got to order the Mole Poblano—Chocolate Chicken Mole. It's beautiful!"

I nod, trying to imagine what the combination tastes like, and reply convincingly, "That sounds great!"

"Yes, my mother makes a real good one. She cooks the pieces of chicken in the sauce, made with lots of ingredients like chilli, garlic, raisins, cinnamon, tomatoes, and of course, chocolate, which is melted into it. I can even try and get the recipe for you if you like!"

And indeed it is truly scrumptious.

Victor's Chocolate Chicken Mole

2 tbsp olive oil, 1 chopped onion, 3-4 crushed garlic cloves, 1 chopped fresh or canned chipotle pepper, 1 tbsp (or more) adobo sauce, 8oz raisins, 16oz canned chopped tomatoes, 3 tbsp smooth peanut butter.

16oz chicken broth, 2 tsp chilli powder, ½ tsp ground cinnamon, 1 tsp black pepper, 2 oz dark chocolate (unsweetened), 1 roast chicken with meat removed and shredded.

For garnish—2oz roughly chopped peanuts (or almonds), 1 tsp sesame seeds and zest of an orange.

For serving—fresh coriander, lime wedges, sliced avocado and flour tortillas.

Place a thick pan over a medium heat and coat with oil. Add onion and garlic to soften for five minutes. Add the chipotle with adobo, raisins, and tomatoes, and stir. Bring to simmer and cook for 10 minutes. Pour mixture into blender. Add peanut butter, broth, chilli powder, and cinnamon. Puree until smooth. Season with salt and pepper. Return mixture to pot and cook for 15 minutes, stirring from time to time. Add the chocolate and stir in until melted. Add the shredded chicken and heat through. Put into a serving dish and garnish with peanuts (or almonds), sesame seeds, and orange zest. Serve with chopped coriander leaves, lime, avocado slices, and warm tortillas. Yum!

By the end of the evening, I've probably had one too many margaritas, but I give the true excuse that I'm in need of a good night's sleep.

14

ESCAPE TO THE HILLSIDES

In order to write about life first you must live it.
Ernest Hemingway

You gotta be joking! It's happening again. I'm woken from my slumber with noises out on the street. My faithful earplugs, which at this moment I'd have given a tortilla for, were back in London where only I thought they were needed. It's well past midnight, and there are raucous youths out on the street below, screaming like they've seen all the ghosts of Baja. The shouting turns to crazy laughs. These kids must be having some kind of sadistic fun in waking paying guests or competing with the howling dogs.

Once again, I slam the luxurious pillow over my head and impatiently count from one hundred backwards, trying to visualize Mexican sheep jumping over sand dunes. And just after dawn my sleep is interrupted, once again, by the windows shuddering from the monster trucks rattling past

Hotel California. I can't help but smile that sometimes even the most decadent sanctuaries can't buy total peace. I'm oh so glad I'd told that little white lie and that I'll be out of here this morning.

With my bags packed, I walk down with them through the beautiful bougainvillea lined courtyards, following the delicious aromas of breakfast. Leaving this place today, my choice, I feel, is ironically rather apt: Heuvos Divorciados or Divorced Eggs. But rather than leave a bad taste in my mouth, they're delicious. Two eggs sunny side up on fried corn tortillas served with ranchero sauce, tomatillo salsa verde, and the obligatory black beans. My stomach is feeling content, which is a step in the right direction from the night's distractions.

I fold the map, showing a tiny section of the town, and head west out of Los Santos to find an almost unnoticeable road, practically on the Tropic of Cancer line, winding narrowly up a hillside to the very top and overlooking the sea. It's not far, maybe just a fifteen minute drive, but it still feels like an adventure. It looks pretty remote, and I'm hoping the small truck can make it up what appears to be a pretty steep, rough road. I'm ready, anticipating that whatever does happen it'll be something dramatically different. The window is wound open with my brown arm resting on it and the foot enthusiastically put down.

Passing in front of Hotel California, I notice a group of tourists making the obligatory stop to take selfies and store digital memories in front of it. But, besides the photographic paraphernalia they're carrying, how can I distinguish they're tourists? It baffles me. I know immediately. It seems they wear different clothes when away from home. Why is this? It seems to be a worldwide phenomena. Baggy, untailored, unflattering shorts, "I've been there" location T-shirts, and "I support them" baseball caps, with a worried but doting partner continually spreading suntan cream over their arms and faces. Unwittingly, they become easy, natural prey for the stall holders and restaurateurs to grab and convince them they need to buy or uniquely experience their offerings.

Travelling solo, I try, where possible, to be a little more inconspicuous, and as an example, avoid carrying the habitual bum bag, which as well as being very unflattering, immediately defines you as an "out of towner." For sure, I'll sometimes carry a hidden money belt under my jeans, but what's wrong with a funky handbag or just pesos and dollars stuffed in the pockets like you'd do back at home? It's maybe called a bit of "travellers' paranoia." That reminds me of when working in Rio and across Brazil in isolated places, with my Brazilian friends always warning me of thefts of belongings of "tourists" and to dress down. And that's exactly what I'd do, walking the streets, dressed with no added travellers accessories. I was never once approached, threatened, or gawped at. I'm all for fitting in wherever I go and not showing off any materialistic wealth that may tempt or invite people to misread you.

I drive slowly past the clicking cameras and out of town, back towards the village of Pescadero. Joy of joys, the road is quiet, and at the first set of traffic lights, I turn off into Barrio San Vicente, which feels like a maze of sandy, rough tracks lined with very modest homes. The whole place has changed from an immaculate, cleanly swept downtown to a very basic neighbourhood, with the habitual loose dogs running across the streets and kids kicking footballs around and into crayon-drawn nets on brick walls.

I drive carefully through the barrio and find myself starting to climb up a small track, which leads me higher and higher, up and over the entire area below. At a small intersection, a small sign points further up to Los Colibris. Not far to go. The track is tiny, narrow, and getting so dangerously steep I'm almost afraid the wheels are going to slide backwards. There's no other option but to continue up, hoping the brakes don't fail. God knows how I'm going to turn round or get back out. At an even smaller V-section there are now only two choices: to climb an even steeper, narrower, rubble-covered gradient with no idea where it leads to, or down a steep but wider dead end. There's a house at the meeting point of these two "goat-tracks," so I'll stop and try and ask someone. It sounds pathetic having to ask, but that's often what travelling solo makes you feel like when there's no one else to dig you out of the hole. The last thing I want is to get stuck on a hill top with no way of getting down.

Fortunately, a couple of friendly dogs approach, wagging their tails, as I walk up the pathway where majestic, uninterrupted views out to the ocean can already be seen from this homely, red terracotta building. Out walks a smiling lady with a large brimmed hat and sunglasses that almost cover her face. With an American accent, she asks, "Hi there. Can I help? I heard the dogs barking when they heard you approaching."

With that, I'm hoping I've arrived. "You sure can! I'm staying at Los Colibris Casitas. I think I'm here and just needed to know where I can park."

"Sure! You're here! And you must be Zoë. I'm Bryon. The boys spoke about you and are at this moment packing to leave. You'll be staying where they've been at "La Chucha Casita." Just drive up the hill a bit, and it's the little yellow house on your right. There's parking next to it. But be careful with the brakes and distance from the low wall, as it drops off down the cliff. Make yourself at home and go check out the poolside until the place is ready for you."

I smile for a couple of reasons. Not because I've made it here safely, but firstly, because of the wacky name of the place I'll be staying at. I always thought "la chucha" meant bitch or f...k, so this must be a f...k of a place to stay! And secondly, her warning on carefully using the brakes when parking reminded me of the disaster I'd had when living in Boston, Massachusetts. I'd only just passed my test and was driving a big automatic Ford Explorer when I mistakenly put my foot down on the accelerator rather than the brake pad and drove straight through the garage's back wall into the kitchen! To say I'm a little nervous in accurately stopping and parking on a cliff face, and then having to reverse correctly back out of possible danger, is a slight understatement.

I intrepidly take off the hand brake and drive up to a thatched casita perched on a steep hillside. Noticing the boys' car, I turn into the neighbouring, tight parking spot, with the dangerous looking slope reaching far below from the front fenders. Let's just hope I switch to reverse when I leave. I get out, calmed to hear the immediate sound of birds singing, and take a deep breath in this quiet, peaceful place high above anything else. It genuinely feels like yet another world, and in such close proximity to a totally different one just down the hill. What a find!

I walk barefooted down to a terrace with a blue pool balancing on the edge of a rocky cliff merging into the sky and sea. Two loungers are pointing out to sea, welcoming me to go and take the views. This place feels pretty special. I wander over, dipping my foot into the warmth of the pearl seashell and blue tiled waters, creating its first ripples of the day. I turn around and up a few steps see a delightful flat palm tree roofed casita. The large terrace window is slightly ajar, where I see two pairs of hands waving and beckoning me to join them.

"Well, good morning, Zoë. You've actually made it to our peaceful retreat! We're just packing and will be leaving shortly to get back to Cabo for the flight back to LA. So all good timing. But before we go, we really must show you around and get the priorities right!"

And so after hugs from the boys, Joseph enthusiastically leads the way into a beautiful, contemporary white-walled room with a massive bed looking out to sea piled with suitcases on it.

Waving his hands around in all directions, he exclaims, "Now just look here. They've got a sound system with a fab collection of music to suit the scene. There's a fridge over there in the little kitchenette for cooling your wine, and there's extra fluffy towels here in the cupboard for bathing. Go take a look in the shower room. The water is always hot."

I walk into the sea-blue tiled bathroom and see a little notice by the toilet: "Please!!!! NO (absolutely none: zero, zippo, nada) toilet paper or other sanitary items of any sort in the toilet—please use trash can—The septic tank will revolt (and that is bad for everybody) Thank you!!" OK, I get it; water is precious here.

"You really won't feel you're missing anything. And out on the roof terrace above, with that chilled wine, you'll see the most spectacular sunsets, as we face directly westwards out to sea. And that's not all. I've a few tips for you to make the stay even better!"

And with that, we all step back out towards the pool. He kindly kneels down to show me some hidden switches. "Now, I'd strongly recommend that one hour before you want to use the Jacuzzi you turn the pump fan and heat switches on. This will warm the water before you get in—so luxurious! There's a little supermarket down along Degollado Road where you'll be able to pick up food for tonight, if you don't fancy going out. This place is so beautiful you probably won't want to move too far away."

We amble towards the beckoning, reclining sun loungers. Garry leans back on one, and Joseph sits at the end of it. I copy Garry on the other one.

For a quiet moment we all look out at the wondrous natural sight of the sea out in front of us. Due to our stillness and silence, out of nowhere three beautiful, red and orange breasted birds, the size of sparrows, fly down to the pool for a drink and to wash themselves in the shallow water-covered step leading down into it. More appear and seem to be flying everywhere.

Garry points to them. "There you go. These are the endangered birds, the yellow throats, we were talking about that survive thanks to the lagoon."

With that, he points over, down below, and across the sandy expanse of beach. "There! Can you see it? The salt and fresh water lake behind those dunes?"

I look down and can't help but see the vegetation around the lake is colourless and brown, and for the most part looks pretty dead.

He continues, "It's incredible, but the eco-system is being slowly destroyed where the fresh water is being diverted to the wealthy homes being built next to it. I'm worried to see what it will look like when we return and what will happen to these birds.

"But don't get me wrong, Todos Santos really still is an unspoilt place compared to other parts of the peninsula. Look out over there. There are septic tanks everywhere by the houses. It's becoming common everywhere. Maybe they'll find a solution. I hope to God there will be. But it needs to be quick. There truly is so much here. For example, the humpback and gray whales visit this area each year from Alaska from October onwards to breed and train their babies for the long journey back in March. Unlike Los Cabos and La Paz, they also say the waters of Todos Santos are still not overfished. Depending on the seasons, the sea here is full of Pacific sierra or mackerel, dorado, also known as mahi-mahi; tuna; bonito, or skipjack; red snapper; squid; cabrilla, that's seabass; and amberjack."

Joseph politely looks at his watch and gets up. "Sorry to spoil the party, but it's time we left. Have fun. The pool will definitely be better than swimming in the sea. There's seventy miles of pristine beach you could walk along, and maybe even go and visit the ruins of the old shipping port of Los Algadones, but be careful! The sea's dangerous, with the waves too strong for swimming at the moment. If it was me, and you're here for less than twenty-four hours, I'd be happy just watching the world go by here. The only thing you may want to do is go and fetch some food."

And with that, they're gone, leaving me the place all to myself. The choice is an easy one. Here it feels, in its tasteful simplicity, one of the most luxurious, exclusive, off the radar places I've probably ever been to. So why would I want to leave it? More birds are coming down to the pool to drink and wash themselves, and humming birds are skilfully hovering back and forth from the brightly coloured flowers. I'll simply go and find the store, stock up on food, and come back.

Not to lose too much precious time, I jump back into the truck, meticulously making sure it's in reverse gear, and wind back down the hill. Just a mile along the main Degollado

Road, or Route 19, a little supermarket appears with people wheeling food-laden trolleys out to their cars. Another mouth-watering feast of food greets and tempts me. As I've already experienced that the best can also be the simplest if it's of the best quality and eaten in a beautiful place—melon, bananas, mango, goat cheese, avocados, tomatoes, crisps, pecan nuts, tin of tuna, a bag of fresh tortillas, fruit yoghurt for breakfast, a bottle of white wine, and a box of pomegranate juice.

That'll do me just fine up until I leave tomorrow morning for one of the trip's longest days. It's going to cover almost 500 miles, across some pretty uncertain terrain. In fact, quite a daunting journey I've set myself. But planning right now can just wait. "Live for the moment" is my motto here and now.

Carrying the bags full of sustenance past the pool, up to the little casita, I'm welcomed by Bryon's family of cats and dogs. I recall her telling me their funny names—there's Juliette the Dalmatian. with Rosie, Zorro. and Charquitos and the cats Tippi, Fluke, Cinco, Fin, Brill Bit, and Biny. Most wander up but quickly disappear under shaded bushes once they've recognised me.

I slide the glass door open and enter the cool room and deposit the food into the fridge. Next to the newly made bed, I bizarrely find just one solitary book next to it. How very apt—*Open Roads Open Minds—an Exploration of Creative Problem Solving* by Steve Uzzell. I lie down and flick it open. The pages, with their photographs of beautiful open, empty roads, read out loud what has been playing on my mind:

"The best place that I have ever found to solve a problem—any kind of problem—is on the Open Road.

"The Open Road never fails to open up your mind. And once your mind is opened, a formidable and boundless power is unleashed. It's called your imagination.

"Open Roads are getting harder and harder to find. I had to find a way to translate The Spirit of the Open Road into an attitude for problem solving. I had to find a way to access this state of mind, whenever and wherever I was, even sitting at my desk."

Just as weirdly, when I flick through the CD pocket of discs, all were either ones I already had or exactly what I would put on. Incredible, and these should all be checked out: Nina Simone—*Essential*, Getzl Byrd—*Jazz Samba*, Sara Evans—*Real Fine Place*, *Joni Mitchell Hits*, Juanito Luis Guerre—<u>Areito</u>, Credence Clearwater—*Revival Chronicle*, Ray Charles—*Genius Loves Company*, Jerome Kein Songbook—*All the Things You Are*, Norah Jones—*Feels like Home*, *The Genius of Charlie Parker*, Diana Karl—*Love Scenes*, *Bebel Gilberto*, John Coltrane—*Giant Steps*, *Earth, Wind and Fire*, Barbara Streisand—*Broadway*.

I sigh smiling, and with fresh tortillas wrapped with fresh vegetables and cheese, I sit by the pool watching the humming birds hover and dart back and forth. There's not a soul on the white wild beach, just the sound of cooing doves, chattering birds, and the distant crashing of waves. I lie back, close my eyes, and feel at peace with the world.

A lot later on, with the light fading, I walk up onto the palm-leafed roof terrace with a glass of wine in one hand, as the boys had so cleverly suggested. I fall into a beautiful, wicker and cream cushioned day bed looking out to sea. The reflection of the sun is getting increasingly larger and diffused across the Pacific Ocean as it slowly comes down to touch and caress the sea. As the sun finally sets, I see dust rising from the beach and can just make out horses slowly walking into the distance.

15

RESCUED

Sometimes I'd rather talk to construction workers than with those idiots who call themselves educated.
                                        Frida Kahlo

The sun was once again slowing rising up over the sea, majestic and spectacular in painting its colours across the horizon, and I was under its spell like it was the first time I'd seen this magic. The palette of reds, orange, green, yellow, and purple were quickly merging, disappearing, and creating the pure blue morning sky.

It was still early, maybe 6:30ish, the car was packed, and with a mug of coffee, I was once again assessing the journey and mileage to be done. The aim was to cross over the peninsula and reach Mulegé, another 350 miles away, and navigating a large part of it on a different route on new, unknown roads. I felt I was taking on a fairly substantial challenge. The plan was to head back up through the remote desert past La Paz

215

and continue up through the middle of the peninsula, where I already knew the excessive, dangerous speeding of trucks was rife. But instead of going back on the road I'd come down on, heading east on the Transpeninsular through Loreto, I'd decided to take an alternative route. This was up along the west coast to then head back inland, a lot further up, to cross over the mountains and down to the Sea of Cortez in close proximity to Bahía Conception.

It would create a more eclectic trip, as I preferred not to take the same , if possible. I had no idea on the conditions of these new roads but thought it all looked fine on my coffee-stained map!

I also still had a batch of tortillas air sealed fresh in their bag, cheese, tuna, and fruit, which at the last minute I thought would be good to take in case I needed some sustenance or it was too remote to find anything. Again, little did I know that this was one of the most important and sensible things I could have done today!

With a little trepidation, the foot is slowly put down, having double-checked I'd slid it into reverse, and reassuringly, it moves backwards away from the cliff. It bumps back down the hillside, through the dusty maze of tracks, and soon back onto the smooth asphalt of Highway 19. I pass sleeping Hotel California for one last time and leaving the town make a 350 peso stop for petrol.

With Todos Santos quickly disappearing from sight in the rear view mirror, I lean back, put my foot down, and place my arm out onto the open window ledge. But it's surprisingly a cold, misty start, with not a lot of visibility out into the distance. Something new again and totally unexpected. But that wasn't the half of it.

Barely ten miles down this silent road, I suddenly catch sight of a big, wild, brown cat racing across the barren landscape on my left and quickly approaching the road. What is this? It has no tail. It's beautiful. It's got to be a lynx, which people have said is quite rare to see. It all seems to happen too quickly, and before I know it, just thirty metres in front, the cat has pelted across the road and disappeared into the sage scrubland. Once again, I'm thinking, what safety would I have had on a bike? I sigh with a sense of joy that I'd witnessed a wild cat roaming freely in its natural habitat.

On this quiet stretch of road, my memory lapses back to the past, remembering another time when I'd come face to face with wild cats, but with a lot more potential to be attacked!

A group of eight of us were endurance horse riding through the Masai Mara reserve in Kenya during the migration season. From the open plains we'd entered a steep canyon, locally known as "Lion Hill," where all of a sudden the horses, acting on their sixth sense, nervously twitched their ears back and forth and whinnied out loud. It was spookily quiet, and the horses knew before us that there were prying eyes looking down from the crevices on the side of the canyon. Bones were strewn on one of the cave's ridges, and the horses were getting ready to uncontrollably gallop away.

All of a sudden, the horses sensed immediate danger and, like real herd animals, instinctively bunched together for protection. It was then I saw at least three lions prowling and looking down at us from the ridges. We were all desperately looking for a way out, in case they came down to attack. The strategy would have been for Jacob to "stand off" the lions with his bull whip, and the rest of us would have fled in the opposite direction.

I blink back into reality, looking into the current misty horizon that, with the heat of the early morning, is slowly clearing. The sky quickly brightens, and along the straight dry lands approaching the capital of La Paz, vehicles magically appear out of nowhere, quickly congesting the road and killing the silence.

I don't want to be stuck in this mess so quickly look down at the map for any alternative route, and as the airport approaches, take a hurried swing to the left and luckily get out totally bypassing the city. Without warning, I'm suddenly once again driving back along the beautiful Sea of Cortez coastline, where I fill up at El Centenario before turning inland and up through this wild stretch of the peninsula.

It's funny how your mind works and analyses things when you've been travelling a while. I feel like my arm has become like a temperature gauge. It's taken me just a few hours to pass La Paz, and the warmth from outside, compared to the chilly start, now feels just right.

It's then I see the familiar "STOP" warning signs in front, and with cars slowing down, it's indicating we've arrived at another police inspection point. For no apparent reason, my heart stupidly starts palpitating, questioning my innocence for what, I don't know! It's my turn. Theatrically, I give the red-faced policeman a happy smile, not quite fluttering my eyelashes but trying to look relaxed. He sternly puts his hand up for me to stop and twists his thumb and forefinger anti-clockwise to indicate I switch the engine off.

He leans in towards me, looking curiously inside, then simply questions me with one word "Plants?"

That was a little unexpected, but besides the pepper, tomatoes, and avocado I've wrapped up in a bag, I shake my head confirming, "No, Señor." I have nothing which would create a problem.

So if I'm not wrong, there probably won't be any other inspections until at least tomorrow. But shortly back out on the highway, I once again witness major road works being seriously tackled. It's reminding me once again that Baja California is undergoing major changes to cope with its development and the surge of increased traffic using the network of roads. It's strange. I'm travelling on the same stretch of road that I'd driven along more than a week ago but coming in the opposite direction, and it all looks totally different, with yet more things to see.

And that's no lie! Out in front, a peloton of serious cyclists appear, rigged out in what looks almost like professional Tour de France biking apparel. It's hot, and with their heads down, they mean business. Quite a Saturday morning workout. I carefully indicate and respectfully overtake, giving them a wide berth as I'd expect when I'm on my motorbike. As to how far they'll be going into the desert is anyone's guess.

The further I get into the immense remoteness of this place the more I can imagine it could be somewhere totally different on the planet. A bit like what I'd imagine the Dakota flatlands must look like—miles upon miles of flat land going out to nowhere. Whatever you may think, there was never a lack of boredom in driving, with the straight roads playing second fiddle to my curiosity in what could appear or happen at any minute. And there, right on cue, I see red flashing lights about one kilometre straight out into the distance, and the guessing game begins on what this means. The lights must be some kind of warning. As I approach, the lights appear out of a massive truck slowly spraying water, and it's there the road starts to climb. The road is narrow, ascending quite steeply, and with no visibility over the other side, so there's no way I can overtake. I'll be here forever.

It's then I notice a guy sitting on top of the lorry looking out and quickly waving for me to overtake them. This is dangerous. I'd seen what had happened with something similar on the way out heading south. This is a silly game of trust. I've got to trust a total stranger with my life that it's safe for me to, not only pass, but have the time to do it. I'm physically feeling the sweat run down my face in quantifying the danger of the situation. He impatiently waves me on again. I close my eyes for a millisecond and suddenly put my foot down to the floor. The truck jumps into life and stoically tries to find extra speed to get past. Reaching the peak, with the lorry behind me, I sigh with relief, but immediately see what could have happened. A coyote is dead on the road.

Then the corners start to appear, and each time I'm going round them it seems I'm closely missing and encountering the monster trucks speeding mercilessly on. I feel like shouting and screaming, "Slow down!" And maybe once or twice I probably did!

I need a drink of water and to calm my nerves so am happy to pull into a petrol station at the tiny pueblo of El Cien. This is also where the road had started to straighten out into flatlands again. Buying some bottles of water, I walk back to the car and notice an old man, proudly standing on his own under the shade of a tree. He's smartly dressed in his Sunday Best, with a crisply ironed blue and white striped shirt, jeans, black polished boots, and what looks like a new white cowboy ranchero hat. His wrinkly skin is as dark as a walnut, and it seems he's waiting patiently for something. The road out into the distance on either side is empty. He looks over to me, and I have an urge to walk up to him, maybe knowing what he needs.

I smile. He politely tips his hat with his hand. In my rough Spanish I state, "I'm heading to Ciudad Insurgentes. Do you need a lift? Do you want to come with me?"

He looks quizzically at me, looking around to maybe see where my friends are. I shake my head negatively and put one finger up, then prodding myself on the chest to indicate I'm on my own. He nods and shyly smiles, indicating he wishes to take me up on the offer. He slowly walks to the car, I open the door for him, and he painfully gets in and leans back into the seat. He looks tiny in it. He must be in his late 70s. I point to his seat belt, indicating that it's probably best he put it on, considering what I've just seen. He stretches behind and secures himself in, with me helping.

I start the engine, and still without a single word uttered from him, we silently set off together as travelling companions.

I have no idea where he wants to go, so again, with faltering sign language and a few words, point to him, then the road, then putting my thumb up to indicate he needs to do the same when he wants to get out. He nods once.

For a few miles there's complete silence. I'll start a conversation to relax the situation. I tell him where I've come from and where I'm going. He nods again just once. I tell him it's a wonderful place he lives in. He nods once. I tell him I like horses. He raises his eyebrows with surprise and nods twice. He seems more enthusiastic. Maybe I'll ask a few questions.

"Do you have horses?"

"Yes, I have some at my farm."

"Where are you going?"

"I'm going to see my daughter at El Crucero."

"I don't know that place; it's not on the map."

"Or Ciudad Constitución. I go most weeks."

I hear this with almost disbelief. Ciudad Constitución is the big farming town I'd passed through coming down. It's got to be at least 100 kilometres further on.

"That's good; so am I. I can take you all the way if you like."

He politely smiles once again and simply nods, but more than once.

"That's good. My name is Zoë. What is yours?"

He splutters a word out that I can't understand. He repeats it, but to no avail. I pass a pen and piece of paper from between the two seats and ask him to write his name down. He shakes his head and states he can't write!

We continue together, mostly in respectful silence, with him once or twice enthusiastically pointing to small farmsteads, which either he must know or which he wants to show are like his.

There are three kinds of ranches in Mexico, and I was guessing which was his; wealthy men ranching on private property, poor men ranching on even poorer property, and the poor man who belongs to an "ejido." This is a group of farmers or ranchers who collectively own the land and farm designated parcels. I'm thinking he's probably part of one of these ejidos.

We pass the famous pink bougainvillea and Christmas bauble-adorned Virgin of Guadalupe place of prayer, where I'd stopped previously after seeing the massive truck accident, and he dutifully crosses his chest. After almost an hour and a half we've safely arrived and drive through the large farming community of Ciudad Constitución, where without any notice, he quickly points to a group of old rancheros standing outside a hardware store. He signals he wishes to get out. He unbuckles his safety belt and puts his hand out to firmly shake mine. I smile, and he slowly wanders over to his friends. Just as I'm leaving, he unexpectedly turns around and, smiling, waves goodbye to me.

A few blocks on, I also stop for a coffee and look out onto the street. There are farm trucks, tractors, cars, and trailers carrying livestock and there are cowboys in every doorway. I'm not surprised that, with more than 37,000 people, this place acts as the hub and gateway to this most agriculturally rich area of Southern Baja, the Valle de Santo Domingo (Valley of Santo Domingo). The colonization of the valley originated only back in 1940. A ranch aptly named "El Crucero" was built on a crossroads. Because of this action, other people started to gather, and it became an obligatory travel stop for the farmers around the area and travellers. And as I'd been told driving here this morning, some locals still call the place El Crucero.

The mainstay of the area is the cultivation of wheat, corn, chickpeas, alfalfa, cotton, asparagus, lemons, oranges, grapefruit, and dairy. But I'd heard back at the beginning of the trip, at the farm near Tecate, that once again, the water levels in the aquifer are dropping about as fast as they can throw up new hotels in Cabo San Lucas, so cotton has now almost been abandoned for crops that conserve more water, like alfalfa.

I continue on for about another twenty miles until I reach the important intersection at Ciudad Insurgentes, where I'd decided to head north on the unknown Route 53, instead of going back along the same road I'd already been on. I stop at the last known gas station and look down at the petrol gauge. It's three quarters full, but I don't think twice about filling it up completely. I take a gulp of water and carefully look down at the map. I'm already slightly concerned, as there doesn't seem to be any signs for petrol for at least 150 miles, and that's somewhere high up in the mountains. If that's closed, I've had it.

I start up and drive out into the unknown. The empty road has immediately narrowed, and now heading directly into the horizon, it doesn't even have a yellow line running through the middle of the grey asphalt. The small farmsteads, with their large metal cereal storage containers, continue to line the road for some distance until they slowly disappear.

Towering green corn cob fields appear on either side and seem to claustrophobically envelope all around me. There's no one here. I glance down at my phone and, not for the first time, see no reception. If I was to break down, what would I do? For no apparent reason, although the tank is still pretty full, I'm just a little anxious.

Memories of a similar experience leap forward and jolt me once again back into another past life.

I'm nervously sitting in the passenger seat of a luxury AC'd sports utility farming truck. It's speeding crazily over dusty tracks through narrow gaps through corn fields. It's mid-summer in central Brazil, near Ribeirao Preto, an agricultural heartland, and the crops are ominously towering over and above the road, almost cutting out the light. I'm putting my total trust in someone I'd met just a few weeks previously.

To say he was an important person in Brazil was no exaggeration. At the time, he was chairman of a well-known multi-national drinks company, and he and his wealthy family owned farms everywhere. I'd been introduced to him by a friend who worked at the British Consulate in Sao Paulo and who innocently thought we'd get on. His macho, dark good looks and strong, tall physique had totally blinded me. He knew I had a few days off from work so had invited me "up country" to attend a cattle auction, where, while sipping champagne, he outbid everyone to buy the majority of the stock. We'd then drive to one of his factories and homes further inland, and the next day I'd fly back to Sao Paulo.

It seemed like a fun idea. But driving horrifyingly fast and all alone with him, along that dusty isolated road, and noticing a gun in the open glove compartment, I was terrified. I had no control. I was totally at the mercy of this powerful and influential person. Anything could have happened in those corn fields, and I'd never have been found. Or at least that's what my head and nerves convinced me to believe. And throughout that sleepless twenty-four hours, I never did feel totally at ease and sighed with relief when I finally stepped back on that plane to Sao Paulo. Power is sometimes not a nice thing to be around.

The giant corn fields along Route 53 fade away, as does the memory, and brings me back into the welcoming open light of flat scrubland, but ever increasing sandy, desert terrain. The road suddenly turns into just a rubbly track with a fallen road sign: "Precaución" lying on the ground at the side. A little further, the road once again finishes with a large barrier signalling "Desviación" and to divert down a sandy, slippery slope, which runs along miles of telegraph poles going out into the distance. More massive road construction work is going on in this seemingly remote area. The whole road looks like it's being doubled in size, with tall metallic fingers pointing up into the sky like they're intending to start a structure for a bridge.

Everything is changing. If I'm to come back, even next year, the place will be different. I look to see how much petrol I've got. It's about half full. I'll need to start thinking about finding that place in that village up in the mountains. I leave the roadworks and look at my watch. It's about midday. I'm really hungry, and I'm dying to pee. There's no one here out on the road. I stop, walk around to the side of the car, and let out a sigh of relief. Heaven. Then back in the car I unwrap one of the precious tortillas and with my knife slice some cheese, avocado, and tomato onto it and wrap it up. I cut part of the mango and eat into the juicy meat. I'm feeling a lot better.

Within almost a blink of an eye, I've headed, where the landscape once again dramatically changes to a remote but lush, green valley with date palms lining the roadside and a stream of water running through the fields at the bottom. This looks like another oasis. Majestic, towering, sandy brown flat mountain ridges line the horizon out into the distance. But more than any of this, approaching the little village of La Purisima, I'm fascinated and dumbstruck in what is bizarrely standing high up on its own in the middle of this lush valley. A large sloped butte, looking somewhat like a volcano or a landing spot for UFOs in a sci-fi movie.

I wind around the corners of this lush, green-sided valley and carefully drive through sleepy La Purisima, positively on the look-out for a petrol sign. Nothing. Nada. OK, I'll continue on to San Isidro, a few miles on. Maybe the map got it wrong. Maybe the pump is there. But little San Isidro seems to have even less going on, if that's at all possible. I need petrol. I turn back to drive down again the only street there is here and right on the other side, that I didn't see coming up the other way, is a tiny hand-painted sign with the magic word *Gasolina*. It's next to a small driveway into a private home. Never! I have no other option. I cross over and pass through the gateway and stop outside a little house, where an old man is watering chilli plants in pots lined along a concrete wall. An aproned lady with slippers on walks out and automatically goes to a small shed with tyres stacked up against it, opens the door, and signals me over. I smile. There's someone here who knows what I want.

"Buenos días, Señora. Do you want to buy a ten or twenty litre drum of petrol?"

Wow. I've no idea. There are no prices anywhere, but I really have no choice. I ask for the largest barrel, "¡El más grande!" She confidently puts a simple, rubber hosepipe into the container, expertly sucks on it, and asks me to unscrew the petrol cap. She takes the other end and tries with all her might to push it into my petrol tank. But it just won't go in, however much we try. This is ridiculous for what should be a really simple thing to do. This new bloody technology! To deter petrol getting stolen and syphoned off, car manufacturers had developed "safety" valves, which don't allow alien pipes in to drain the petrol out. As I didn't drive a car at home, it's something I'd been totally unaware of.

God, an extra thing I didn't need! Stupid thoughts start flying through my mind. With no petrol how would I continue, and would any sort of emergency assistance come to my rescue in such a remote location? I'm feeling somewhat despondent and helpless. She sees my worried look, smiles, and shouts out towards the house, "¡Ross! Ross! Ven aquí!"

A pretty young girl with long plaited hair, in her early twenties, walks out of the house and approaches us.

"This is my daughter, Ross. She's an English teacher here at the village school. There's another house that sells petrol in the next village, which may have the right funnel end to get into the tank. Ross can accompany you to show you the way."

I'm shocked with another offer of generosity and wildly nod my head in acceptance. But before leaving, I politely ask if I can relieve myself and use their bathroom. I'm kindly shown through their house, and even given a small clean towel to wipe my hands.

Ross and I jump into the car, where the conversation immediately flows.

"This area is beautiful. It's so green."

"Yes. It is. We like living here. This is so good to speak with an English person. I've never met one before. You are the first. Your accent is so different to when I watch American TV. This will be good practice for me for teaching the children. San Isidro was established in 1719 because of the underground springs that could support small areas for cattle farming, and now these watering holes and the cliff side aqueduct still provide water for our citrus, mango, and date trees. The palms are also dried here for palapa roofs and fences."

I point questioningly over to the "*Close Encounters of The Third Kind*" rock.

"Oh yes, that's called El Pilón. You can see it for miles when you drive through the valley. Where are you going exactly?"

"I'm going to continue through the mountains here and drop down to the coast on the other side to Mulegé."

She unexpectedly looks at me in horror and animatedly waving her hands around in the air explains, "That's not a good idea! No, that's not good. It's impassable. There's been a recent landslide. There are basketball-sized boulders everywhere. It's very unsafe. There's no way for you to get through. Even if you drove a Baja-prepped race vehicle or rode a donkey!"

I look back at her in horror but believe she's telling the truth. That means I've got to retrace my arduously slow journey of this morning, which will represent an extra 140 miles and a lot of it through construction work at a snail's pace. But one thing at a time. Let's first get the petrol sorted.

Driving through La Purisma, the Godly word *Gasolina* once again appears on a hand-painted sign. We turn into a sandy courtyard where there's a little blue and white painted shed with what I can only describe as a small box standing on steel legs with a rubber tube coming out of it and a manual lever on its side. But it has the correct nozzle and fifteen litres fuller or 225 pesos poorer I gladly hand the money over.

Due to these entrepreneurial villagers having to purchase the fuel at the standard retail price from a petrol station and then transport the drums all the way up to these remote places, the petrol is slightly more expensive, but who cares. They're providing an essential service to the community and travellers here. I remember seeing something similar in the remoter places of New Mexico, where people stood selling barrels on the sides of the roads. With just eighty miles to get back to ciudad de Los Surgentes and onto Highway 1, I'll be fine. Conveying my sincere gratitude, I happily take Ross back to her home.

So the mountain route has been jettisoned, and before too long, I've passed the sparse lands, turning into corn fields and farm lands, and leaving Highway 53 and am back onto hot, dry Highway 1. This will lead me down to the cooling, inviting sea that I can soon imagine immersing myself into. It doesn't take long.

Entering the beautiful landscape of Bahía Conceptión, with mountains on one side and the blue turquoise waters on the other, I bumpily drive down a sandy track to Playa El Coyote. I stop on the beach, almost up to the lapping waters. Besides a few people throwing their lines out to fish and wading out a little, the place is incredibly peaceful as I quickly rip off my sweaty jeans and jog to the sea. I slowly immerse myself in the cooling water and let out a sigh of true happiness. Another beautiful moment in time.

I'm not worried about drying myself or changing. It's mid-afternoon as I jump back into the car with just my T-shirt and bikini bottoms on. I put the shoeless, sandy foot down and know I've not far to go.

Driving up and then down into a valley, palm trees and verdant landscapes once again magically appear out of nowhere. I turn into an arched entrance and find myself driving through narrow, antiquated streets of a small rural town. I stop on the side and, now totally dry, reach over for my shorts and discreetly wriggle into them. Mulegé is another oasis, tucked away on the lush banks of the Río Santa Rosalía, which flows into the Sea of Cortez. It's desperately empty and lifeless as I approach the old centre and Plaza Corona in search of the Hotel Hacienda.

After driving round a second time through the streets, I find myself back at the same square and then see the old colonial-style building dating back to the 1770s, with its thick walls and high doors. I've arrived.

I walk through into the silent, spacious courtyard lined with bougainvillea, colourful plants and potted flowers, wooden rocking chairs, old plastic chairs, a small pool, and up to an old bar counter, which seems to double up as the hotel reception desk. It all feels a bit rough at the edges and from a bygone age. Perfect!

A young girl with long dark hair is sitting behind the bar dreamily looking at a thick, old computer screen. She looks up from her probable boredom. "Hola. Bienvenido. Welcome."

After the introductions, Teresa hands me a key and points to a door opposite facing into the courtyard. For just twenty dollars, I'm not expecting much, except for a peaceful night.

"So, what would be good to see here? I've driven a long way, but it would be nice to stretch my legs and wander around."

She seriously mulls the question over like it's the most difficult one ever asked, then truthfully replies, "Well, I don't know. There's really not much happening. I suppose you could walk up along the river to see the lighthouse. Most people come here for the beaches along Bahía Conceptíon or to go fishing. But my father, Cuesta, will be here later, and he can tell you more. He takes people to visit places, like seeing the Indian paintings. And of course, there's the mission up on the hill out of town."

She looks down at my bags, which reminds me, "Thank you. I think I'll go for a walk. But I have some food and drink in these bags. Could I possibly leave it all in that fridge over there?"

A nod is given. "Yes. Make yourself at home. If you want to prepare your food, you can use the counter here in the kitchen. No one else is staying. You'll be here on your own tonight."

That's not the first time I'd heard that. I walk across the courtyard and place the bags, minus the food, in a simple room, which has seen better days. I go and do the two most important things. I test the mattress, which is thin but will do, and turn on the tap, which runs water. But the place is quiet, which is probably more important.

I stroll out into the mid-afternoon sunshine and wander aimlessly around the tree-lined square, believing I'll see a welcoming café terrace serving chilled Mexican drinks by a smiling moustached waiter. In my dreams! I walk around it again, just for something to do. Everything is closed. I turn round and pass the hotel and down the empty street, where the few small bars and eateries are also closed. It's true, there's really not a lot happening here. Walking along the same palm-lined road, the river appears alongside it and looks like it's flowing out to sea at the very end.

On the opposite side of the river are what look like fairly well-heeled holiday homes, with boats parked outside on trailers and a number of camper vans. I already knew this was a popular holiday destination for Americans coming south through the border, but peak season had come and gone and it looked like they had too. At the very end the road merges into a stony beach with an old white lighthouse perched on the top of a high, rocky cliff face. There's nothing more to do than walk over and try and climb up to it. The rubble pathway is steep and slippery, and only halfway up there's a barricaded wall with no further access. But even here the view is pretty spectacular, looking out over the estuary to the Sea of Cortez and behind, the flowing river coming to join it. The name *Mulegé* is apt, derived from the Cochimi language, meaning "Large ravine of the white mouth."

I slide back down almost on my bum and, brushing the dust off it, return back along the empty road and into the Hacienda's courtyard. Nowhere is open to eat for dinner, so I know what I'm having—again. I pull up a white plastic chair by the small pool and watch flies systematically drop into it. Not because of that, but because I need a drink, I walk back to the now empty reception bar area, go behind it, and pour myself a glass of wine from the bottle I'd put in the fridge. With the chilled glass in my hand, I sit back outside and reflect on the day's events.

It's then I hear a large echoing sound coming from over the wall on the other side of the courtyard. I'm curious. I get up and walk over to inquisitively peer through a convenient hole in the wall. On the other side is an indoor sports hall where a small projection screen has been put up and a handful of children are sitting on the concrete terrace steps starting to watch a film. What the film is I've no idea, but the children seem enraptured. I wander back to my chair, and this simple place reminds me of an infants' school playground with the classrooms around it—I could be in Cuba.

With the sun slowly setting and the daylight disappearing, it's time I had something to eat. That tortilla sandwich on the dusty lost road earlier in the day seems a lifetime ago. God, I'm glad I'd bought that extra food. So for the fourth consecutive meal, I'll have had tortillas, cheese, and my salad stuff. But at least I can open that can of tuna tonight, and at least it's healthy. I grab some cutlery, a plate, the food, and wine and sit back by the pool.

Pouring a more than generous but well-deserved glass, I hear footsteps come up from behind. A bespectacled, smiling gentleman with gelled back hair approaches the pool.

"Good evening, Señora. Welcome. Theresa, my daughter, had mentioned you'd arrived earlier. I'm the owner. My name is Ciro."

His English is pretty good, and it's nice to have a chat with someone as he drags another chair to the poolside to sit down.

"I've had a really long and difficult journey today. It was almost 500 miles, due to a long detour I had to make with the mountain roads blocked."

"Yes, up in those remote areas that sometimes happens."

"It's quiet here in Mulegé. I'll be glad to have a good night's sleep in this lovely place."

He smiles. "Yes, parts of this hacienda are about 230 years. It was originally an adobe and is the oldest building in town. It used to be a mission, a school, a military building, and a hotel with my father since the 1950s."

He then politely coughs, as though he's got a little more to say and add to the subject. I nod in appreciation, like I'm happy to hear more.

"Well, Señora, I do hope you sleep well, but there are a few stories about this place." He points over to one of the rooms.

"Lots of strange things happen here! Over there, in Rooms Six and Seven, people have seen a ghost child brushing her hair in front of the mirror. We believe it to be Dolce Maria."

The hairs on my arms stand up on end, hoping she won't come into my room, but I nod again to hear more, refilling my glass and taking a gulp.

"I'm not lying when I say this, why should I? But sometimes in the middle of the night, from over there in the corner, you can clearly hear horses' hooves walking through the courtyard. My wife has seen a man on a horse, and we've heard chains loudly clanking."

He gets up, smiling with an expression on his face as if to say "but please don't worry" and salutes me good night, disappearing into the dark.

I'm left on my own in the warm evening watching the dark night clouds sweeping over and brushing past the bright stars. I then unexpectedly jump out of my seat with fright! A woman's scream resounds through the courtyard! But it's alright. It's no ghost. It's just from the cinema over the wall.

16

OPEN YOUR EYES!

*Maybe that's what life is . . . a wink of the eye and
winking stars.*

Jack Kerouac

Despite the thin mattress, I'd slept amazingly well, except
for sweating in bed and then stumbling into the bathroom
at one in the morning to take a quick, cold shower from the
unbearable heat in the airless room. But with the rising sun, I
was also now getting up ready to leave. I'd heard a kind knock
on the door and the words *café en la cocina*.

I wander across the shady courtyard, and Ciro is already
pouring fresh coffee into two mugs. I pull up a stool and spread
the map out. He also curiously leans over to take a better look
and asks, "So, where are you planning to get to today?"

I explain by silently tracing my finger up from Mulegé,
over, and across to the remote Estero El Coyote (Wolf
Estuary), which then flows into El Bahía de Bellenas (The Bay

of Whales). For the last leg of this incredible trip I'd tried to find one of the most remote places, but which still represented another unique perspective to this beautiful peninsula. I'd found an old, solitary fishing campsite which welcomed fishermen, and they'd confirmed, through an intermediary based in Ensenada, who'd asked for a deposit, that I could stay for a few nights in one of their basic fishing huts. It sounded perfect.

"I'm travelling about 200 miles to the southern part of El Vizcaíno Biosphere Reserve. I know it's a huge area, the largest wildlife and marine reserve in Mexico with UNESCO recognition, but I've found this isolated fishing place through the desert and on the tip of the Pacific coast, which I'm going to try and get to. I think it's called the Wolf Campsite."

He nods, looking like it sounds like a good plan. "But Señora, are you maybe going to drive up quickly to our mission on the top of the hill overlooking the river? It's only a couple of miles out of town, so it shouldn't take up much of your time. It also explains a bit of the history, from the Indians to the padres who came and settled here. Or up the hill there's the old prison that had no bars and where the inmates were free to work in the village during the day, but now it's our museum. But it's too early to be open."

I nod. "You're right. It's still early, so yes, I'll drive up and just take a look at the mission."

We shake hands, and I say farewell to the "Ghost Hotel." At just after 7, I've driven under a bridge, up a dirt road, to the top of a hill, and stopped in front of the austere but beautiful Misión de Santa Rosalia de Mulegé. It was founded by the Jesuits in 1705 and Father Juan Manuel Basaldua as a mission to the Indians. The construction was completed sixty years later, in 1766. But less than 100 years later, the Americans tried to occupy long stretches of the West, such as California, Baja California, and New Mexico, which were then all part of Mexico. This became known as the Mexican-American War of 1846-1848. The people of Mulegé and neighbouring areas along the coast defeated the Americans. So the town was rewarded with the official title of "Heroica Mulegé," which is still its official name.

I look down at my watch and see it's just 7:30, which is perfect. I also glance at the petrol gauge, which indicates I have enough. So I descend down and navigate through the empty, sleeping streets, back out onto the green, lush hilly road leading away and north up the coast. Almost immediately, the emptiness of the narrow mountainous road starts curving and winding in and around and along the dry, steep, gritty slopes. I need to be careful.

I'd checked on the map that just a few miles out of town I'd find a petrol station where I could fill up. But I was driving further and further away and into more and more barren desert with the tall cactus increasing in numbers. I felt I was already in the middle of nowhere. There is certainly no gas station here. I was learning that these petrol signs on maps are either not one hundred per cent accurate or sometimes a little unreliable. I had to make a decision. My mind starts racing. The next possibility to fill up, even if it is there, is probably too far away. I am somewhat of a gambler with things but can't afford to continue or risk it here.

I have to get onto a straight piece of road to feasibly turn. A mile on, emerging onto the flat desert, I put my foot on the brake, sharply pull the steering wheel round, and swing back. I drive the ten miles back to Mulegé to find petrol. By just after eight, when I roll up, the little town has woken up, and the only gas station, hidden up a tiny road, has just opened. It might have been an extra twenty miles I've just done, but here filling the tank, I was sure to have enough petrol now until at least Santa Rosalía. Hopefully, I was now leaving this palm-lined desert oasis, with Baja's only navigable river for one last time.

Away from the lush tropical valley and the twisting, torturous mountain bends, the road descended and opened up once again to this vast expanse of the wild Transpeninsular Highway. At first glance, the desert, for lots of people, must surely seem monotonous, but on closer inspection, it somehow to me always felt different. This morning was no exception, and the wispy, hardly visible clouds high above caste no or little shadow on the dry rubbly land. Stately clusters of the giant cardon cactus stretching fifty or sixty feet up into the sky were the only objects slightly obliterating a perfect view of the horizon. This tough wood, as I'd now seen in so many places, was a survivor in the most extreme conditions to intense heat, dust storms, and hurricanes, and as a permanent feature and intrinsic part of life here, was often used for the construction of beams and housing by the hardy ranchers.

The sun piercingly struck into the black tarmac road and enhanced the brightness of the canary yellow line cutting through it. With my arm out on the window lapping up the racing breeze, I quickly get into the rhythm of this long empty road. But out in the distance appears a black solitary object, which doesn't seem to be moving. And the closer I approach, the more I realize it is at a standstill. It's a bus that had stopped at an army military check point. I drive slowly up behind it and respectfully stop, waiting for my turn, but the sensation of uncontrollable palpitations is, once again, rearing its ugly head.

The desert camouflaged soldiers seem to be out in force on this early morning and seemingly in no particular rush. Before too long, two jean-clad girls have stepped out of the bus and are walking to the side of the road carrying two suitcases. They are ordered to open them on the ground, with the soldiers then searching through them. This seems quite extreme. Without any explanation, the soldiers simply nod, the girls stuff everything back in again, and then quickly jump back into the bus, which slowly moves away.

It's my turn. The rifle-carrying soldiers slowly approach, and a stern wave is given that I stop.

"Buenos días. Please step out of the car and open the back."

In situations like this, it's probably best to agree on everything. I walk around to the back of the truck and lift the rear door up. The tallest soldier, with what looks like the biggest rifle, points at my suitcase. "Please bring it out and open it. We need to see inside it."

I dutifully heave the suitcase out, with the soldiers looking on, and onto the hot tarmac open it, hoping that at least some of my cleaner clothes are on the top. The soldier with the big rifle approaches, peers in, and literally rifles through it. With no success in finding what he's looking for, he simply nods, indicating that all is well. I gladly shove everything back in again, unconcerned of the mess it's created.

A surprising smile appears on his austere face and he signals me to leave. Without questioning or asking to take a souvenir photo of him and his rifle, I speed off. But before I've even had the chance to put my arm out of the window and go into fifth gear, the massive bus with the two girls appears just in front out on the road. Seeing me approach from behind again, the driver kindly slows right down on the straight stretch, and his hand comes out at the same time as his right indicator to wave me past.

Without any further interruption, the coastal drive up to Santa Rosalía is beautiful. Passing Isla San Marcos with its seal colony, and just one of more than fifty islands in the Sea of Cortez, it looks so remote and isolated in the shimmering ocean. Approaching the town, between the fragile rocky sides with its homes and huts awkwardly balancing on its edges and the deep blue water lapping on the other side, I make a bee-line for the old, tumbling down mining towers close to the port. I stop in front of antique, copper-mining machinery, smelters, and an old steam train. Everything here looks to be in decay from a bygone era.

A man appears through a gap in the fence from the old port and approaches, noticing my curiosity. He kindly suggests that if I wish to learn more about the town's mining history, El Boleo Museum is well worth a visit, now housed in the old mining offices and a bit further up the hill. It's hard to believe that when they started exporting the copper to Europe in 1872, it was mainly to Swansea in Wales. Due to that and the discovery of gold, by 1880, the small scale mining had come to the attention of the Rothschilds, who provided money to the French company "El Boleo" to buy the mining rights. They then went on to create a town with a very French flair and constructed 600 kilometres of tunnels, built a dock, a hotel, homes, and even stores for the workers to buy supplies. Even the foundry was shipped from Europe. In the heyday of this place, in the 1920s, El Boleo had a steamboat that would bring people from La Paz, where they would come to party and dance ballroom-style.

But by the 1950s, with falling profits, the pits were sold by the French to the Mexican government with little activity. Since 2004, work has now been undertaken by a Canadian mining company to re-open the mine and bring the place back to life.

Leaving Santa Rosalía, the road once again starts climbing back up into the mountains, looking out onto the desolate and barren valleys, with its ever-increasing number of roadside crosses warning of the dangers. It all opens out again, and I'm joined by the cactus troops marching out on this rugged beautiful landscape to the distant horizons. It's hot, unimaginably hot, and the thirsty intake of water into my dry mouth tastes like nectar.

Passing the junction that leads to the oasis village of San Ignacio, I'd remembered there was a petrol station a bit further up. I'm crossing my fingers, as it's a Sunday. But with a sigh of relief, it's open and a last opportunity to fill the tank. Funny how the small things can make you happy. Where I was going was at least another hundred miles on an isolated road and the only other "Gasolina" sign I'd seen on my map was in the village of Punto Abreojos, which was my final destination.

Continuing on, I'm now diligently looking for the small road I'll need to turn into, which I know from the map I should soon be approaching. But with no road number, I'm hoping it'll at least provide reassurance in showing on a sign the name of the place I'm headed to. All I notice on the next turning is a small sign for San Ángel. I check and see it's a small settlement on the road I need to take. I smile and cross over onto the remote Carreterra Campo Fisher—Punto Abreojos.

I gasp, not quite believing what I see. Almost immediately, the road has narrowed and become one with this flat, gorse-covered sandy desert, disappearing for limitless miles into the unknown distance. The sand has wildly blown up, across, and over the asphalt, almost camouflaging it. The mountains behind me slowly sink lower and lower the further I travel, until they've also completely disappeared from view. The sky feels like it's becoming bigger and bigger, and the road and myself becoming smaller and smaller in this massive, silent wilderness, putting everything into perspective of our importance here.

I have a simple job. All I need do is look out for a sign in about seventy miles for Campo René. Seventy miles comes and goes. Nothing. I pass seventy-five miles. Nothing. Eighty miles is eaten up. Nothing. This is getting worrying. Then I quickly notice a small gap off the road and the sight of a building out in the distance. There's no specific track, but just about enough space to drive and zig-zag through gorse shrubs on the bumpy and rutted, sandy terrain. Is that it? With no other option and still feeling this isn't right, I drive down the sandy slope and literally slide from side to side. Surely not. There's no life here. I'm worried. This isn't even a pathway! The wheels could quite easily get stuck in the soft fine sand, and then what would I do with no phone reception? I approach a half-built terracotta home empty of all life. This is definitely not it!

I've no other option but to somehow turn round and drive back. The truck scarily seems to take control of itself and, with no real grasp of the ground, slides in every direction but forward and drops into every sandy hole it finds. I draw breath with relief as we reach the road again. Now what? The place should be here. With just another ten miles to Punta Abreojos, I decide to continue on to hopefully ask someone the way.

The remote fishing village of Punta Abreojos, which looks half asleep, appears with a welcoming gas station. I pull in and walk over to a fat guy sweeping the courtyard on this quiet Sunday lunchtime.

"Hola. Estoy buscando Campo René. ¡Estoy perdido!"

It's true! I am looking for Campo René and I am also lost!

He leans on his brush and looks at me like I've asked a silly question.

"Well, it's only about fifteen miles from here. There's an entrance on the right of the road, with big stones on either side. Yes, it's a small sign, but it does say, "Campo René." They have no phone, but it is open.

Well, that's one less thing to worry about, as I'd already paid a deposit. If the worst comes to the worst, I imagine I could always ask for help and get him to show me where the place is. I love having contingency plans. I continue down the tiny one-street place and stop at the seafront. It's empty. I park and get out and breathe in the wild, salty air. Down on the white sandy beach are at least ten large fishing boats pulled up on trailers. This is a working place, but what a beautiful sight. They are all painted as brightly blue as the sky and as white as the sand beneath them. But there's not a single fisherman in sight. Next to the boats and the rippling, white frothy sea are hundreds of seagulls Sunday promenading out along the beach, with a handful of pelicans twice their size also paddling and looking out to sea for their next beak-full of fish.

That reminds me. I need to find a place to grab a bite, if that's at all possible. I wander further along, and standing right on the side of the beach is a beautiful canary yellow and white Catholic church with a tall bell tower. It looks totally out of context with the sand blowing up to its yellow walls and tatty, broken wooden fences with agricultural equipment stacked up next to them. Colourful, stained glass windows reflect the bright sunshine. This really is a find, and totally unexpected.

I turn back along the shoreline towards my four wheels and notice, across the road from it, a small, meek-looking café, which besides a few men sitting quietly inside, looks agreeably open. Maybe something simple is still on offer. I respectfully sit at a small table next to the four men, who somehow look like fishermen, with dirt-stained T-shirts and wide-brimmed straw hats. There's no menu, and although it looks like the place is closing, with tops being cleaned, the lady who comes to my table nods when I say, "¿Pescado?"

The men curiously look over to me, knowing I'm not from this place. I smile, acknowledging them. They smile back.

"I'm sure the fish here must be very good!"

The one closest to me, with a burly build that no doubt comes from years of hauling lobster traps and fishing nets, nods, "Yes, it will be from this morning. Where are you from?"

I like the inquisitiveness, which gives me the excuse to find out more. "I'm here travelling through Baja. But I'm fascinated by this place. It's so remote, and I've still got to find Estero El Coyote."

He nods, also seemingly keen to strike up a conversation with a total stranger, "Yes, the town's main money earner is fishing for spring lobster and abalone. We only have about five hundred houses, but we do have a few grocery stores, an airstrip, a fish packing plant, a hardware store, schools, and our church."

A simple plate of pan-fried fish and rice appears. It's delicious, and I contentedly smile to the fishermen, wondering if it was them who'd caught it.

"It's good that you're curious and interested. This place, Abreojos, means "Open Your Eyes" and refers to the dangerous conditions with the many rocks and reefs here. The fishermen and sailors have to be careful, but there are several lighthouses, and the high hill behind the town is a good landmark for us. I'm sure you'll learn a lot more about our fishing co-operative when you arrive at René's. There are some interesting stories!"

I thank them for their company and, with crossed fingers, hope that this time I'll find Campo René in the Estero El Coyote. Almost exactly fifteen miles down the sandy road, as the guy at the garage had said, I see a small sign: "Campo

René" standing in the earth. That's why I hadn't seen it. There wasn't one facing the other way. I'm excited not knowing what to expect. I turn onto a vast flat expanse of sand, which has a few wheel tracks running straight ahead. Then I notice a track appear, created with simple large stones on either side and just delineating what is sand and what is the track. Continuing on, there is still nothing else here.

At least a mile or so further on I enter a small, sandy parking area with a few ramshackle white cabins on one side, two palm topped huts on the other, and out in front, a cream painted building with wall paintings of whales, dolphins, turtles, birds, and a solitary howling wolf in a cactus desert. The sign above reads "Restaurant Bar—Campo René—Estero El Coyote BCS". The doors are closed. The whole place looks closed, except for one solitary truck parked outside. I get out of the sand-covered car and walk towards the door at the side of the building. I stand still, look a little further out, and am dumbstruck and amazed with the views I see. There's a massive, beautiful expanse of quiet, still water, which looks like a lake with green rich vegetation sprouting up from little islands in the middle of it and large white heron-looking birds perched in the large trees. A large red canoe has been pulled up by the pebbly shoreline.

I knock at the door. There's no reply. I hear shuffling inside and then a loud shout: "¡Sí, un momento!"

That's good. Someone is here. A large, well-built man with a blue stripped apron and knife in hand comes to the door. "Can we help you?"

"Yes. I'd contacted you to stay in one of your cabins for two nights."

His quizzical expression looks like it's the first time he's heard anything about it and, shaking his head, simply says "I'm sorry, but we've got no booking. This is low season, and normally we don't get people staying, besides those wanting to use the place for their camper vans and the odd boat coming in to get meals."

That's good. We're off to a good start. I desperately explain "I can assure you, I even paid thirty dollars. I've come a long way!"

I think he's starting to see I'm telling the truth. "Well, Jesús, who looks after this place, is coming later. You can speak to him then, but he shouldn't be long. But we can still make up a bed for you in one of the wooden cabañas overlooking the estuary. We can also get you a beer if you want."

I sigh with a little relief by his friendliness and walk back to get my stuff. Just a little further, overlooking and right next to the verdant watery landscape, are two round huts that look like they've been built with mud and wood and covered with beautiful palm-lined roofs. These are the cabañas. Next to them, is a rickety, old, wood-stepped tower with, incredibly, a massive nest at the top with at least two sea ospreys looking out onto these watery marshlands.

I put my luggage on one of the steps and walk back and around the side of the restaurant to sit on a stool on a terrace looking out to the quiet water view. The tide looks like it's out, but all of a sudden I notice fish jumping out of the water and quickly back in again out of sight. Large grey herons are nested in the trees out on the islands, and further around the shoreline is a sandy beach with some kind of fishing activity going on and a couple of small boats and buildings. I'm wondering what I'm going to do here all on my own for the next few days. Taking a greedy gulp of chilled Modelo beer, I hear a vehicle arrive, and then footsteps come up behind me.

But instead of expecting a large fisherman to welcome me, I turn around and see a smiling, slightly-built guy daintily approach with his hand extended out to shake mine. Jesús is bejewelled with rings, bracelets, and necklaces and wearing a pair of black trousers and a crisp, ironed blue shirt.

In almost perfect English he starts, "Hello. You must be Zoë. Ricardo said you had arrived. I'm here to welcome you."

And with that, he pulls over a stool and sits down next to me, and I try to explain, "I think there's been a slight misunderstanding, but I can assure you I'd booked and even paid a deposit by PayPal to someone's account in San Diego!"

He looks startled and, in theatrical shock, puts his delicate hands to his cheeks. "Oh my God! They've done it again! We have a problem. Not your problem. Our problem! There's a terrible man in Ensenada. The thieves stole our website, got our domain name, and have been getting our clients to pay a deposit without telling us. It's a scam, and you've been caught in it."

"Wow! Yes I did pay thirty dollars, so I guess I won't see that back. But is it still OK to stay for two nights?"

He smiles, "Of course it is! And I will make it up to you. I can guarantee."

At that very moment, I see the fish jumping out again, and he points to them. "Yes, those are molet. All the fish you'll eat here are fresh from the lagoon and our oyster farm over there . . . well, I'm sure you'll eat those too. In fact, I'm going to ask the fishermen, as an apology to you, to take you out on one of their boats tomorrow to see the estuary and how the oysters are bred and grow. I know, having worked on a cruise-liner for many years, that customer service is very important!"

I smile and can see his genuine wish to please me. "Thank you so very much. That's wonderful, and it'll certainly more than make up for that horrible man's actions."

"Yes. He's come before to also poach fish and hunt rare wild ducks with a gun. But you must enjoy yourself here. Go walking around the coastline. You'll see more tomorrow. Please use the kayak if you want, although in the afternoon you must be careful, as the current is a lot stronger. The place here is now very quiet. These fishing camps are the outposts of Baja's remote coastlines, and although we're quite seasonal, we still offer opportunities for people who come by boat to purchase cooked or fresh seafood. We're very proud of this special place. There's a lot for you to see here. I promise tomorrow I can tell you a lot more."

I nod enthusiastically "Yes, I met some fishermen in Punta Abreojos earlier on, and they said this place had a lot of stories."

"They're right. We have all day tomorrow, and I'll then tell you the amazing story about René. I've just started working here and want to make it good to help sustain the place, so any suggestions would be gladly received. My father is retired from the co-operative, and my grandfather was one of the founders of it. So I guess you could say I'm part of the belief in helping the whole place succeed. The co-op needed someone in the tourist business who spoke English to run the place. I feel we can improve the look of the restaurant and bar. It looks so old. In the next three years I plan to try and totally renovate the place! But be reassured, we don't want to totally change the special character of this lost place.

"We have some regulars who come here for the fishing on their private planes and land near those small old huts from San Francisco, Argentina, and Los Angeles! One man who I know is very rich and brings friends. His friends stay in the larger newer cabañas where you'll be, but he's just as happy to stay in the old, smaller, and simpler huts next to his plane. They all don't want change. That's why they come here.

The world is changing too much! Ricardo will cook you some fish tonight. Just let him know what time."

And with that, he gets up to go, theatrically waving and putting his thumbs up that we're going to have fun tomorrow with the fishermen.

After that interesting little interlude, I walk back up to my cabaña, which has now been made ready, and find a beautiful but simple round room built with local timber and earth, with doors open on either side leaving the cool air to breeze through. Through a little door is a small shower. The open door at the back leads to a small terrace, wide enough for a stool to look out to the marshlands ultimately leading into the Pacific. Lost perfection.

I walk out, around the lagoon, and across the large sandy landscape to the wide estuary and coastal shoreline. The warm breeze plays games with fluttering the fine sand and leaves into the air and pushing it all out and over the vast expanses of this white remote beach.

Then, like a ghost, along the soft waved estuary out at sea, a large, abandoned fishing boat appears, standing on its own on the empty white beach. I approach it. It's just a skeleton of its former self, and I wonder why it's never been moved. Sea eagles appear and dive down into the water nearby, bringing fish back up in their strong clawed feet.

This place is truly magical. It feels so special. I walk to the edge of the water and sit down on the sand, looking out to sea. And then just a few yards out, some fins appear above the surface, and then a handful of dolphins playfully swim around, almost reaching the beach and then disappearing out of the estuary and into the sea. The place feels so isolated; no tracks, no sun worshippers—nothing. Wanting to further beachcomb tomorrow, I'll definitely walk further then and discover more of the coastline I see past those sandy hills out along the beach in the distance.

This evening a massive, orange and red full moon travels up and over the lagoon's horizon, accompanied by shining stars magically appearing one by one. But strangely, the wind also gets up, making the place feel a lot colder. And mysteriously, the electricity is no longer working, so with a small torch I feel my way back into the pitch-dark cabaña. With just one, thin cotton sheet covering me, I reluctantly put on my jeans, zip up my hoodie over my nightie, and pull the sheet up under my chin.

17

BEACH SKULLS AND SKELETONS

As you get older, the question comes down to about two or three. How long? And what do I do with the time I've got left?

David Bowie

The early morning sunshine is seeping through the closed shutters. With no idea of the time, I walk over the bare wooded floor and open them to be greeted by a hazy sun bouncing off the mangroves and white dazzling water. Besides the beautiful calming sound of tweeting birds, the place is peacefully silent.

But out in the distance there is something. I'm having to listen hard. Rumbling. Is that traffic? Normally, my senses would have confirmed this, but the harder I concentrate the more I realize it's simply just the strong, continuous pounding of the ocean. Just below me, the marshland waters have dramatically receded, showing sandy, slimy mud among the roots of the plants.

I'm also amazed I slept so well, considering I'd put most of my clothes on to keep warm. I wander over to the sink in the corner of the dark room to clean my teeth and lean over to turn the light switch on. But no light comes on. I try all the wall switches and even flip the electric socket on and off but to no avail. I guess it doesn't really matter, as I'd only use the socket to charge my phone, and that's pointless, anyway, as there's no reception or Wi-Fi here. Thankfully, the torch came to the rescue last night for just a bit of light.

Leaning over to the other side of the bed, I slightly open the other door facing out onto the sandy parking area and curiously peer out. It's totally empty, with no cars except for mine. I'm guessing no one, even the chef and his family, had stayed here last night, so I was all on my own. That's besides the osprey neighbours lodging next door. I walk barefooted into the fresh day, over the sandy parking area and out to the quiet terrace behind the locked-up bar overlooking the marshes and sleepy waters.

The harsh cold wind from last night has now totally dropped to just a slight warm breeze. The orange and yellow shark wind chime, with its fins uncontrollably whizzing around, gently rattles over one of the tables. I go and sit on a stool and quietly look out to the best Monday morning office view ever! I peer down below me and see grey crabs the size of small feet come out of their holes in the muddy sand banks and run comically sideways then quickly disappear back into other neighbours' homes.

Everything is waking up. A sea osprey flies and hovers over this perfect hunting ground, with the fish jumping out, making it an even easier job for him to catch his breakfast. And this he does. He swoops down into the water, his sharp talons gracefully grab a fish, and flies back out, landing on the top of a palm covered roof, where his beak grabs and pulls his catch, quickly eating it all up.

After about an hour in this idyllic "with nature" peace, I hear a rattling truck pull up. The chef, his wife, and son have arrived. And then a massive sound erupts. The noisy, rumbling generator supplying the electricity, which yesterday had almost been a silent unperceived background noise, has been turned back on. I understand now. I'm such a city person not to have understood. That's why I had no light. The TV on the wall in the restaurant is immediately turned on, and the little bespectacled crew-cut boy, Enrico, sits silently transfixed in front of it. Noises of pans crashing onto surfaces, and the chopping of food is coming out from the kitchen. The world has come to life, and the few hours of serenity this morning have somewhat disappeared.

I don't mind. But it's the graveling, sinister, continuous energy generator out in the distance which symbolizes for me the noise and distractions that a city brings, and which can so easily and quickly overtake, deafen, and monopolise the serenity and natural sounds of everything else.

Maria walks out smiling with a menu card and hands it to me, "Buenos días. A beautiful day. We're going to cook you a good breakfast. What would you like?"

Without hesitating, I quickly point to one item, and she nods wandering back to the kitchen. The heightening sun is now streaming down onto my laminate wood-covered table and the turquoise-painted cement floor. The water is rapidly rising over the mangroves and sandy bottom from the tidal sea coming back in again. Then with the mug of coffee, I sprinkle in some Coffee Mate and take a sip from the bottle of pomegranate juice I'd brought with me. Looking out, while eating my delicious huevos rancheros, even more ripples are being created from the jumping fish, and the water's surface sparkles and glitters from the strong morning light.

I stretch my arms up over my head, feeling the need for some exercise and to take a walk out over to the beach and estuary shoreline. Maria returns and smiles at the empty plate.

I appreciatively smile back. "When will Jesús be here? He'd mentioned we could maybe go out with the fishermen today."

"Yes, he'll be here shortly, probably by the time you've had your walk. I know he'd spoken to them, and with the tide, they were going to come and collect you around lunchtime."

My smile broadens even further. "Really? That's great. I'll come back in a bit and might even try to get that kayak out for a paddle!"

"That's a good idea. Just be careful with the current."

I head back towards my cabaña and sadly notice some beach litter stuck in the water's vegetation. The horrible plastic cola and beer can holders, with their deadly holes that birds can so easily get strangled in. I pick up all I can see and throw them hatefully into a big bin. How can people do that, and particularly in a place like this? The swimming costume is put on, and I walk the short distance down the pebbly waterside, dragging the heavy double-seated kayak into the shallows. The paddle only has one blade, which means I'll need to row for two people and swap it over every so often to even go straight. Not very practical.

I stoically paddle out, alternating the blade from one side to the other, but surprisingly there's quite a strong current flowing and ripping against me. It's a bit too much like hard work to get anywhere, and after a while, I jettison that idea. My feet step out onto the shallow, pebbly, muddy floor, and I pull the heavy boat safely back onto the stony shore and proceed to wander back over the empty sandy expanse to the estuary beach, where I'd seen the playing dolphins.

The soft, dry sand feels good running through my toes, and I wantonly kick it up into the air, where it flies away into the warm breeze. On the edge of the estuary, I pass the ghostly wrecked and stranded fishing boat where the beach dramatically opens up and widens. The golden brown leaves are scattered like confetti on the sand, but I also notice other objects with them of the same colour. I kneel down. Multitudes of empty red, orange, and golden lobster carcasses and skulls have been washed up. White clam and giant, black mussel shells are also scattered everywhere. In fact, there are so many clam shells leading from the sea that it looks like they're marching up the beach.

Approaching the high dunes, I walk around them and am confronted with an amazing spectacle. Up on the beach, against the dunes and almost as high, are literally stacks and stacks, and layers and layers, of massive clam shells layered in between the sand and stretching along the beach for a couple of hundred metres. There must be millions of these large, thick white shells, averaging five inches in width, most bigger than my hand, and some of the shell hills are more than my height! The ocean must have swept them in, and with few if no people ever coming here, they've just collected and amassed over time; something I have never before seen. I pick one up and stroke my fingers over it. The sea has worn it so much that all its ridges have worn away, leaving it smooth and silky in texture.

And flung out across the beach are massive mother of pearl "upside-down ice-cream cone" shells. Some look like they've been there for so long that they've weathered away into miniature cracked versions. The wind is continuing to sweep across the long, flat beach, making beautiful drift patterns and lines. The beach is so flat and wide that I'm unsure where it merges into the sea. I once again kneel down onto this virgin beach and with my finger write one very large word across it— LIFE.

Standing back up, I notice a beautiful long and smooth oval, grey-brown pebble with water weathered holes on its surface. If I was to take one thing back with me to remember this place, it would be this stone. I bend back down again and go to pick it up. Amazingly, the "stone" splits, breaks, and crumbles in my hand. It's only sand! Maybe it's telling me how delicate and fragile this place is and how we can't take it with us. I carefully place the crumbled "pebble" back down and walk away, up and over the dunes.

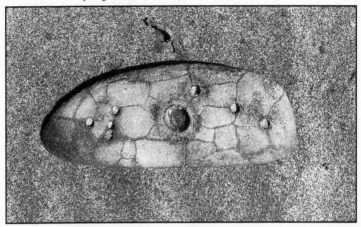

Walking down, I see the same phenomena—a massive hill of sun-bleached crabs. With the hot sun their shells have turned orange, as though they've been cooked.

The fishing lodge comes back into view, and I notice Jesús's van is now parked up outside. The smell of fish being cooked wafts out from the kitchen as I wander round to the terrace. Jesús is seated at a table with a mug of coffee. He stands up when he sees me and, with a smile, indicates the seat next to him. I join him.

"So, how are you? It's very exciting. The boys from the Co-op are going to bring the boat over in an hour or so and take you out to see their oyster farm!"

I smile. "That's fantastic. I hope it hasn't put them out too much. But you must come too! It would be fun, and you can help translate if I don't understand."

He looks down at his trousers, smart ironed shirt, and polished black shoes, probably thinking they'd only get smelly and dirty in the fishing boat, but gladly nods his agreement. He automatically pours me a mug of coffee without me asking.

"So Jesús. Please, do tell me more about this place before we go out with the fishermen. I'm all ears!"

After taking a gulp from his mug he says, "Well first, please call me Chuy. That's what everyone calls me."

He sits back and looks up into the cloudless sky like he's thinking how to best tell the story. "Well, it's like this. I'll try and tell you all about René. But first come into the bar and look at some pictures."

We walk into the dark unlit bar, whose walls need a bit of a tender loving care paint job, and behind the counter are two dusty framed photographs. They don't look like they've seen the light of day or been moved for a long time. One is of an old, white haired man with an open shirt and a healthy looking belly flopping over the top of his trousers and crazily steering a motor boat through a choppy sea. The other is him standing near an old palm-roofed hut holding a giant lobster while a few people look on. He resembles some sort of adventurous Hemingway.

"That's René back in the '70s. Let's go back outside."

Both contentedly seated and looking out to the quiet waters with the elegantly long legged white egret heron birds flying over, he continues with the story: "René came from the mainland and fell in love with this part of Baja. He met a local woman, and they married. He first visited this place in the 1950s and already had a vision. So he bought some land here and built a simple weekend retreat, just for his family. But even then, in this wild place, he saw the potential for fishing. The locals got to hear about him and would come and visit. They liked the place so much that at weekends they would bring their own food, and it was all shared by everybody around large tables.

"It all started with humble beginnings—just a simple straw hut. But people started to talk about the place and wanted to stay. I remember when I was just a small child, I would also come here with my family to eat with everyone. It was wonderful. We would prepare and cook the fish, octopus, clams, and make the ceviche, all with local recipes. And it would all be shared. Very quickly, René saw this as a possible business and opened a shop here selling just soft drinks and beer. Then he built two or three small cabañas. But it was very different then. He worked hard and cleared the stones here and cleaned up the swamps to make it more accessible for people. Yes, I suppose he really was a businessman. He also had another shop in town selling beer and co-operated with our fishermen."

He stops, and I can see he's trying to remember everything, "Yes, that's right. He built it all himself with only a little help. It was a simple place here for thirty years. But then he died in the '80s, and his wife was left it, with no children to help. Very quickly, her brother, who worked at the salt company in Guerrero Negro, said he'd help turn it into a proper business, obtain the permission for planes to land, and get all that kind of stuff to start a proper bar and restaurant. So the brother hired Ricardo here to run it. It was hard work. For seven years Ricardo did everything on his own. He cooked, he served the food, he did the cleaning—everything!

"René's wife was living near Negro and slowly, as she and her brother-in-law were both not really in the tourist business, believed it to be a bad investment. She tried to sell this place to anyone with money to buy it. It was difficult. But in 2010 our co-operative heard about it. They were already concerned about finding ways of protecting the rich biodiversity of this area. They already had the oyster farm here, over on the other side of the lagoon. So finally, they bought it. They are solid and strong and have been operating for seventy years."

I ask inquisitively, "What is the co-operative exactly?"

"The Punta Abreojos Co-op is a union of about a hundred local people and fishermen, who all jointly own it. It's a local consortium. They own the oyster farm. But the main money makers are the lobsters, which are fished and processed between October and March. The lobster season is four or five months, and when caught, they're mainly exported to America and Japan. We have a hi-tech plant in Abreojos, which employs the local people from the town. Then after the lobster, the abalone divers arrive, and that season starts from March and runs to July. They dive and strictly only take by the correct size."

I'm fascinated knowing I'm soon going to be out on the boat and let him continue.

"And our fishermen help to stop the terrible poachers. This is a problem. We have to stop the black market, with them taking the sea turtles, lobster, and abalone, to conserve the fishing resources that our people depend on for their livelihoods. You may be lucky and see some turtles later. Our co-op has been successful in being a model for fisheries conservation. We have exclusive control of this place through a government concession, which means we can ban outsiders from fishing here. We want to look after this place for a long time, and at the moment, that's possible!"

Lowering my hat to further shade my eyes I ask, "That's such good news, but walking the beach earlier I saw lots of dead lobsters and crabs washed up. What's all that about?"

"Well, that's probably a different story all together and also something else to worry about. Many scientists are pointing their finger to El Niño as a culprit of these freak events and considering this year was such a strong one. Although it peaked some months ago, its effects are still being felt. One of them is the El Niño effect, which alters ocean temperatures, warming the sea surface and currents here in the eastern Pacific. It's forcing lobsters to higher latitudes, due to the water being too warm here. They say beaches further up in California are seeing lobster and masses of small crustaceans like crabs, crayfish, and shrimp washing up on their shores. These are usually found here off these coasts, but with the current, warmer water temperatures, they've drifted further up the west coast of America!"

Smelling wafts of food seeping from the kitchen, I ask what time it is, and Chuy smiles. "Yes, it's that time, and we may also have another surprise for you today. Let's see if it's ready, and then the fishermen will be here."

He trots off, and before long, he's come back with a beer and a massive plateful of oysters simply accompanied by limes chopped in half.

"These are for you. They're fresh from this morning—enjoy!"

I have to admit, I don't normally like oysters, but this occasion was too good to miss, and thank goodness! Under the rays of sun reflecting off the water's surface next to me, and picking them up with my fingers and letting them slide from their shells into my mouth, they were sweet and delicious, tasting totally of where they'd come from. René would have been happy.

As I ate the oysters with their strong taste of the sea and their faint metallic taste that the cold white wine washed away, leaving only the sea taste and the succulent texture, and as I drank their cold liquid from each shell and washed it down with the crisp

*taste of the wine, I lost the empty feeling and began to
be happy to make plans*
Ernest Hemingway, A Moveable Feast

While then tucking into prawn tortillas in their soft, crispy batter, I notice a small, shabby-looking motorboat slowly approach. The engine turns off, and a hooded sweatshirted guy with long shorts jumps out of it and wades up the stony beach. Another taller guy, just as scruffily dressed with cut-off jeans and a ripped sleeveless T-shirt, casually follows him from the boat. I'm hearing deep, rough American voices.

"Hey, dude. Watta we gonna get? Howz about tacos de camarones? And lets stock up on beers!" He crazily laughs and walks up to the kitchen to place the order.

The taller "dude" notices me, maybe reckoning it's his day, and casually wanders over. Without asking, he plonks himself on the seat opposite, obviously curious in seeing a single female alone in a remote and isolated place like this in the off-season. My hackles rise slightly, and I don't have a good feeling.

"Hey, ma'am. You travelling here on your own? We've got a real good boat. This place is great to explore. You'd never believe it, but they're shooting a film around the cove at the back. You wanna take a ride with us?"

I'm sure if a film was being shot around this area, Jesús would have said something. Before answering, the other, rougher-looking hobo joins us, drinking out of a beer bottle. I don't like what I see, and I don't totally believe what he's just said. He probably thinks I'm some kind of naïve female tourist, gullible to everything. Thank goodness, I have a valid excuse.

"Thanks for asking but . . . "

With what sounds like a drink or drug induced slurred voice, the beer guzzling individual interrupts. "Oh my, she's got an English accent. How cute is that!"

My sixth sense is kicking in. I don't feel at ease with them and, quickly continue emphasizing I'm not on my own, "Thanks for the offer, but we're all getting out on our boat with the fishermen pretty shortly . . . and I'm waiting for my friends."

"Huh, well, if that's what you want!" With that, they take more slurps of their beers and stumble back to their boat and chug out into the estuary. I hope I never see them again.

I hate exaggerating or telling little white lies, but sometimes it's a question of getting out of awkward situations as painlessly as possible. I didn't like what I saw in their actions and mannerisms, and I was already hoping that they weren't thinking about returning later on tonight, when I really would be on my own!

A short while later, smiling Chuy comes back to join me. All he's done to prepare himself for the boat ride out is to roll his sleeves down to probably protect himself from the sun and put on a pair of trendy sunglasses. He's still got his shiny shoes on.

It's then I hear the rumbling of a heavy-duty engine, and a blue and white boat appears, coming towards us from the beach where the co-op's fishing huts on the other side of the shoreline are located. Two burly, but friendly-looking men, one in orange and yellow heavy-duty, rubber waterproof fishing overalls and "long to the elbow" rubber gloves, and the other with shorts and baseball cap and the same navy blue long rubber gloves, painlessly jump out of the boat smiling and push the big boat close to the shallows.

One lifts out a metal mesh-looking sack and drops it onto the sand next to the boat to use as a step for us to get back in. I look closer and see it has oysters in it. They both smile and jovially put their thumbs up and say in unison, "¡Hola y bienvenidos!"

Chuy also smiles and introduces me to them, "This is Jesús Villa Vicencio and Luís Zuniga. But I call them the "Oyster Farm Boys"! It's more fun!" All of a sudden, he points excitedly down, wanting to grab my attention to several crabs running along the muddy shore from out of their holes. "Oh, quick! Look! Look! Look!"

He then delicately negotiates by putting one foot on the oyster sack and carefully steps over into the deep-hulled boat with some water swishing around in the bottom. He sits on one of the narrow benches, putting his feet up on it to avoid getting his feet wet. I do the same. Jesús gets in at the helm by the engine, and Luís pushes the boat back out. Almost immediately, we've picked up speed and are motoring across the salty waters to the oyster farm.

The metal-netted sacks are floating in long, long lines tied down, and each section of the sea has sacks with different sizes and ages of oyster in them. The boat stops, and Luís leans over the boat and pulls out a sack, unwinds the metal ties at the top, and puts his rubber gloved hand down into it, delicately taking out a handful of tiny little oysters, not more than half an inch each long, which he shows me on the outstretched palm of his hand.

We make another four stops, and each time he does the same to show us the growth stages of the oysters. Each time the heavy bags hold even bigger oysters until the last stop is, without exaggeration, holding enormous, at least six-inch, prize specimens!

Chuy points at them. "This is a big process for our co-op. The oyster grains are cultivated in La Paz, and then you've just seen them at nursery, then in the kindergarten, the university, and then they're ready to go off out to the world! We cultivate three million oysters a year in this lagoon!"

Luis throws the last sack back into the water, looks behind his shoulder, and shouts out something. All of a sudden, Chuy dramatically points, out a little way from the boat, laughing out loud and quickly shouting, "Look, look! It's dolphins with their young swimming up by us. They swim in through the lagoon entrance and come here for the warmer water and to play."

I lean over, stretching my fingers to almost teasingly touch the water's surface and the oh so close dolphins. Then almost immediately, our farm boys stop the engine and also quietly look down over the boat. Leaning further over and down through the blue clear water, I see two enormous sea turtles slowly and calmly swimming together with their flippers moving in perfect unison, like some form of strange water ballet. Nature's theatrical performers continue to entertain us when sea eagles swoop and dive for the small fish that the bigger ones have chased up to the surface.

I spontaneously stumble up to the bow of the boat and crazily sit on the tip of the boat with my legs swung over it, and as the boat moves and jumps forward, so the waves crash over them. I'm on such a high from everything I've seen that I feel I've smoked a joint, like I'd once done with fishermen in Jamaica who'd left me to maniacally steer their boat, which ended going in just crazy circles and them holding on for dear life! The boat passes white shell beaches within the massive lagoon that had been out of sight from René's. I'd be surprised if anyone had even stepped foot on them.

It sounds stupid, but this spontaneous unique experience with the generosity of these good people makes me feel very emotional, and I have to hold back the tears. The time disappears, and we've all of a sudden arrived back. The boat slides to a stop on the muddy bottom, but the tide has already started to rise. Without thinking, I simply jump out of the boat and barefooted walk up the wet, sandy shore. I turn around and can't help but giggle out loud, as Chuy has asked for a piggy back. He's gripping tight around Jesús, with his arms firmly around his neck, or otherwise his black shoes would get wet. He's carefully dropped back on dry solid ground.

We thank and wave the boys goodbye as they motor off, back across the lagoon. What kind hospitality. These are not tour guides, but workers, and it was something they hadn't done before. I do hope this place, like so many people before me have said, stays the way it is.

Later that afternoon, along the quiet beach, I see wind twisters out in the desert beyond the lagoon. This really has to be one of the best days ever. Walking back, I notice a solitary camper van parked up at the end of the old row of cabañas by the entrance. Walking to the kitchen to ask for a drink, I notice a guy is collecting some food. He's a German trucker, who works for a year and then in the alternate years travels with his camper van through Baja, which he leaves with friends in the US when he's back working in Germany. Without hesitation, he says this is a place which always surprises him with its beauty.

With beer in hand, I sit out on the terrace and, once again on my own, think back about those two crazy gringos. Chuy walks up and sits down.

"Oh, I'm glad I've seen you. I'm afraid those two guys that moored up earlier may turn up later when you've all gone!"

"Don't worry, Zoë. Ricardo and his wife check the place and are just at the end of the road by the entrance, sleeping in their caravan."

I sigh, feeling somehow it'll be alright, but these sort of thoughts from time to time pop up when you've been travelling on your own for a while. "Thank you so much for an incredible time. I'll never forget it, and I hope the co-op will continue to look after this place and be successful."

With that, the wind once again starts to blow a cold, strong breeze across the marshlands. Even the few flies from the heat of the afternoon have disappeared due to the temperature drop.

"That reminds me. Is there any chance for an extra set or two of blankets? It was freezing here last night."

"Sure. We'll bring some over. Ricardo probably has some spare ones in his caravan. Let me know how the rest of your trip goes. I'm also hoping I'll be here for a long time."

With that, we give each other a hug and say our heartfelt good-byes.

That evening after Ricardo's delicious plate of seafood and a few beers, I feel saddened I'll be leaving this very special place so early tomorrow morning. But I have an incredibly long journey, through some new, unchartered, difficult terrain and roads which will hopefully lead me back across the peninsula to the Sea of Cortez and San Felipe. The generator stops, the lights go out, and everything becomes silent again. With torch in hand, I wander back to my little hut.

With a lot more blankets on the bed, and both doors firmly shut and locked, it's making the place feel warm and cosy. With the cold, gusty, wind howling outside and just a torch lighting up the dark wood-panelled room, it feels more like a mountain cabin retreat than one by the beach in the tropics.

18

ON THE ROADS
LESS TRAVELLED

*Life should be not be a journey to the grave with
the intention of arriving safely in a pretty and well
preserved body, but rather to skid in broadside in a
cloud of smoke, thoroughly used up, totally worn out,
and loudly proclaiming "Wow! What a ride!"*
Hunter S. Thompson

That occasional feeling of vulnerability in the middle of
the night being a lone traveller is still the same, whatever
transport you use. You're on your own, and the senses are
amplified on what's around you.

Jotting some diary notes in the dark with just a torch,
I was worried the crazy lone wolf gringo was somehow
prowling "out there," even though I'd been reassured Ricardo
would keep an eye out from his caravan. I was also worried

about petrol. When and where should I get some? Should I make a twenty-mile detour back to Punta Abreojos, just to pacify my worries, or simply just leave and travel the eighty plus miles back up onto Highway 1, hoping the gas station at the intersection will be open? Annoyingly, my stomach is also very queasy, which means that me and the toilet seat were up for most of the night! I was feeling very weak and was just hoping I'd be alright to travel.

After tossing and turning for a few more hours, I sense it's time. It's still dark. Jesus, my stomach and the pain! I'll just have to eat very simply until it goes away. But today, of all days! It's energy and concentration I now need for a difficult journey that will cover more than 400 miles.

I walk out into the early, starry-skied morning, load the car, and with the headlights on full beam set off from this beautiful, secret place. I've actually got plenty of petrol, so I'll take the risk and fill up when I get onto Highway 1. Out in the darkness, the empty straight road disappearing into the barren land's horizon looks even more like passing through a lunar landscape. The full moon overhead is strongly radiating its white light onto the asphalt but quickly drops and disappears into the horizon to show the sun's first rays of light.

And like magic, before the fiery planet has even appeared, the ever growing horizon's light is changing colour from dark midnight blues, to purple and amethyst, to layers of oranges and bright yellows highlighting the outlines of the tall, marching cacti and the black, jagged mountain ridges far, far away. Once again, this is one of the most beautiful jaw-dropping sights I've ever seen that words just cannot explain. But I can now better understand the Eagles lyrics: "It's just another tequila sunrise . . . " Besides a couple of "get up at dawn" camper vans trundling towards me in the opposite direction, the beauty of this wild road is totally unspoilt.

It is truly an untamed, eternal landscape that puts the duration of my life into perspective. But it's maybe also being in these wild places that allows the traveller to thankfully sometimes act or think in wacky or unorthodox ways and to come out of our comfort zone. How many times have I approached total strangers and so many times been amazed or surprised by the outcome? How many times have I decided to take a risk and opt for an alternative route and been so happy I'd decided to take the unknown or more difficult one?

With the sun risen up over the mountains, the beautiful road has now been totally driven, and I approach the T-junction to turn left back up onto Highway 1. Before long, I'm passing the 28th Parallel and El Aguila (Eagle), the 150 foot, steel sculpture monument that marks the boundary between the states of Baja California and Baja California Sur. My watch also goes back an hour. Well past the salt flats, on this quiet and isolated road, a red and green Pemex sign tells me it's time for the obligatory fill up. I'm so glad to see it's open so early. Not immediately seeing anyone, I get out, and a cute, wrinkly-faced, Labrador puppy mongrel waggingly ambles over and flops down, imploring his belly be scratched. His chocolate liquid eyes curiously watch me until I've patted him for one last time before leaving.

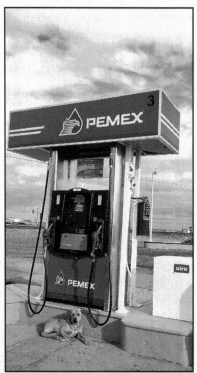

The Transpeninsular continues directly north across this straight, barren desert landscape. The only respite from the flat, sandy views are the unique cirio cactus that I'd first seen when riding the horses with Raúl on his ranch south of Tecate. They're tall and slender and twist in every possible shape and direction, growing to over fifty feet high. They're endemic to Baja and the State of Sonora and seem to look like a thin, upside-down carrot. After rain they come to life, with a trunk that sprouts leaves, wavy tentacles, and yellow-cream flowers at the very top. And I'd been lucky enough to see them in full bloom up in the mountains at the ranch.

Not more than twenty miles further on in this remote place, I see an ominous sign. Orange road cones are barricading the road, and military trucks are parked on the side. A couple of desert-camouflaged and bullet-proof vested soldiers approach me, both carrying automatic rifles slung over their shoulders. This looks like a fairly serious military checkpoint. They unexpectedly ask me to get out and stand on the side of the road with my suitcase and bags. My palpitations uncontrollably come to the surface, and once again the past comes back to haunt me . . .

I'm in the back of a car with my Lao boyfriend, Jean, driving from Chiang Mai to Bangkok with our Thai friend and driver, Prawat. We can't be both more than twenty years old and still very naïve. Somewhere along a road, in a remote part of the northern Thai countryside, armed police appear from nowhere and flag the car down.

Without any smiles, we're ordered to get out of the car. There's no doubt they're looking for drugs, and mercifully, my two Thai-speaking friends try and reassure the police that we're just tourists visiting. But to no avail. They throw the bags out and literally empty everything onto the road. Then incredibly, with an iron bar they wedge into and force open the inner front passenger's door to see if drugs have been hidden in the cavity. We'd already been warned by Prawat that drugs could so easily be "dropped" into or under unsuspecting travellers' cars, and he had meticulously checked before we'd left.

It was looking serious that they would continue destroying the car. But for some unknown reason, Prawat and the police start talking like they're negotiating on something. He walks back to the car and, from under his seat, pulls out an unopened box of 200 cigarettes and hands them over. The police immediately stop searching and simply wave us on. Thank God, we'd been with someone who'd known how to bribe the police from further searches and stress.

But here in Mexico, I think offering "gifts" would be the last thing to do. This young, serious-looking soldier has started a massive search of my bags and inside the car, from opening the glove compartment to rummaging under the seats. It's been made clear to me by other people that their purpose is to capture the bad guys involved in drug trafficking and other illegal activities but will, from time to time, search tourists. And particularly, I guess, those with American registration plates, as the possession of guns and ammunition is totally illegal in Baja, and there are no excuses. I smile in a pleasant way, which I think helps things.

Thankfully, all is good, and very soon I've left them behind. With still a weak stomach, I grab and bite into a Mars bar to also calm my nerves. The drive continues unrelentingly through the arid land, and my only friends out on the road with me, that I see from time to time, are the massive white "Los Pinos"

trucks carrying their tons of tomatoes and vegetables up and down the peninsula.

It's surely not far now, here in Baja's Central Desert region, that I'll be leaving the highway to take the small unknown route that will head eastward and up along the unfamiliar stretch of coastline along the Sea of Cortez. I've already seen on the map that part of this 150 mile route looks almost like a one lane track up to San Felipe. But surely, if it's on a map it should be navigable! People have warned me that it's under construction. The only landmark I'd been told to look out for was an old garage out on its own called "Chapala." The road should be opposite. Am I doing the right thing, instead of taking the main Highway 1 all the way back up to the border? At this stage, I don't really know, but it's going to be interesting.

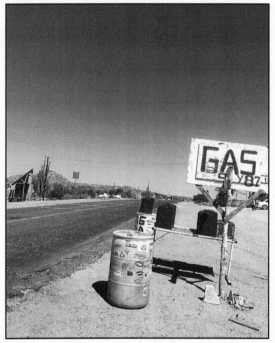

But when I finally get to La Chapala and the turning up onto the unknown, unbuilt road, I drive past it, as once again, I need to fill up. So I continue on for at least thirty miles until on the side of the road at Catavina I thankfully see a table with four red metal cans on it and a painted "GAS" sign propped up against it.

A lady in jeans and blue sweatshirt approaches me and, seeing my US registration, simply points to one of the cans with a quizzical look. I nod. She lifts the jerry can off the table and inserts a plastic hose into it and somehow forces the other end into the truck's tank. She lifts the heavy can over her head and pours the liquid in.

"So, Señora, where are you going today? To Ensenada and Tijuana?"

I smile, as I'll be turning round and heading in the opposite direction. "No. I'm going back to Chapala and then up along the unbuilt section of Highway 5 and along the coast to San Felipe."

She does a double take, which isn't the first time I've seen someone look at me with that same shocked expression. "Really? You do know that the majority of that road, at least up to Puertecitos Hot Springs, is wild and under construction! It'll become the rest of Highway 5 but is now just a rough sandy track and must be like that for at least fifty miles. It's a major, national government project to open up that area of coast road from San Felipe. It's one of the last remaining areas in the peninsula that hasn't got links onto the Transpeninsular Highway. Every day, we ask the drivers passing by how much is left to be done until it's finished. Be careful through the desert and up into the hills. It's dangerous with all those trucks, muddy roads, and steep ravines and cliff sides. The roads are rocky, and no one is there to help, except for maybe some of the workers who camp up in the hills." She takes the hose out and adds, "That'll be 240 pesos."

Oh lovely! That sounds great! I look again at the map. I'm having serious second thoughts on whether the route is actually that safe and even navigable in what I'm driving. But ideally, I don't want to repeat the route I'd already taken three weeks ago coming down. Surely if the worst comes to the worst and I can't get through, I'll just turn back and abandon getting to San Felipe.

Blindly rummaging through my bag for peso notes, the second, tatty old envelope, which I'd brought from London, strangely falls out. I'd totally forgotten about it but had brought it knowing it was another courageous story of venturing into the unknown. It was written by Steve, my godfather and best friend to my father. Both had travelled and been to places at momentous times in history. Steve was a Jewish Hungarian who'd escaped the Nazis and fled across Europe, finally arriving in Britain. Both had been in the RAF, Steve in Intelligence and Dad as an aircraft engineer. I want to read it here and now. I walk over to the shade of a small tree and sit on the sandy floor with my back leaning against the trunk.

I carefully unfold the sheets of old, manually-typed paper and from in between them slips out a handwritten letter that I'd never seen before. I start reading.

Hi Alan—Birthdays! It used to be a time to look to the future now it's a time to remember. I was rummaging through an old suitcase full of papers going back to the war and came across an old diary that I thought might interest you since you must have had similar experiences when dressed in blue. My pals have no doubt followed their own destinies in various corners of the world and the girlfriend referred to is now no doubt a fat grandmother in the north of London but somehow the taste and smell of these days is still there. It had been a long and arduous task getting into the RAF for I was a foreign national but I managed to join up eventually to start my career as Stefan Gyalai. After half a century it gave me a strange feeling to reread lines that I had written and to think how young how very young we were . . .

Extracts from Continental Diary, July 17th 1944. We left Uxbridge at 6 a.m. and as the old lorries rumbled out through the gates all the nurses were there to greet us and wish us well. They're sweet things, almost without exception, and will no doubt be lonely without us.

Was tired after guard and slept on my kitbag during the first half of the journey. Arrived at Old Sarum— what a name! We're in a vast concentration area here that is most effectively sealed off from the outside world—no letters, no telephone, I doubt if we'll even get papers here. Tents neatly lined up in long parallel rows and thousands of new faces. We've been issued with 200 paper francs each and they look just like the old francs one knew. Funny to think I'll be in France in 48 hours or so. I have not seen France since April 1939. The horrors of war then were but the distorted visions of a few incorrigible pessimists, people thought and spoke of war but neither knew nor believed in its reality. I was eighteen, very young. We stood on the threshold of events we knew would be frightening in proportions, overwhelming, unprecedented. We knew and we did not care to know.

July 18th. There are some Poles in the next tent and I went over to talk to them. They are a strange mixture and difficult to consider collectively; some have been in Russian captivity or Siberia even and these are naturally no pro-Russian enthusiasts and many have outspoken Fascist leanings, yet quite a few surprised me by their strong democratic opinions. All of them seem to agree that there is no going back to the notoriously corrupt structure built by the Becks, Smiglys and their like.

July 19th. On the move heading for Portsmouth but the destination was kept secret. Got our landing rations, biscuits, two bars of chocolate, 20 cigarettes plus a thoroughly worn life-belt. I hear we'll be on the upper deck—what no invasion barges? I don't think we can expect serious interference from Jerry planes, U-boats and mines are our only enemies. But I suppose it will be quite a convoy.

July 20th. Still here and nothing to do but wait and play cards. In our spare moments we watch various outfits parade fully loaded with their cumbersome webbing and kit, sweating like horses and on their faces a devilish grin. Let's go. This isn't England any more this wretched sun baked camp on the south coast. No, England is the very antithesis of this barbed wire desert—the open, green fields, the plush seat of the Underground, the music of Geraldo, the buzzing lobby of the Queensbury Club. England is independence, freedom, the lights of the Paramount and the Sunday

crowds in Hyde Park. This is no man's land. Let's go,
for Christ's sake.

July 21st. We get dragged out of bed at 3 a.m. and after
a parade in pitch-dark we're moved about two miles to
our lorries. It was pouring as we headed slowly towards
our mysterious embarkation port. It turned out to be
Gosport. On the way we heard about the attempt on
Hitler's life—looks like things really are brewing in
Germany now. The first glimpse we had of the sea was
thrilling. I remember having felt the same mixture of
awe and amazement each time I saw its vastness, its
endlessness whether in San Remo, Nice or Blackpool.

Perhaps it is simply that only in meeting the infinite
are we conscious of our own insignificance and cannot
but bow to things the dimensions and beauty of which
are manifestly on a higher than human plane. The
ships around us—all lying still like ourselves are
a magnificent sight: ships, nothing but ships, big
and small, some fairly new and flying strange flags,
some of them obviously bearing the scars of previous
engagements and exhaling thick columns of smoke.
Our own LST must seem nothing more than an
insignificant particle of this sea armada.

July 22nd. At about 4—we have been sailing for
twelve solid hours—we saw land. Steep cliffs, sandy
beaches and soon American ducks passing up and
down the beach in an apparently unceasing flow.
France! We are in Normandy! Somehow it didn't feel
real—this was more like a business or pleasure trip
than a fighting expedition. Soon we left the ship and
were driving up the narrow muddy road, and soon
we clearly saw the church of St. Combes visible in the
distance. This is a couple of miles further inland from
Arromanches where we landed. Now that we are in

Normandy and saw not one Jerry plane on the way we have little doubt that they were wasting their time. Nothing is going to stop us now: we've simply got the stuff and they haven't.

Little Marcel, aged thirteen, working on this field was the first French civilian I talked to. A bright little fellow with big blue eyes and a sadly undernourished body. He told us his father and mother worked on a farm, too; he himself worked 12 hours a day for his keep. What struck me most was not the remarkable measure of Vichy social justice—one hardly expected anything else—but the painful sight of this boy not having enough to eat in a rich food producing district like Normandy. There must be millions of kids like Marcel all over Europe and the thought of it hurts: somehow seeing misery is different from hearing about it. The boys who crowded around while I was talking to Marcel insisted on the translation of his every word and soon Marcel was carrying home more chocolate than he had seen in his life time. I hardly care about tents tonight I am so tired I could sleep under a lorry.

July 23rd. Went to see the people on the neighbouring farm. The farmer and family were reserved but not unfriendly, we were offered to taste their cider and pretty terrible stuff it is. We duly declared it was ce qu'il y a de plus excellent!

Bayeux seems hardly touched by the war though its roads see thousands of lorries and jeeps roll by daily and its pavements were crowded by allied soldiers to a point defying description. Even special RAF Police have made their unwelcome appearance to add to the variety of uniforms: commandos and marines, airmen, soldiers, Free French and Canadians compete for Bayeux's attention and living space. No, nobody is especially interested in the latest batch of newcomers in blue battle dresses: we are certainly no novelty here.

Another Sunday away from Hyde Park and all the other cherished things that come to mind. There are many things Bayeux can't make up for. Yet I am quite happy in France. I think I'll enjoy it more and more as we advance.

July 24th. The kids are the most interesting things to see in Normandy. In spite of their undernourished condition they are cheerful and friendly: there is none of that self-consciousness and timidity one finds in English kids, as a rule. The story one of them told me was so pathetic that I was determined to set it down (I have now had it confirmed beyond doubt). Louis told me his mother got sentenced to three months' hard labour for calling a German "Boche." She denied the charge and had no trial. She works on a farm with her husband: there are six children in the family. Fascism unadulterated. I am only beginning to realize how severely the local French population was hit by our bombardment. At least half the population in Bayeux is made-up of refugees who have lost all, or nearly all, their possessions, sometimes they mourn the death of their family. In trying to justify these bombardments I usually refer to "military necessity" but I would be hard put to determine just where the line is to be drawn. But most of these people are wonderfully reasonable: "D'abord il faut chasser le Boche." I hope they mean it.

July 25th. We had been with two other units but today we moved to another field. We are on our own from now on. The idea, I imagine, to make it harder for Jerry to spot us. We never worried on this score as our camouflage is as near perfect as it can get. Last night we were awakened by the sound of a tremendous barrage reminiscent of the London blitz. If we did not realize how near the front line we were, we certainly are beginning to know it now. If we know something about Monty, a powerful new offensive can't be far distant.

July 28th. Met the first French girl today. She's the type I remember—dark, vivacious and warm. She works in a jewellers shop in town and fixed my watch bracelet in a mere forty minutes. She would not accept any money and looking at Gorgeous' pictures in my wallet thought she was "tres jolie." We're due to move any time so there is not likely to be a sequel.

July 29th. This morning we moved further to the front line . . . but have no idea where we are but it is rumoured we might be near St. Lo in the American sector of the front.

July 30th. Probably not far from the fighting judging by the fireworks last night. The village is ugly: its two focal points the church and the brothel, if, differing in moral purpose equal each other in hideousness.

July 31st. I'm back with the "C" watch boys—a nice bunch, yet somehow I am not pleased: I suppose if people are together too long they cease to be of interest. But to these boys lying beside me on the soft grass of Normandy I belong more fully than to any RAF outfit I have been with: Lofty the over 6 ft. tall Scotsman from the Highlands, cheerful, strong like a bull and with a perpetually friendly grin; Howard Shaw "baby face" a lively boy from Stafford with a lively sense of humour and somehow less "English" than the others, Angus Armet, another Scotsman from Edinburgh, a bit of a grumbler and notoriously selfish, yet quite a good and honest companion, Dick from a London suburb, the eternal Cockney, quick witted and skilful but too hopelessly attached to Bermondsey to be happy amongst foreigners; finally Rony Lemmon from Cambridge, intellectually on the highest level, conscientious humorous and ever reliable, mad on chewing gum, cricket and Joyce his fiancée (in that order). No I must not grumble. And who said living in tents and eating bully was not healthy anyway?

August 1st. Just heard that while we were in Cussy an airman in the next field shot himself accidentally by leaning on his loaded Sten while on guard. A tragic thing—the telegram from the War Office must have closely followed on this first card announcing he landed safely.

August 2nd. Thank God we're on American rations: from now on it's delicious coffee for breakfast and peanut butter with tea. Instead of 20 players and 20 Woodbines it's 160 Chesterfields or Camels a week—free. And are they good! In England cigarettes accounted for a lion's share of my expenses; here we accumulate paper francs and wonder what to spend them on. My expenses so far: view postcards, Normandy cream (lovely cream that reminds one of Swiss Yoghurt) and baby powder for shaving. The Red Army is still 60 miles off. I am trying hard not to think.

August 3rd. On watch tonight. It must be about a year since I last touched a Morse key.

August 4th. The news is sensational, almost too good to be true. The Yanks still advancing have almost entirely cut off the Brittany peninsula. With the ports of Brest, Lorient and St. Malo in our hands—apart from the importance of depriving the Nazis of their U-boat bases—we'll be able to ship over men and materials in unlimited numbers. The Germans sure enough built an extensive system of defence fortifications on and immediately behind the coast but they simply failed to reckon, or to deal with, so massive an onslaught. Meanwhile the Russians are hammering at the gates of E. Prussia and Warsaw. Surely there could be no plainer writing on the wall for Germany's panic-stricken war lords.

September 4th. It was hard re-joining my own unit and hard saying goodbye to the M.S.U. boys. They were a splendid lot. I shall not forget any of them. All of them friendly, open and generous. I liked them from the moment I joined them; first good impressions were confirmed when hearing I was not English and were not bothered about details of my biography at all hours. I feel it's wrong that they're staying—they all long for action while we're to move on. I wish I could have managed to hide something of the triumphant joy in me when they asked where we were heading. There must have been something cruel in hearing me say: Brussels.'

I briefly close my eyes, then carefully fold the old notes and get up to continue my own journey into the unknown. This has actually made me feel on a bit of a high for the next challenge, so I enthusiastically drive back down the highway until I get to the unmarked, dusty, untarmacked turn at the one-building-place of Chapala. I stop, get out, and wander across the road to see how rough this new route currently being constructed really is. The sandy, rubbly track goes straight out into the hilly, bumpy horizon, where dusty clouds are rising up in the distance from vehicles driving along it. Yes, for sure, it looks a bit stony and uneven, but if it's only that, then I'll be fine.

I jump back in, wind the window up to escape the imminent choking dust, and enter up onto the muddy, rutted, untamed, bumpy, unfinished, hardly two lane wide, you name it, track. I also check I've got my water bottles and snacks within easy "hand grabbing" distance. I've stocked up somehow on extra supplies for this unknown expedition and route, not really knowing what I'll encounter and not even sure I'll get there. After a rattling, back-jolting, bouncy, and lurching ride across the desert track, I catch up with the dust and slowly pass the big trucks, and soon reach the start of the mountain range, where the road is being built over and through. The route slowly climbs, and with increasingly narrower and sharper bends, its surface is also getting ever more uneven and rougher.

This new part of Route 5 is a massive project, and the terrain is becoming harder to navigate by the minute, with the inability to exceed any more than just a measly ten to fifteen mph. I hope to God my little vehicle will be alright and not slide down the edge. With the ever larger stones appearing, scattered all over the track, and no one else in sight, I really will be in extra trouble if one of the tyres decides to burst. My palpitations are uncontrollably returning to haunt me in this vast, empty expanse of nowhereness, and I'm starting to fear I may not have enough petrol to cover the last 180 miles to San Felipe further north along the coast.

True to the woman's word at the Jerry Can stop, there are, indeed, small tented settlements up here in the hills, but nothing seems to be happening, and there's no one in sight. The massive trucks and machinery are just standing silently around waiting for the next job. After every bend and twisty turn I'm hoping it'll be the last one. But of course, it's not. The road is becoming so narrow round these bends that I feel I could almost fall off. This is not fun. Then after forty unrelenting miles, crawling at the speed of a snail, the muddy treacherous road magically turns into a pristine, brand new highway. It's running parallel to the azure Sea of Cortez, which almost disappears into the sky's horizon, so similar they are in their deep blue tones. I feel proud of myself having navigated such a rough unbuilt section of Highway 5. In just a few months, this rough section will probably have disappeared and been replaced by another "easy to drive" highway. I'm glad I did it now.

I feel exhausted from the concentration I've put in to just get here, but smile when I see a little palm-covered shack on the roadside selling water and facing the island of San Luís. This seems like a perfect place to get out and stretch my legs. This part of the northern coast feels even more arid than elsewhere further south. Sparse, bushy terrain disappears somewhere down to the ocean. There is no luxuriant or healthy vegetation here or even resilient tall cactus. It's all pretty barren.

Just a few miles down this brand new road and void of any traffic except for me, I strangely encounter another military checkpoint. Once again, the soldiers signal for me to stop.

"¿Habla Español? ¿Adonde va?"

Yes, I speak a little Spanish, and I'm travelling to San Felipe. But once again, there's a massive search through my bags and throughout the truck. Memories flood back. It's certainly not as terrifying as when I was detained, questioned, and searched at the airport of the Jewish city of Tel Aviv, due to having just flown in from Istanbul, Turkey, a majority Muslim country. This made the plane leave late. But I'm feeling here that this is more of a procedure they have to do, and I just need to be patient. They shut the doors, nod, and all's good again.

Just fifty or sixty miles from my final destination, private residential "estates" with funny names like "La Playa" and beach homes sprawling along the coastline start popping up. But sadly, most look fairly decrepit and poorly looked after. I'm hot and would love a swim to cool down. But there's no chance to swim here. I do manage to drive down one little track and walk down to the water's edge. But the sea has dropped so dangerously steep, and the water is so cold that I just can't be bothered. I continue on, increasingly encountering more and more small beach settlements with RV camper vans and small homes dotted along the coast, which is a popular location for retirees from north of the border.

The road is now so totally different. It's brand new and velvety smooth and a joy to drive along. But before entering San Felipe, there is one last hidden place I want to try and find. I'd heard about this place—The Valley of Giants. Just four miles out of town is a part of the desert scattered with giant, ancient cardon cacti that has some of the most ancient on the peninsula. Apparently, some are more than 1,500 years old and fifteen metres tall. It's now a private reserve, and I'd need to park and pay to get in. That's not an issue if it's to see something interesting and unique. I can do that. But easier said than done.

A small roadside sign appears, and I steer off onto a little dusty track, stopping at a gated entrance. There's no one here. I call out "¡Hola!" and only after a long few minutes, a roughly shaved guy saunters up, looking like he's just slept for a day. He silently looks through the grilled gate.

In my best Spanish, I smilingly say, "Good afternoon. I'd like to visit. Can I come in?"

He curtly replies like he doesn't really care, "That's 170 pesos or ten dollars."

I look into my purse. I only have 140 pesos in change or a 500 peso note. I show him what I've got. He looks at both options and shakes his head.

"No, no Señora, that's not possible. That's not enough, and I don't have change for the note. I can't let you in."

I stand back in shock. I can't believe what I'm hearing, that this cactus guy isn't letting me in for the sake of thirty pesos.

"I'm sorry, but I've travelled 600 kilometres today to visit this place. Surely you could make an exception?"

He adamantly refuses, point blank, and I almost detect a small snigger. I'm angered by his actions. I bet ninety-nine per cent he's not the owner. If he was, he would have talked to me in a different way, like I've experienced everywhere else. I conclude that this guy must be on a power trip, rejecting the gringo woman's money and pleas. F . . . you! I've probably seen better elsewhere! Without giving him the pleasure of seeing my disappointment, I politely smile then turn back on my heels, driving out as quickly as possible, wanting to quickly forget this unpleasant episode. But that feeling of what I've just seen and heard somehow continues for the rest of the day.

Approaching San Felipe, my first impressions of what was once a remote, tiny, fishing village and frontier town are not good. With more RV camper vans, old weather beaten buildings, a sprinkling of tourist postcard shops, lines of taco restaurants, a few bars with people staring with a look of boredom out onto the street with beers in hand, and a few overweight people dressed in baggy shorts ambling along the streets, it looks a little dismal and rough around the edges.

But it can't be that bad. I have, after all, booked a night at the well-rated Hotel El Cortez, with a room overlooking the sea and right on the beach. I drive a little further and park up and walk into a silent reception area.

The place feels dead. A massively overweight Mexican guy behind the desk looks up from a comic magazine he's been reading. He doesn't look very friendly. With an American twang, he drawls, "It's quiet here. Off season. We're doing you a real good deal today for seventy dollars. You'll be in room Sixteen, round the corner. Make sure to leave on time tomorrow, or you'll be charged."

Why is he saying that? It's not a deal. It's what was advertised online a while back. It's expensive, from what I've paid anywhere else. I don't think so! The red-lipsticked and nail-painted girl sitting next to him nods in agreement and impatiently looks at her watch like she's finished her shift and is ready to go home.

I sigh and drive the handful of yards to a little terracotta cement box with two doors, iron-grilled windows, but gratefully on the edge of the beach. Door Sixteen is on the left, and with difficulty, I unlock it, entering a sparsely furnished room with two massive beds. The bathroom has seen better days, with the tap dripping. I have that untold feeling that I'll need to keep the door locked for the safety of my possessions. But I'm here, and there's only an hour or so of daylight left, so I'll drop everything and crash out on the beach, which is just a few steps away. But things seem to go from bad to worse.

I amble down to a small sandy slope in front of Number Sixteen, but this sand is different from anywhere else. Instead of the fine crystal white grains I've seen in so many places along the peninsula, it's coarser and looks like the grittier orange beaches found in the tourist package destinations on the Costa del Sol. That's not a problem, but the sand is strewn with old plastic plates, cigarette butts, dog do-dahs, and old rusty beer caps. I still can't quite fathom why people do this and why they can't respect these so-called places of beauty. I can do nothing else but kick the litter away and lay my towel on the beach, as there are obviously no loungers at this place.

Even the sea looks dirty from the paradises I've just come from. It's the pink-orange sand and the churning waves that are making the water look so unappealing. Close by, there's a family group of about eight people squashed under a palm covered parasol, who don't look too happy. Noisy water scooters crash over the waves, and a few guys are walking up and down the beach touting T-shirts and hats. Even the sparse number of seagulls pecking at the sand look weather-beaten, with tatty feathers, and there's no sound of any birds singing up in the trees.

I'm going to close my eyes, soak up the sun, and not let what I've just seen spoil everything I've experienced over the past month. But they do say one negative experience can obliterate a hundred positives. That I will not allow, as my positives ran into the thousands. So I settle down on my narrow towel, but unsurprisingly, my peace is soon disturbed by two Chihuahuas being led up the beach, loudly barking and growling at me. They continue until only a few feet away and within biting distance. The woman quickly sweeps them up, putting one under each arm.

After a while, the only thing of interest I can see are a cortège of about nineteen rowing boats; eights, quads, double and single skulls rowing out across the sea and towards a big grey mountain rearing its head at the end of the bay. It looks quite a challenge with the current against them, and most of the rowers look pretty novice, like at any moment they're going to be pushed and drifted onto the beach. But what is funny is the colour and design of their blades—black, yellow, and green—almost identical to my old rowing club at Walbrook, in London, where I spent so many wonderful summers rowing along the Thames.

With no surprise, the hotel bar is closed when I wander back to finally grab a drink and bite to eat. The first taco joint along the beach pulls me in, and after a good piece of fish, I wander back, curiously noticing an increasingly widening beach and disappearing sea under the starry sky.

19

BEER AND COWBOY HATS

*Walk tall, kick ass, learn to speak Arabic, love music,
and never forget that you come from a long line of
truth seekers, lovers and warriors.*

Hunter S. Thompson

A little tabby kitten is brushing up against my legs as I raise
my hand to shield my eyes from the bright early morning sun
to view in amazement that the sea has almost disappeared out
into the far distance. With a cup of coffee I sit on the hotel
terrace and see that all that remains are little shallow inlets
where the water's been trapped and a wet sandy ocean floor
bottom. The spectacle is incredible. Where has the water
gone?

It's here, in the upper reaches of the Sea of Cortez, that the
sea experiences the world's third largest tides. Water rushes up
through the gulf, rising higher as it travels north. At La Paz
it's about four and a half feet, but here there are fluctuations

303

of about twenty feet, and the water can recede to about half a mile into the distance by mid-afternoon. I'm guessing this shallow, flat beach makes the low tide even more pronounced and impressive. The Cook Inlet in Anchorage, Alaska, is the second largest tide, but it's Canada's Bay of Fundy which is number one, where the tides regularly reach forty-five feet, meaning the tidal bores fill the wide, river valleys in moments.

And talking about water, that reminds me. Before I leave San Felipe, I really must find a car wash or somewhere to clean my incredibly dirty, muddy, and dusty truck before I hand it back tomorrow in Los Angeles. I certainly don't want to incur any surcharge or penalty for its current abysmal state. I just hope the mud isn't hiding any stone scratches on the paintwork from climbing all those hills and mountains over the past month.

I look over the map one last time, reckoning it's about a 200 mile journey up through the salt flats, past Mexicali, over some mountains, and down to Tecate, where I'd decided to stay overnight. Purposely, I hadn't booked a room, thinking I'd just "wing it" when I got there, knowing it was a transitory border town where there must be a lot of cheap accommodation.

I load the truck, drop the key off to Mr. Fatty, who grunts his thanks, and drive out along the main street, which is still Highway 5 and which will take me directly north. Little taco stands are serving early morning workers, and in between them is a blue, covered awning next to a garage with hoses and buckets on a watery floor. I smile, having found it so easily. I drive in and turn the engine off, where a man wearing rubber boots immediately approaches with a sponge in his hand.

"How much?" is my first question.

Without hesitation he replies, "Eighty pesos!"

I reckon for a couple of quid that'll do nicely and leave him to get on with it, expecting no more than a quick few minutes' job. But this guy is so meticulous and careful, taking out sponges, different size brushes, hundreds of mysterious cleaning products, towels—you name it. After about fifteen to twenty minutes, with locals also coming to stop and have a chat with him, the car looks fine, but he shakes his head and starts again, now polishing the wheels. Looking at my watch after forty long minutes, and just a little exasperated it's taken so long, he backs away from his work and proudly looks at the result. A shining, glisteningly, clean set of four wheels. I gladly give him his eighty pesos, along with a little tip. He smiles and waves me goodbye.

Hardly half a mile out of town, and already hot and not yet eight o'clock, the place has once again transformed itself back into a sandy desert. The tidal sea on my right has gone out so far I can hardly see it. It looks like it's floating out on the horizon across the empty, sandy sea floor. But it's not quite as empty and desolate here. Surprisingly, almost everywhere on the sides of the road are signs for "Lots of Land For Sale."

A windowless, empty concrete "Seguridad" officers box, between road accident cross memorials, is in the middle of it all, but with no sign of any security officers chasing people away from stealing the land. Miles and miles of telegraph poles follow me along the road. It all looks and feels so desolate and barren that even a little motel I pass with a rusty broken gate is gaudily enwrapped with tatty electric cables from the pylons above, without much care or aesthetic thought.

Bizarre, frugal dwellings in the desert appear including a group of rusty camper van shells stacked together and with a grubby hand painted board kicked into the sandy ground calling itself the "Ranch." Out in the back is a pile of lorry wheels that are maybe providing some form of existence in this nowhere land.

The desert is eating everything up, including the non-existent vegetation, and soon the floating, watery mirages appear at the end of the long, long road. I need to remember this feeling of solitude, tranquility, and warmth. I lean over with one hand and try and jot down a few words in my notebook. It's not easy, and the car starts to zig-zag across the road. Just at that moment, having not looked in the rear mirror for a while, a black police car speeds up, overtakes, and disappears. God, I thought he was going to stop me, thinking I was drunk!

Not more than thirty miles further along this mesmerizingly straight road, another military checkpoint appears at El Chinero (La Trinidad), next to the salt works. The well-known, waving hand flags me down to stop, and I read a warning notice: "During the inspection: Take all valuable things with you (wallet, jewelry, cell phones, etc.)

and watch the activities of the military personnel. At the end of the inspection make sure you have nothing lost. People who refuse to be searched or insults the military authorities fall into crimes of 'resisting an officer' or 'against the authority'." I'd better behave.

Just one question from the armed soldier: "Where are you going?"

I smile to myself, as it seems a bit of a silly question, as along this road there are no turns and nowhere else seemingly to go except to the big border town and Baja's capital of Mexicali. How much do I need to say? Best to keep it simple.

I smile. "I'm driving on to Tecate, then over the border tomorrow to catch a flight back to London."

He's done his job. He nods and waves me on. No searches. Nothing. Good. But I don't rush off immediately. It's here I also see the desert peak of El Chinero and can't help but shiver from what I'd read. It's named after Chinese labourers, who in the early 1900s came to work in Baja on the railways and the rich agricultural areas around Mexicali. They were trying to cross the San Felipe desert. Left stranded, the 160 ill-advised workers started to head across the desert to Mexicali, about 125 miles away. A lot never got past this hill, and none of them reached Mexicali.

I want to leave and get out of here. I put my foot down and turn the music up. Jimi Hendrix's *All Along the Watchtower* blasts out: " . . . there must be some kind of way outta here said the joker to the thief." I push my foot harder down . . . 80 . . . 90 . . . 100 mph.

There's no respite here, and I thirstily drink the warm water. Out in the distance is a dust twister turning the mountain on the horizon a dark shade of pink. But the nearer I get to this red earth-blown landscape, the clearer I see it's no tornado but just dust from working mines. It's all manmade. Heavy machinery up in the hills of Sierra Las Pintas is ruthlessly digging into the mountain sides and then transporting the rocks along moving rail carriages down to the valley.

Coming round a tight bend, massive, white salt flats begin to appear, from La Ventana going far out into the distance and deeply reminding me of the iconic Bonneville Salt Flats I'd ridden out to just four years previously. These I follow for a long, long way, until crossing over the Laguna Salada, the flat, salty terrain once again turns into desert, with the black asphalt road running away and disappearing over the horizon. It's all quite majestic, but there's no vegetation of any sort, no hard surviving cactus and it's very different from anywhere else.

But no more than twenty minutes further on from this wild place, I'm starting to catch glimpses of the Rio Colorado teasingly appearing from time to time running parallel to the road. The whole landscape once again incredibly changes. Immediately, there are green fertile grass banks on the side of the road. Rich green fields full of crops stretch luxuriously across the valley to the protective hillsides. Here in the valley are farms and people actively working the land. It's all change here, and you can feel the vibrancy of the area. And without notice, the traffic also increases, and the remote Highway 5 turns into a full-scale, multi-lane motorway, indicating we're getting closer to civilization.

The speed and frenetic pace is fast, approaching the capital city of Baja California. I need to concentrate. I need to find the turning westwards onto Highway 2, instead of potentially getting trapped and lost through Mexicali and its 700,000 people.

With a millisecond's notice before passing it, I see a sign for Tijuana Highway 2 and career off and up and over onto this new road. I wipe my brow. That was close. I almost missed it. Highway 2 now follows the US and Mexican border from Tijuana all the way over eastwards to Sonora and continuing to the Gulf of Mexico near Matamoros, 1,200 miles away. I'll be on it for just seventy miles, heading to my final destination of Tecate.

But before anything else a stop for the two "Ps" is essential—a pee and petrol. A couple of miles on and my wish has been granted as I pull into a gas station. Nothing strange about this stop, except for one thing, and another money earner that I'd never seen before, but which is also trying to promote environmental friendliness. There's no cost for using the toilets, except there's a machine on the wall, not to buy what you think, but to buy toilet paper for one peso. I try it, slot my coin in, and out spurts a metre of soft white roll. I fold the remaining valuable piece into my pocket. The other pesos I've stuffed in my pockets are then shortly used to pay seventy-five pesos for the highway charge to get me to Tecate. And it would have been just forty-five pesos on a bike.

Again, throughout this journey, I'm thinking about how not once have I encountered any long distance bikers on any of these roads, which I find a bit strange. I'm continuing to think I made the right decision in not doing this trip on two wheels, but surely there must be other people out there riding to or from somewhere in Baja. It would have been good to talk to them about their experiences.

I put my foot down and set off on this last leg of the trip along the empty highway. Without exception and without disappointment, this road feels the same—quiet, straight, smooth, and disappearing out into a mountain range with sandy, gorse-laden terrain on either side. This last morning is gifting me with another pristine blue sky and not a single cloud—something which is not a common occurrence back in Britain!

Just twenty miles down the road, a military checkpoint comes into sight. I do the dutiful thing and stop as the familiar hand waves me down. By now, the well-searched suitcase is automatically heaved out once again and curiously looked through. A simple nod is given, and I heave it back in again. And this, hopefully, for the last time.

I hate the anticipation of journeys of any kind almost coming to an end. But I can still afford to drive in a leisurely way and soak in the landscape and atmosphere. This trip through Baja California has exceeded all my expectations, bringing surprises from around almost every corner. Yes, Baja California is uncompromising, but that's good. This 800 mile strip, which feels independently suspended between the US and Mexico, with its wild desert and cactus, with the Pacific Ocean on one side and the Sea of Cortez on the other, thrashed by strong winds, beaten by gigantic waves, and almost unbearably hot does, indeed, feel like being at the "end of the world." At least at this time of the year it seems overlooked by most tourists, and for this reason, makes it feel even more authentic. But as I've seen, things are changing rapidly, and now, I feel more than ever, was the right time to discover this mysterious and extreme place.

The road is gradually climbing into the mountains and large monster trucks are once again becoming increasingly visible, careering towards me down and round the bends, as well as the crosses appearing, stuck in the cliff sides. But the views, the higher I climb, are becoming more spectacular, looking out to the arid cactus plains and desert below.

I need to stop to soak in the majesty of this vista, which I may not see for a long, long time or maybe never again. Gratefully, there are laybys. The next one seems to be almost at the top of a summit. Two massive trucks are parked up there too. I indicate and pull up in front of them. I walk to the cliff's edge and look out and over to a vast expanse of rocky, sandy, barren lands far below and mountains that reach out to join the sky's horizon. It's totally beautiful. Well, actually, I'm going to go back on that statement. It's *almost* totally beautiful. I peer down, and a long, long way down in the rocky gulley are, strangely, hundreds and hundreds of black truck tyres that have been indiscriminately thrown down there. Piled up and dotted everywhere, they look like bizarre extra-terrestrial insects creepily trying to crawl back up the slope. Again, another challenging question I can't answer. Why are they chucked just here, and surely the truckers could take them with them to dispose of elsewhere.

I turn and notice behind me one of the guys has the bonnet of his white truck open, and he's diligently sponging it clean. Next to his registration plate is another plate, maybe indicating his name: "M. Lopez, Mexicali, BC". He courteously smiles but is too engrossed with his task to talk. I walk past and am left speechless by the enormity of this other truck. It's bright blue with silver metal fenders, two massive chimneys at the back of the cabin, and hauling what looks like tons and tons of rocks. This guy wearing an oil-smeared T-shirt over his fat belly is also fiddling with some kind of maintenance job but turns round and smiles. I immediately feel no threat with this guy in this empty place, and I walk towards him, showing my curiosity. But he's probably also asking himself why a woman is approaching him in the middle of nowhere.

"Morning, Señor. Beautiful truck!" Well at least that's a one-line opener for a chat.

For some reason, this conversation also just naturally starts to flow. Standing up, he wipes his hands with a cloth and puts one out to shake mine, introducing himself as Guillermo. He offers me a chewing gum, and as long as that's not drugs, then that's very kind.

"Morning, Señora. You're not from around here, are you? Yes, this is a 1996 Kenworth, which has done over one million miles with me! It cost me $17,000. I'm carrying scrap metal westwards and then get to go back to see my wife near Tijuana. The truck has done me good. I have everything I need here to stay on the road for a long time—bed, TV, fridge."

I'm fascinated by this other kind of traveller. I'd never seen or had the opportunity to look into a "monster" so can't resist it.

"Guillermo. I know it's a strange question, but could I look inside where you drive and live?"

He smiles and walks round to open the driver's door that feels like it's about six feet or more up in the air. With him pointing, I tip-toe and peer inside. It's enormous, with a massive, wooden steering wheel; a black leather-embossed and padded ceiling with speakers; a wood laminate dashboard with hundreds of chrome speed, petrol, or whatever dials; and a gear shift which looks like the height of a dwarf with high heels on. Everything is massive in scale.

He points behind the driver's seat with an open curtain. "That's where I sleep and where the TV is."

It looks like a fairly decent area to chill out in. I look at him, and he knows what I'm thinking and nods. I literally climb up into the truck and sit behind the giant steering wheel. I peer over it and look through the tinted, narrow window that I'd seen approaching me ominously from behind so many times. How they drive these vehicles I have no idea! I jump back out, we smile, we shake hands, and we wish each other a safe trip, with Guillermo kindly giving me his last piece of chewing gum and me getting back into what now feels like a toy.

I continue climbing up and along the stony, rocky, cliff side, with views that are now extending out to a hazy horizon of infinity. I have no other wish but to park up once again and indulge in the sight of this highest 1,117 metre stop. With the winds so strong up on this unprotected peak I can hardly open the door without using my own brute force. Far below, winding up the mountainside, are large blue pipes. This is, in fact, from what I've read on the shuddering windblown panel next to me, an amazing structure. It's a 125 kilometre aqueduct reaching an altitude of 1,061 metres, coming from the Colorado River in the valleys below and supplying the essential water to Tecate, Tijuana, and the beaches of Rosarito on the Pacific Coast. Quite a feat!

But the danger of this place is not forgotten, and once again, this earthly promontory has several stoic memorial crosses cemented permanently into the rock.

Then out of nowhere in this windblown place, a solitary man with a rucksack and walking stick appears from below the steep hillside, slowly and bravely heaving himself up. Where he's going is anyone's guess. He's a long way from anywhere, and he doesn't look the youngest or spriteliest of people. Hopefully he won't come across a Puma, which are said to stalk this mountainous region.

A lovely sign with pictures confirms this fact and indicates that other animals such as the ram, white tail deer, the California condor, rattlesnake, mice-hunting eagle, red tail hawk, and the grey fox are also found here. In fact, as it goes on to explain, the California condor had disappeared from its natural habitat, and it was only in 2002 that five condors were re-introduced in the San Pedro Mártir Mountains. And in 2009, a hatchling named "Inyaa," meaning "Sun" in the Kiliwa dialect, was born, keeping the breed alive.

It's cold. I slam the door shut and slowly descend, with white wind turbines peeking out over the crests of the rocky hillsides. The stony slopes change and sweep down to rugged, green moorlands as the darker clouds also start to sweep in. The first sights of dwellings come into view out in the distance as I approach yet another set of mountains rearing over and above Tecate.

The border town of Tecate is still pretty quiet from when I left it all those weeks ago. There're a couple of things I want to find while I'm here. A bed, a hat, and some beer! I park opposite McDonalds and under the grey, cloudy sky wander into the town's square. Surely there must be a cheap but pleasant place to stay and put my head down for the night. But there's nothing visible, with no hotel, inn, or motel sign displayed anywhere. I walk into a little convenience store to get a bottle of water and tell the girl stacking shelves that I need an inexpensive, centrally located, bolt hole for the night. She considers what should be an easy question carefully then points me in the direction of a small narrow street off the plaza.

I've got nothing else to do but go and investigate. I find it, but already this place looks suspiciously like a dive. Barred iron windows look out onto the street, with a small metal door leading into a dark room with a shabby counter. A Chinese man shows me two so-called rooms, one for 250 pesos without a bathroom or 350 pesos with wash facilities. Both rooms don't have windows. They are boxes at the back of the building. With their tatty décor and miserable looking, flat beds with stains on the covers, they look more like an Asian "one hour" motel room. It's an option, at least, but I'm not sure. It won't be much of a memory for a last night in Baja.

I tell the Chinese guy I'll return within an hour if I decide to take the luxury option. I continue wandering around the side streets, looking for somewhere else to stay, with it getting ever cloudier and colder. I need a hot brew. I return to the square and notice the strangely named place "Paris Patisserie." Walking in, I'm dumbstruck with the authenticity of the place, which feels like I've walked into a café on the streets of Paris, with its large array of luxury chocolate and creamy cakes out on the counter. A smartly suited guy, with a tie and smoothed back hair, carefully makes a cappuccino and creates an artistic heart on the milky froth.

He points his finger to his chin in serious thought when I ask the question, "Where can I stay tonight that ideally has windows?"

He smiles, like that was easy, "Why, upstairs of course! Walk around the corner, into the taco shop, and someone will take you upstairs to the reception. It's the Hotel Tecate."

As simple as that. And that I do, walking through a mouth-watering taco eaterie with a woman carefully chopping cooked meat on a hot griddle and spooning out rice and vegetables from terracotta pots. Within a few minutes, I'm standing in front of a counter and a sliding glass-paneled window looking into a sofa filled living room. I ring the bell. An old woman in a zimmer frame slowly approaches. She puts her hand to her ear, obviously showing she can't hear me.

But I hear her shout, "I don't know what you want! You need to go back downstairs and ask for my son."

So that I do. The son wipes his hands on his apron and back upstairs provides me with a key. Once again, I've kindly been given two options, one room with a TV and one without. I don't need a TV, so I take the cheaper 350 peso option, and amazingly, this basic room is also looking out onto the square. This is a no-brainer. I run back to McDonalds to collect the car, finding my way back past the church, all the taco stands, and up the one-way street, where the son has kindly moved his truck from directly outside to let me park in his place. Carrying the bags back into the simple, street taco bar, the woman at the griddle is still busy making lunches, cutting and chopping meat and vegetables.

The smell is just too tempting, so I have no other choice but to drop everything next to a table and point to what looks the most mouthwatering. The pork and hot chilli sauce, rice, beans, and tacos are heavenly. Perfection on a plate and just seventy pesos, or a couple of pounds. I search for the money to pay. I've lost my wallet, with all my stuff in it, including my credit cards, and I have no money in my pockets! Where is it? With a feeling of sudden panic, I put my hand up, indicating I'll return, and with a rolled tortilla in one hand, rush back to the café next door, but the barman shakes his head. I race upstairs and run around my room like a headless chicken, searching high and low for that damn wallet. Mercifully, I find it simply hiding under some dirty T-shirts that I'd thrown on the bed. I apologetically give the taco girl her money with a good tip. She generously smiles like it happens all the time.

So now I've found the bed and a deal for just twelve pounds, it's time to find the hat! Since being with the rancheros, I'd fallen in love with a beautiful flat Panama hat one of the girls had worn at the farm, and they'd all mentioned a famous place here called "La Tienda de Sombreros Vaceros"—the perfect shop for authentic cowboy hats. Down a little alley, I walk back in time, opening the rustic door to a shop which has thousands of hats stacked and piled on every conceivable shelf and wall. Cowboy and ranchero hats of all styles, colours, and sizes, from pink silver-banded girls' stetsons for rodeo day to working men's white Stetsons with traditional leather bands.

An old man standing on a ladder at the back of the shop, with pointy black cowboy boots, is carefully stretching up to place more hats on the shelves. He turns around, "How can I help you?"

"I'm looking for a flat Panama hat. Do you have anything?"

He shakes his head, as unfortunately, it's not a typical Mexican style, but my eye is caught when I notice intricately braided, handmade horsehair bands, which adjust to make any sort of hat fit that bit better and look just that bit smarter. I smile, as a couple of these will make perfect presents for horse loving friends, as well as one for my O'Farrell Stetson as an authentic memento from the trip. I gladly pass the notes over the counter and walk out with my pockets filled with more than just peso coins.

And now my third job, to find the beer. Walking across the square, I pull a sweatshirt over me, as it's getting even colder and the clouds getting thicker. It almost feels like winter! Around two stone tables, and seated on stone benches around them, are two groups of elderly men, playing what looks like a mix of draughts and cards with stones. Most are wearing the traditional, white straw Stetsons and thick warm jackets. In deep concentration with the tactics of the game, they don't seem to notice me curiously looking at them as I walk past, heading away to find probably one of the most famous places in Baja California, the Tecate Brewery.

I'd seen the familiar red and gold symbol with an eagle almost everywhere; hanging from every market, restaurant, and bar where the famous beer is sold. Most believe this to be Mexico's best brewery, which produces millions of litres every month to quell people's thirst.

Studying Tecate's street map in the tree-lined square, the brewery seems to be about half a dozen blocks away. It turns out to be a good walk down quiet streets, with most shops now closed for siesta.

I come to a crossroads, and stopping at the red lights, my eyes are drawn upwards to see an incredible, giant pink bougainvillea plant that has somehow managed to climb and creep around to the top of a massive pine tree at least forty metres in height. There is nothing higher in the whole area, and the bright, coral rose-covered tree dominates everything around it. Once again, beauty in the most unexpected places.

Walking around the streets for a bit to find the brewery, I pass women selling colourful bunches of flowers on the sidewalk and school kids with their heavy shoulder bags coming back from school, I somehow find the gates to the big factory and decide to simply walk through them to find a reception area and ask about going on a tour. I'd heard most were on Saturdays, but surely they could make an exception for little old me!

Before I can even step a foot through them, a uniformed guard stops me. "Hola. How can we help you?"

With my very best smile, "I'd love to come and visit the factory and see how the beer's made. I've come a long way!"

That's not a lie. I had walked a long way and was thirsty to drink a good chilled beer.

He kindly smiles, but officially shakes his head, indicating this won't be possible "I'm very sorry, Señora, but since late 2015 we're undertaking a two-year project to build an eight-storey visitor building to show our beers and history, and with the factory behind it. It's a massive job, and there are no visits today."

I turn back, disappointed, but I'll make a point to stop along the way at a bar for a taster of the famed Cerveza Tecate.

It's all been quite a day to end this amazing journey, but with the sun setting, I'm feeling tired, and my poor stomach once again feels weak and fragile. I know I'm losing some of my strength. I crash out on the bed and without effort drop into a deep sleep for a couple of hours. By the time I've woken, it's dark outside, and the street lights in the square have automatically switched on and are streaming into my room. I look out, and the emptiness the place outside feels like everybody has gone home. My stomach still feels somewhat delicate, but I also feel I need something homely and comforting to eat. I'll take a short wander.

It doesn't take me long, as most places are quietly closed, and so I walk into Lola's Cantina, just next door. The understated room with half a dozen tables and small bar at the back is empty except for an old man sitting quietly at a table behind me with a beer in his hand. I pick up a menu on the table resting against a small ceramic statue of Jesus, but don't see anything that can tempt me for how I'm feeling. The old man is watching my dilemma and helpfully leans over.

"I'd recommend the Bohemia Obscura beer. It's rica!"

I nod, "Thank you. But I'm also not feeling very well. I want to eat something, but very light."

He looks over to the dimly lit counter, where an older lady is wiping its top, giving the impression she's finishing for the day.

"You should ask Elena who cooks here! . . . Eh, Elena. ¡Ven aquí, por favor!"

A grey-haired, smiling lady carefully folds and puts her towel down and walks over, also kindly placing my uncapped bottle of beer on the table. "I overheard what you said about your poor stomach. I have the perfect suggestion. I'll make you a sopa de ajo. I do that for my children too."

Just fifteen minutes later, Elena proudly places a steaming hot bowl in front of me. The smell is wonderful, and with the comforting tastes of the warm garlic, hot rich chicken broth and eggs mixed into it, there's no question it's the perfect choice. Even little "saladitas," crisp bread croutons, are kindly put on the side of the bowl to add to the soup. I scrape the bowl clean, feeling a lot better, and before the end of the evening, the little garlic soup recipe has been written on the back of a beer mat for me.

ELENA'S SOPA DE AJO TECATE
(ENOUGH FOR 6 PEOPLE)

Prepare a half litre of good rich chicken stock.

Drop a good knob of butter into a pan and warm through the cloves of 2 peeled bulbs of garlic until soft and golden. The cloves should be cut or chopped very roughly and not too tiny!

Add to the cooking broth for about 30 minutes.

Then when things smell good, break 7 eggs, using mainly just the whites, and drizzle into the hot broth for the eggs to cook.

At the end, maybe add a small amount of garlic salt.

The same recipe can be made with onions, and the bowls can be filled with bread croutons, avocado slices, and any sort of cheese that melts well, like goat's or sheep's. Top with roughly cut coriander leaves.

What a wonderful gift to take home. I'm feeling stronger already. I walk out to the chilly night and back upstairs. With only one naked bulb hanging from the middle of the room, I walk over to the bed fully dressed in jeans and tops to keep me warm and to avoid any flea bites. But I'm more than ready to just crash to be refreshed for the journey back to Los Angeles tomorrow.

The early morning smell of freshly made tacos teasingly wafts up into my room, and before long, and for one last time, I sit down on the narrow pavement, looking out, and devour a plateful of deliciousness.

Finally crossing the border on this chilly day and fast approaching the congested metropolis of Los Angeles, which feels like another world from the silent, peaceful wilderness I'd come from, I strangely notice vehicles emblazoned with their names: Escape, Explore, Sierra, Expedition, Armada, Highlander, Rogue, Odyssey. Almost everything I had done! I smile, knowing that each day out on the road was a unique and priceless experience and adventure that could never again be exactly repeated by me or anyone else.

There's so much I'll remember on this road trip odyssey, but above all, I'll never forget all the kindness of the Baja people—their genuine smiles; their warm hospitality; their generous nature in never asking for anything in return; the incredible and diverse landscapes, which changed so often; the wonderful, eclectic food, from mouthwatering meats to sweet, tender seafood and fish, and the ever present hot chillis that created the warmth and life to it all—without ever forgetting the other river of life of the warm, flowing, golden tequila!

Appendix

Baja California Norte is 6 hours behind from London GMT; Baja California Sud is 7 hours behind from London GMT.

Terra Peninsular Conservation Projects; Conserving and protecting the natural ecosystems and wildlife of Baja California. More information; www.terrapeninsular.org

Reading companions—

Notes from a Small Island by Bill Bryson, *Barbarian Days* by William Finnegan, *Murder in La Paz* by Murdoch Hughes, *Into A Desert Place* by Graham MacIntosh, *Baja Legends* by Greg Niemann, *The Rough Guide to Mexico* by John Fisher, Daniel Jacobs, and Stephen Keeling

Baja California "on the roads less travelled" route, with approximate mileage to each destination—

    Day 1 - London to Los Angeles

    Day 2 - Los Angeles, via Tecate to Rancho La Bellota (200 mi.)

    Day 3 - Rancho La Bellota

    Day 4 - Rancho La Bellota to Valle de Guadalupe (20 mi.)

Day 5 - Valle de Guadalupe to Guerrero Negro (400 mi.)

Day 6 - Guerrero Negro to Loreto (260 mi.)

Day 7 - Loreto to La Paz (223 mi.)

Day 8 - La Paz

Day 9 - La Paz

Day 10 - La Paz to La Ventana Bay (47 mi.)

Day 11 - La Ventana Bay

Day 12 - La Ventana Bay to Cabo Pulmo

Day 13 - Cabo Pulmo

Day 14 - Cabo Pulmo to Todos Santos (102 mi.)

Day 15 - Todos Santos

Day 16 - Todos Santos

Day 17 - Todos Santos to Mulegé (353 mi.)

Day 18 - Mulegé to Estero El Coyote, Bahía de Bellenas (200 mi.)

Day 19 - Bahía de Bellenas, Campo Rene

Day 20 - Bahía de Bellenas, Campo René to San Felipe (256 mi.)

Day 21 - San Felipe to Tecate (200 mi.)

Day 22 - Tecate to Los Angeles (161 mi.)

Accommodation following the route taken—
Los Angeles Airport - Travel Lodge LAX South, El Segundo
1804 East Sycamore Avenue, El Segundo 90245

Rancho La Bellota - www.bajarancho.com
rancholabellota@yahoo.com, t.+52 646 172 7773

Valle de Guadalupe Wine Country - Terra del Valle B & B
San José de la Zorra Road, Ejido El Porvenir
terradelvalle.bb@gmail.com,
t.+52 1 646 117 3645, +52 1 646 117 2508

Guerrero Negro—The Halfway Inn
Carretera Transpeninsular Paralelo 28, Guerrero Negro 23940
t.+52 615 157 1305

Loreto - Iguana Inn, Juarez s/n, at Davis
iguanainnloreto@yahoo.com, t.+52 613 135 1627

La Paz - El Angel Azul Hacienda
Independencia 518, Zona Central, 2300 La Paz
www.elangelazul.com, t.+52 612 1255130

La Ventana - Ventana Bay Resort
Carretera El Sargento, Número 1045, 23060 La Ventana
www.ventanabay.com, t.+52 612 114 0222

Cabo Pulmo - Hotel Cabo Pulmo (Beach Resort and Dive Center)
Conocido Cabo Pulmo, Cabo Pulmo 23406
www.cabopulmo.com, t.+52 624 141 0726

Todos Santos - Hotel California
A.P. 48 Calle Juárez e Morelos, Todos Santos 23305
www.hotelcaliforniabaja.com +52 612 145 0525

Todos Santos - Los Colibris Casitas
88 Calle Guaycura, cerro La Poza, 23300 Todos Santos
www.loscolibris.com, t. +52 612 145 0189

Mulegé - Hotel Hacienda
Madero no 3, Col. Centro, 23900 Mulegé
HaciendaMulege@gmail.com, t.+52 615153 0021
Punto Abreojos, Campo René, Estero el Coyote
www.camporene.com (check this website!)

San Felipe - Hotel El Cortez
Avenida Mar de Cortés, 21850 San Felipe
www.elcortezsanfelipebaja.com, t.+52 686 577 1055

Tecate - Hotel Tecate
Calle Presidente Lazaro Cardenas y Callejón, Libertade s/n, 21400
Tecate, t.+52 654 11 16

Note—
Exchange rate in May 2016; M$100 (Mexican Pesos) = £3.82

Other Books from Road Dog Publications

Also by Zoë Cano

Bonneville Go or Bust[12] *by Zoë Cano*
A true story with a difference. Zoe had no experience for such a mammoth adventure of a lifetime but goes all out to make her dream come true to travel solo across the lesser known roads of the American continent on a classic motorcycle.
I loved reading this book. She has a way of putting you right into the scene. It was like riding on the back seat and experiencing this adventure along with Zoe.—(★★★★★ Amazon Review)

Southern Escapades[12] *by Zoë Cano*
As an encore to her cross country trip, Zoë rides through the tropical Gulf of Mexico & Atlantic Coast in Florida, through the forgotten back roads of Alabama and Georgia. This adventure uncovers the many hidden gems of lesser known places in these beautiful Southern states.
…Zoe has once again interested and entertained me with her American adventures. Her insightful prose is a delight to read and makes me want to visit the same places.—(★★★★★ Amazon Review)

Other Authors

Motorcycles, Life, and . . .[12] *by Brent Allen*
Sit down and talk motorcycles, life and . . . (fill in the blank) with award winning riding instructor and creator of the popular "Howzit Done?" video series, Brent "Capt. Crash" Allen. Here are his thoughts about riding and life and how they combine told in a lighthearted tone.

The Elemental Motorcyclist[12] *by Brent Allen*
Brent's second book offers more insights into life and riding and how they go together. This volume, while still told in the author's typical easy-going tone, gets down to more specifics about being a better rider.

A Tale of Two Dusters & Other Stories[12] *by Kirk Swanick*
In this collection of tales, Kirk Swanick tells of growing up a gear head behind both the wheels of muscle cars and the handlebars of motorcycles and describes the joys and trials of riding

Beads in the Headlight[1] *by Isabel Dyson*
A British couple tackle riding from Alaska to Tierra del Fuego two-up on a 31 year-old BMW "airhead." Join them on this epic journey across two continents.
A great blend of travel, motorcycling, determination, and humor.—(★★★★★ Amazon Review)

A Short Ride in the Jungle[12] *by Antonia Bolingbroke-Kent*
A young woman tackles the famed Ho Chi Minh Trail alone on a diminutive pink Honda Cub armed only with her love of Southeast Asia and its people and her wits.

Asphalt & Dirt[12] *by Aaron Heinrich*
A compilation of profiles of both famous and relatively unknown people who ride, dispelling the myth of the stereotypical "biker" image.

Thoughts on the Road[12] *by Michael Fitterling*
The founder of Road Dog Publications and Editor of *Vintage Japanese Motorcycle Magazine*, ponders his experience with motorcycles and riding, and how those two things intersect and influence his life.

Northeast by Northwest[12] *by Michael Fitterling*
A personal story of dealing with stress and depression by heading out on the back roads of North America on a motorcycle, where the author rediscovers the kindness of people and the beauty of North America.
…makes you feel that you are on the journey yourself. The book shows how inexpensively a rider can tour America! Buy it, read it, and you will not be disappointed.—(★★★★★ Amazon Review)

In Search of Greener Grass[1] *by Graham Field*
With his game show winnings, Graham sets out solo on his KLR for Mongolia and beyond.

Eureka[1] *by Graham Field*
Graham sets out on a journey to Kazahkstan only to realize his contrived goal is not making him happy. He has a "Eureka!" moment and turns around and begins to enjoy the ride as the ride itself becomes the destination.

Different Natures[1] *by Graham Field*
The story of two early journeys Graham made while living in the US, one north to Alaska and the other south through Mexico. Follow along as Graham tells the stories in his own unique way.